From Fire to Flood

FROM FIRE TO FLOOD

A HISTORY OF THEATRE IN MANITOBA

KEVIN LONGFIELD

On the cover: Megan McArton, Arne MacPherson and Maire Babb in Shakespeare in the Ruins' production of *The Tempest*. Cover photo by Paul Martens.
Cover design by Terry Gallagher/Doowah Design.

Thanks to the University of Manitoba, Winnipeg Tribune Collection for the following photographs: First Theatre Royal (PC 18/6453/18/5370-195); Second Theatre Royal (PC 18/6453/18/5370-194); Walker Theatre, exterior (PC 18/6453/18-5370-198); Dominion Theatre (PC 18/6453/18-5370-191); Rainbow Stage (PC 18-1360-001 neg); John Hirsch (PC 18-1833-001 neg); MTC Opening (PC 18/4510/18-4510-032); Cercle Molière (PC 18-4395-001 neg).

Thanks to the Provincial Archives of Manitoba for the following photographs: Corner of Portage and Main (Winnipeg—Streets—Main 1872 1-3); Winnipeg Opera House (Winnipeg Streets, Notre Dame 1, N8974); C.P. Walker (Walker, C.P. 1) Harriet Walker (Canadian Women's Press Club, N14825); Walker Theatre, interior (Winnipeg—Theatres—Walker 9, N13272)

We acknowledge the financial assistance of the Manitoba Arts Council and The Canada Council for the Arts for our publishing program.

Printed and bound in Canada by AGMV Marquis.

Canadian Cataloguing in Publication Data

Longfield, Kevin
From fire to flood: a history of theatre in Manitoba

Includes bibliographical references and index.
ISBN 0-921833-79-2

1. Theatre--Manitoba--History I. Title.

PN2305.M3L65 2001 792'.097127 C2001-903653-1

Signature Editions
P.O. Box 206, RPO Corydon, Winnipeg, MB R3M 3S7

To all the people who volunteered their time to helping make theatre happen in Manitoba. Their gift of time has helped to create a priceless resource—our collective consciousness.

Contents

Acknowledgments

Creating this book would have been impossible without the assistance so many people generously offered me.

My family helped me both materially and by patiently taking up the domestic slack. The professional theatre companies responded quickly to my requests for information, even when I did not request information close to the deadline. Their websites were also a valuable source of historical data. The University of Manitoba archives helped me find numerous invaluable documents. The libraries at the University of Winnipeg, the University of Manitoba, and the Winnipeg Public Library all offered assistance. In particular, Margo Charlton of Theatre Projects, Laurie Lam of the Manitoba Theatre Centre, Grant Guy of Adhere and Deny, and Cherry Karpyshin of PTE were very generous in loaning me archival material. Thanks also to Shakespeare in the Ruins for permission to use their poster art on the book cover.

Eileen Shewchuk gave me some valuable insights into the historian's craft and to the immigrant experience in Manitoba. Fred Narvey shared his experiences with the labour theatre movement of the 1930s. B. Pat Burns, Richard Howell and Brian Richardson gave me many first-hand accounts of theatre in the 1970s and 1980s. Brian also helped me find much of the information I used about the time before and just after Manitoba was a province. Cathy Enns helped fill in some blanks in the community theatre scene. Rory Runnells offered invaluable fact checking. My publisher, Signature Editions, was far more patient with me than I deserved.

Finally, thank you to all theatre artists and administrators, past and present, for making our lives a little more bearable—and for giving me something to write about.

Introduction:
It's All a Matter of Perspective

"Never look back; something may be gaining on you."
—Satchel Paige

Sometimes looking back is a good thing. It can tell you how far you have traveled, and it can tell you where the bumps in the road are, so you can avoid them next time.

In a previous life, I did process engineering for a high-tech company. My job was to find ways to improve product quality as printed circuit boards rolled off an automated soldering process. It can be pretty discouraging.

Like all human processes, manufacturing is subject to error and random variation. Some days it seemed as if I were making two steps back for every step forward. Some problems are harder to solve than others, and it is easy to magnify the time spent on these problems and minimize the triumphs. As Einstein said about relativity, a minute sitting on your lover's lap seems much shorter than a minute sitting on a hot stove.

One day, though, when making slides for an annual report, I saw the result of months of effort. There in front of me was a graph showing a steady decline in defects. I felt a sense of accomplishment that focusing on the daily trials had obscured.

At the same time, I saw that the progress made was still short of the end goal, a process that stood alone without needing outside influence to succeed.

What did all that have to do with theatre?

Looking at Manitoba's theatre scene today, I see many problems. Actors (most of them, anyway) do not make a living wage. We have some great playwrights, including possibly the most talented playwright in Canada, and yet our playwrights often wait years between premieres. Local directors have a hard time cracking the big stages. Artistically sound theatre companies struggle to survive, and often fail: Popular Theatre Alliance, Primus, 40 Below Mime, and Agassiz are all defunct.

On the other hand, when I look back ten years to when I first became involved in theatre, much has improved. Two important new theatre companies, Theatre Projects and Shakespeare in the Ruins, started. Primus, although gone, left a lasting impression. That small, dedicated theatre company put Winnipeg on the map as a place for top-level avant-garde theatre. The Winnipeg Fringe Festival became a major tourist attraction, and helped launch many careers. Several small professional companies give Manitobans unique theatre experiences. Winnipeg actors appear on local stages much more frequently. A growing film industry has resulted in further opportunities.

Ten years ago, an actor who had two gigs in a season (amounting to perhaps 12 weeks of work) could boast of a good year. Today, actors are cast three or even four times a year and use film and commercial work to earn a limited but livable income. In the early days of the Manitoba Association of Playwrights (MAP), a major problem was finding experienced directors to workshop new scripts. Today we have almost as many talented directors as we have actors. When MAP started, it was with the conviction that we had talented playwrights who just needed a few breaks to arrive on local stages. Today we have a sizable list of published playwrights, enough to warrant an anthology (*A Map of the Senses*). Three Manitoba playwrights have been nominated for the Governor General's Literary Award. Ian Ross has won it.

What we do not yet have is an integrated theatre. For all the strength of the individual parts, we have not yet produced a great theatre, one that translates the particular experience of Manitoba to the larger world. We do not have the equivalent of Elizabethan England's Globe Theatre, or Louis XIV's Comédie Française, or Dublin's Abbey Theatre. These were places where playwrights, actors, and a public came together to create art that transcended borders and time. The pieces are there, but how do we put them together? Is it even possible that a place such as Manitoba could spawn a great theatre?

This book looks at approximately 150 years of Manitoba theatre history, from the first theatre performance in Winnipeg, in which a fire nearly destroyed the city, to the present flood of theatre activity. It attempts to explain how we got to where we are today, why we did not go somewhere else, and how we might make the leap from a respected regional theatre centre to a revered source of greatness.

1

Theatre Comes to Winnipeg: Where Did It Go?

"Not to go to the theatre is like taking one's toilet without a mirror."

—Schopenhauer

Theatre history is full of people warning us about the dangers of theatre. Theatre's detractors call it an immoral force that will cause society's ruin. Winnipeg's theatre debut, however, came closer to causing mass civil destruction than in any other place. Live theatre nearly killed Winnipeg before the city properly started.

Winnipeg's first recorded theatre event took place in September 1867.[1] Manitoba was not yet a province. Winnipeg was not yet incorporated as a city; the town's population was about 100, with perhaps 1000 people living in the area that would become the unified City of Winnipeg in 1971.

Even in those early days, Winnipeg was proud of its people, and ready to celebrate any achievement. When George "Dutch" Emmerling opened the George Hotel, therefore, some enterprising citizens planned a night of "dramatic readings and recitations, a pianoforte solo and a comedy skit" in honour of the new business. They booked an empty room above a general store and dubbed it the Red River Hall.

The intrepid theatre artists set about securing props, costumes, and a grasp on their lines. The city streets were not yet paved, so they set some sandbags on the gummy mud in front of the hall's only entrance, and laid planks on this foundation to make a crude walkway.

The first to arrive was a man on horseback, bringing the lamps to be used for footlights. He parked his horse astride the entrance and unloading began. A short time later the company learned that the horse had become stuck in the gumbo. They would have no audience unless they could free the horse.

In the grandest theatre tradition, all hands put themselves to the task, including actors already in costume. After a great effort that included the destruction of some costumes, they freed the horse. The show could now begin, although some of the actors were forced to wear street clothes.

The audience trooped in, including the beaming Mr. Emmerling. He had put candles in every window of his new establishment down the street, to better advertise the subject of the night's show.

The first warning of potential doom came when the stage manager announced that the floor was dangerously overloaded. (An overflow crowd amounting to more than half the town's population had shown up.) He therefore asked the audience to refrain from applause, lest the added stress on the structure should cause it to fail, destroying the building and quite possibly themselves.

The show proceeded, with the finale being a slapstick version of the reception the first customer might have at the George. The skit featured exploding candles, disappearing shoes, and numerous topical references, many at Emmerling's expense. (Emmerling, despite fears to the contrary, and displaying a forebearance that today's leading citizens would do well to emulate, took the jibes with good humour.) Winnipeg's first night of theatre therefore included an original Manitoba script. The reception was wild: as Hargrave says, the "...applause [was] of so violent a nature as severely tried the frail supports with which the flooring was upheld and was in consequence 'speedily suppressed.'"

Latecomers are a bane of audiences everywhere, but on this night one literally saved the town. As he hurried towards Red River Hall, he noticed that a candle in Emmerling's hotel had ignited the curtain, putting the entire hotel in danger. He rushed inside and doused the fire before crossing the street to disturb the performance.

Since Winnipeg was then a tight collection of wood buildings, it is likely that, had the latecomer not saved the hotel, the fire would have razed the town. Since Red River Hall had only one exit, it is also likely that most of its citizens would have perished, since they would have been trapped in the building by the single, narrow exit.

A population made of less sturdy stock would have thought themselves fortunate and banned future theatricals as a precaution.

Not so Winnipeg. The theatre group promised a return engagement the next week, leaving the store owner seven days to frantically prop up the second floor with poplar logs. This return engagement had to proceed without the "principal actor and organizer." Upon returning to the stage to fetch a forgotten item, he stumbled in the dark and severely gashed his leg on the tin reflector of a footlight. The injury required surgery and several weeks of bed rest.

This was the start of a lively theatre community that would soon have more splendid facilities and performances. Within a few years Winnipeg would have a hall with a capacity greater than the population, and performances of both classics and scripts by local playwrights.

Later, when the Anglican Church approached Alexander Begg, the building's owner, about using Red River Hall for Sunday evening services, the structure did double duty. Sunday evenings it served the faithful who did not want to walk to St. John's Cathedral. This congregation became the founding members of Holy Trinity Anglican Church.

As chronicler Alexander Begg put it, "Out of the theatre therefore grew the church."

While theatre in Manitoba has a history dating back almost 150 years, a Manitoba theatre has not dawned yet. No theatre has created Manitoba plays that express the Manitoba experience so well on our stages that they overflow our borders and time, as the great theatres have in other parts of the world.

Our mark in the greater world is faint. A small comfort is that the Canadian theatre's mark is scarcely more vivid. A search of some world theatre books for Canadian references yields disappointing results.[2]

Novelists such as Margaret Atwood, Michael Ondaatje and Carol Shields regularly win or make the short list of such book prizes as the Pulitzer and the Booker. Meanwhile, Canadian theatre artists do not so much as strut and fret our hour upon world stages. We scarcely make it to the wings.

Manitoba theatre's place on the Canadian scene is a microcosm of Canada's in the world.[3] Outside of our role in establishing regional theatre, we do not seem to have made much of a mark on the national scene.

If writers outside Manitoba place little importance on our theatre, writers inside the province pay scarcely more attention to it. Reading the classic texts on Manitoba history reveals little impact for theatre.[4]

2

Mommy, Where Does Theatre Come From?

"All the world's a stage."
—William Shakespeare, *As You Like It,* Act II

A common misconception today, governed as we are by people with strong financial prerogatives, is that artistic expression is something that people do in idle moments, when all the "necessities" of life are secure. History does not bear this out.

The suggestion in the last chapter that Manitoba history represents a missed opportunity for a national theatre might on the surface seem ridiculous. Still, it comes from strong evidence that the artistic impulse is one of the most powerful human drives.

The first Canadian play, Marc Lescarbot's *The Theatre of Neptune in New France,* had its first performance at the Port Royal colony in 1606, during a harrowing winter in which many colonists died.

Almost 300 years later, William Wallace's 1880s epistolary account of settlement in the Shellmouth region reveals that music, recitation, and even theatre began before the settlement was anywhere near what we would call civilization.[5] In one letter home, Wallace asks his sister for a loan so he can make up the difference he needs to buy an organ from a family who is returning East.

This event proves two things:

1. One family thought enough of music to bring a cumbersome instrument into the wilderness, at the cost of leaving other "necessities" behind. (Everything they brought had to come by oxcart. Often an oxcart would make only a few miles in a day, so only the most vital necessities would go on a cart.)
2. Although life on his homestead was still precarious, Wallace's need for artistic expression was strong enough that he would

go into debt to find an outlet. (His letters show a strong reluctance to borrow money, as one might expect from a stereotypical Scot.)

These two events are not isolated examples of exalted spirits cast into the wilderness. Within a year of settling, the Shellmouth area had regular artistic events. Wallace found his popularity enhanced by his ability to do recitations of Scott, Dickens and Twain. (He writes disparagingly of an invitation he received to join a dramatic society. This shows two things: his Presbyterian attitude towards theatre, and the existence of theatre before the settlement became firmly established.)

Just What Is a National Theatre, and How Does It Develop?

While theatre, like the thistle, tends to establish itself wherever people settle, and is difficult to eradicate once established, great theatre is not a natural or inevitable result of a group gathering to produce a play. A quick survey of places that established great national theatres shows some common characteristics.

(I stop here to reiterate what I mean by a great national theatre. It is not just the literary works of a great writer who created some great scripts, and it is not the best theatre that happened in a political entity during a set period. A great theatre results from a gathering of gifted theatre artists who collectively create drama that expresses the local perspective in a way that transcends time and borders. People who view later theatre events, great or small, can discern the influence of a great national theatre in those productions. One can draw a more or less straight line through Greek and Roman comedies to *commedia dell'arte*, Molière, the Marx Brothers and, finally, to its palest imitation, the TV sitcom.)

Let's look briefly, then, at some great national theatres and the conditions that spawned them, in approximate chronological order.

Greece

Greece, the "cradle of democracy," also gave birth to Western drama. Greek Drama grew out of the Great Dionysia, a religious festival in Athens (part of ancient Attica) celebrating wine, revelry, and fertility. (This is probably the start of the unsavoury reputation actors have to this day.)

Greek drama predates democracy slightly (drama received official recognition in 534 BC, while democracy arrived about 508 BC) but it was during the golden age of Greek democracy that its drama flourished.

Also in 508, the competitive aspect of Greek drama began. As part of the democratic movement, Attica was divided into ten tribes, and these tribes competed by entering plays in the Great (or City) Dionysia. Each playwright was to enter four plays (three tragedies and a satyr play) and a winner emerged through a complicated balloting system. An archon appointed wealthy patrons for the three playwrights chosen for the competitions, and the actors were state employees. Greek comedies were also part of this festival, judged separately. Aristophanes (c. 448–380 BC) is the only comedian whose complete plays survive.

The three great tragedians were Aeschelus (c. 523–456 BC), Sophocles (c. 496–406 BC) and Euripedes (c. 480–406 BC). All three were active at the same time, and all three wrote most of their plays after the Greeks ended their wars with Persia in triumph around 479 BC. (Sophocles is said to have first won public attention in his victory dance following the defeat of the Persian fleet.)

It is noteworthy that Greek drama grew out of a conscious state decision to promote and sponsor it. The government of the day saw drama as an essential part of a mature, thriving society, and paid to support it.

Athens was one of two leading city-states in ancient Greece, the other being Sparta. Greek drama went into decline with Sparta's victory over Athens, although performances continued well into the Roman period.

England

English theatre's golden age started in Elizabethan times (1558–1603) and carried through into the early years of King James I (1603–1625). This period coincides with England's greatest period as a nation (with the possible exception of Victorian times).

During Elizabeth I's reign, England became the world naval power, following the defeat of the Spanish Armada (1588). Afterwards, William Shakespeare (1564–1616), Christopher Marlowe (1564–1593) and Ben Jonson (1572–1637) flourished. This period gave us Shakespeare's canon (c.1590–1611), Marlowe's *Edward II* (c.1592) and *Dr. Faustus* (c.1604), and Jonson's *Volpone* (1605).

The period also enjoyed the work of some great actors, most notably Richard Burbage (c. 1569–1619) and Edward Alleyn (1566–1626). Jonson and Shakespeare, of course, were actors as well as playwrights. Inigo Jones' designs graced Jonson's masques.

Since then, England has had several dramatic renaissances, and has given the world some of its great plays. The terms Restoration drama and Victorian melodrama describe two such periods.

Even today, playwrights such as Stoppard, Shaffer and Pinter see their plays produced around the world.

While "playing the provinces" is a time-honoured tradition and apprenticeship, London is both England's political and dramatic capital. Playing the West End means a theatre artist has reached the profession's top rung.

France

The great age in French theatre took place while Molière and Racine (and to a lesser extent, Corneille) wrote. This was during the reign of the Sun King, Louis XIV (1643–1715). The Thirty Years War, one of the planet's bloodiest and most destructive conflicts, ended in 1648. In the years following this war, French playwrights produced such enduring plays as *Phaedra* (Racine, 1677), *Le Tartuffe* (Molière, 1664) and *Le Misanthrope* (also Molière, 1666).

Great French actors included Molière, Mlle Du Parc (1633–68) and Mlle Champmeslé (1642–98). (Unlike the English court, the French allowed women to be actors at this time.)

Paris, the capital, is France's theatrical centre, although Molière and others honed their craft in the provinces. The king's court, though, was the mark of success for any playwright. In spite of France's wealth and power under the Sun King, theatres were constantly in dire financial straits. Louis often had to bail out the Comédie Française.

Germany

Prussia emerged from the Seven Years War (1756–1763) as a dominant power under Frederick the Great (ruled 1748–1786). Frederick was a friend and admirer of Voltaire, who called Shakespeare's work "barbarian." Official German drama therefore aligned itself along French lines, with its stronger allegiance to the three unities (time, place and action) than Shakespeare followed. German theatre achieved greatness only after it abandoned the French model for Shakespeare's.

The Sturm und Drang school emerged later (about 1776) and dominated European literature, ushering in the Romantic Age. Goethe (1749–1832) and Schiller (1759–1805) became leading Romantic figures, although they later founded the classical movement. Weimar, where Goethe moved in 1775 and where Schiller had many plays produced, became a focal point in 18th century arts. The Weimar state theatre was home to Goethe's *Faust,* and many works by Schiller and Herder. Goethe's Weimar School and his *Rules for Actors* had a long-term, world-wide effect. Germany regards Schiller as its national playwright.

A second high-water mark came in the 20th century with Bertolt Brecht (1898–1956) and his epic theatre. Working with such actors as his wife Helene Weigel (1900–71) Peter Lorre (1904–64) and composer Kurt Weill (1900–1950), he revolutionized 20th century theatre. His plays and his theories have had a profound effect on Western drama. His Berliner Ensemble, with Helene Weigel and many leading actors and directors, explored and expressed his concepts of acting and directing, and especially his epic theatre.

Unlike many other theatre movements, Brecht's epic theatre grew out of national defeat and turmoil in post-World War I Germany, and developed during a period of forced exile for Brecht in Europe and the United States. The Ensemble started in Soviet-occupied East Berlin in 1949.

Although Brecht was a socialist with Communist sympathies, he kept an Austrian passport and a West German publisher. His drama is global rather than national in outlook, and outside rather than within prevailing social forces.

Norway

This slender Scandinavian country hugging the North Atlantic shoreline produced one of the giants of dramatic literature: Henrik Ibsen (1828–1906). His *A Doll's House* (1879), *Ghosts* (1881) and *Hedda Gabler* (1890) electrified and outraged audiences in their day, and still provoke strong reactions. Ibsen and Bjørnstjerne Bjørnson (1832–1910) established Norwegian as a dramatic literature in their country. Through their direction at the Norwegian Theatre in Bergen and the Christiana Theatre in Oslo, they established a tradition of excellence for Norwegian actors and other stage artists.

Norwegian literature was slow to emerge on the world scene. Until 1814, Norway was part of Denmark, and Danish was the official language. Norway then came under the political influence of Sweden until 1905, although it had a separate monarch.

Ibsen and Bjørnson therefore did for Norway what Shakespeare and his cronies did for England: establish a national literature and language. In 1864 Ibsen moved to Rome, where he stayed for 27 years. Bjørnson's influence was more direct: he stayed in Oslo, made a mark as a journalist and took an active part in politics. His son Bjørn (1859–1942) joined the Christiana theatre in 1884. His influence was also enormous. He introduced naturalistic acting and staging, and directed many classic works, both domestic and foreign. His energies resulted in the founding of the Nationaltheatret in 1899.

Norway's dramatic roots are therefore geographically diverse, spreading from the capital (Oslo) to its former capital (Bergen) to the continent, where Ibsen wrote his master works.

Russia

Where would modern theatre be without Stanislavsky? The formation of the Moscow Art Theatre (MAT) in 1898 led to a period of theatrical output that influenced theatre all over the world. Performing the plays of Gorky (1868–1936) and Chekhov (1860–1904), Konstantin Stanislavsky (1863–1938) and Vladimir Nemirovich-Danchenko (1858–1943) founded a theatre and school that lasted into the Communist regime. Much of their reputation rests, however, on Chekhov's four major plays: *The Sea Gull, Uncle Vanya, The Three Sisters* and *The Cherry Orchard*, all performed before 1904. Stanislavsky's written works on theatre, although often poorly translated, have become standard references for theatre artists.

The Moscow Art Theatre arose during the end of the czarist period in Russian history. During this time a growing middle class was becoming stronger, and ever more impatient with the last three czars (Alexander II, assassinated in 1881, Alexander III, and Nicholas II, assassinated in 1918). None of these three men made a mark for their intellect. Their authoritarian regimes both discouraged artistic expression through censorship and spawned it by the outrage they fostered in the intelligentsia. If a little learning is a dangerous thing, these czars' ignorance was an absolute terror, but a vital spark to great art.

Although Moscow became Russia's capital after the 1918 Revolution, St. Petersburg (later named Leningrad) was capital from 1712 until the end of the czarist regime. Throughout its history, however, Moscow has been a cultural, religious, and economic leader. Its apex as a cultural centre was 1890–1910. After the revolution it became the political capital and home of the labour movement.

Unlike most other great European dramas, therefore, Russian theatre flowered in spite of, rather than because of court influence. Indeed, the climate of the times dictated that the great Russian drama occur away from the capital city.

Ireland

Ireland, as it does in so many ways, defies ordinary logic when it comes to drama.

Although Irish playwrights have given the world many great plays, they often had to do so outside their native land. Goldsmith (1728–74), Sheridan (1751–1816), Wilde (1854–1900), Shaw (1856–1950) and Beckett (1906–1989) all made their mark in London or Paris. Where other theatre movements followed a successful time of national trial, Ireland's preceded it.

Like Russia, Ireland has named a period "the troubles," and as it does for Russia, that name could apply to much of the rest of its history. For centuries subject to the British crown, Ireland achieved at least partial independence in 1922, when Britain relinquished its claim to all but six counties of the northern province, Ulster.

The time leading up to independence included the brutally suppressed 1798 rebellion, the potato famine of 1845-49 (which saw one-third of its people either starve or emigrate), the Fenian movement (a period of armed resistance), and the Home Rule question of the late 19th century and beginning of the 20th, in which the Irish patriot Parnell and the British attempted a political solution. This movement failed, resulting in the Easter Rebellion of 1916. Other world events, such as the trade union movement, also had their effect in Ireland.

During this turbulent time, the "Irish Renaissance," an outpouring of literary and artistic expression that celebrated Irish heritage, started. The theatrical expression of this nationalist sentiment found a home in Dublin's Abbey Theatre, which grew out of the Irish Literary Society. Starting in 1899, the theatre produced plays by W.B. Yeats (1865–1939),

Lady Gregory (1852–1932), J.M. Synge (1871–1909), and (later) Sean O'Casey (1880–1964).

These plays often had an inflammatory effect. Yeats struck an audience member trying to stop a production of O'Casey's *The Plough and the Stars* (1926), knocking him off the stage. "You have disgraced yourselves again," he chastised the audience.

Despite the sometimes hostile reaction O'Casey's plays caused at home (and elsewhere), his gritty portrayal of lower-class life became a model for playwrights around the globe.

The United States

This country's history seems like a heartbeat compared to others'. While short, American history has had a profound world influence. The shot heard around the world in 1776 started a series of republican and democratic revolutions that spread to France and South America, and echoes today in such diverse places as South Africa and the Philippines.

Not until after World War I, however, did American theatre have an influence on the world. The United States emerged from the conflict as the dominant economic, political, and military power.

In the post-war euphoria, Eugene O'Neill (1888–1953) in serious drama and the Algonquin Round Table (Moss Hart, George S. Kaufman, Dorothy Parker, Robert Benchley, Edna Ferber and Alexander Woolcott) in comedy and musicals wrote timeless drama that traveled the world, most notably with the Marx Brothers.

The Round Table lasted from 1919 until 1929, but not even the Great Depression could dampen America's hold on the world's stages. Lillian Hellman (1906–84) wrote *The Children's Hour* and *The Little Foxes.* She and others wrote the plays the world saw and discussed. After World War II, writers such as Arthur Miller (1915–) (*Death of a Salesman, The Crucible*) and Tennessee Williams (1911–83) (*The Glass Menagerie, A Streetcar named Desire*) Sam Shepard (1943–) and David Mamet (1947–) carried the standard.

New York City is the theatrical capital of the United States, challenging London for the world title. While not a political capital, New York is the business capital of the world, a city synonymous with leadership in trend and fashion. A person who has not succeeded at The Big Apple cannot claim to have been a success on the world stage.

Drawing the Threads Together

Naturally, this survey does not comprise all great playwrights, or all great ages in theatre. It does not describe Noh theatre of Japan, *commedia dell'arte* in Italy, Roman, Spanish or Chinese theatre. Part of the justification for these omissions comes from space limitations, and part from relevance. Since theatre in North America draws primarily from the Western European tradition, examples from other cultures, however worthy the art may be, did not seem to offer much relevance.

What conclusions can we draw from this brief survey? The survey shows two models: one, theatre as an expression of pride in empire (Greece, England, France, Germany, Russia and the United States), and two, an expression of pride in an emerging nationalism in a former subservient existence (Norway and Ireland).

A second very common feature is a powerful benefactor, either the state, as in Greece, or a monarch, as in England, France, and Germany, or individuals such as Lady Gregory or impresarios in New York.

With the possible exception of Russia, great theatres emerged in cultures that embraced and valued artistic expression. Ancient Greece was probably the world's greatest experiment in self-improvement. Elizabeth I (and her father, Henry VIII) were both highly intelligent people and skilled writers. (Some conspiracy theories attribute some of Shakespeare's canon to Elizabeth.) Both father and daughter enjoyed pomp and glamour. Louis XIV, the Sun King, was in his youth one of the finest dancers in Europe and an assiduous patron of the arts. Frederick the Great had Voltaire as a mentor, wrote poetry, and was skilled musically. The Weimar court was a cultural oasis. Theatre flourished in Norway and Ireland during a cultural renaissance. In Russia, theatre artists at least enjoyed neglect from the dimwitted czars' court.

In only one case (Brecht) did a great theatre emerge from a national tragedy, but Brecht's theatre was more international than national in outlook. Besides, it emerged during the 1920s, a buoyant time.

All countries had theatres that either presaged or reacted to times of great national change resulting from a national crisis.

At a first glance, the survey does not seem to offer much hope that Manitoba could become the seat of a great national theatre. Manitoba, (or Canada, for that matter) does not offer much promise of establishing a military or cultural empire. Our great and mighty do not cascade financial and moral support on theatre.

A more likely model is provided by Norway and Ireland. Their theatre was an expression of pride in an emerging national identity. The theatre that emerged from Quebec during and after the Quiet Revolution (Gelinas, Tremblay, and LePage) expressed the same sentiment.

Almost as important as what this survey points out is what it does not. National optimism and a nurturing attitude to the arts are not enough. Despite enormous support, Napoleonic theatre produced little of lasting importance. The ideal climate seems to be a combination of financial support and artistic neglect.

Great national theatre lagged behind the American revolution by more than a century. Italian reunification in the 1860s did not result in great theatre. While some Italian actors gained worldwide fame through touring, their playwrights did not give them plays they could take with them.

Great theatre cannot travel on mediocre plays. The question arises, then, what circumstances create great playwrights? Let's look at their social status first.

Evidence suggests that the Greek playwrights came from the upper classes. The English playwrights (Shakespeare, Jonson, and Marlowe) all had fathers who were "in trade": a glover, bricklayer, and shoemaker, respectively. Jonson and Marlowe had a university education; Shakespeare probably did not. Corneille's father was a government official who could afford to give his son a Jesuit education and training in law. Racine was an orphaned Jansenist divinity student. (His father was a tax official.) Molière's father was a well-to-do upholsterer, working in the French court.

Goethe and Schiller both had a good education and standing as leading intellectuals in other fields. Schiller's father was an army captain, while Goethe's was an Imperial Councillor. Ibsen and Bjørnson were working theatre professionals as well as writers. Gorky came from an impoverished peasant background and was self-educated. Chekhov, like Schiller, was a doctor, the son of a small merchant. (Ibsen apprenticed to an apothecary after his family's financial ruin and also studied medicine.)

O'Casey came from a lower-middle class background and received much of his early education from a Protestant priest and self-study. Synge was well enough off to travel Europe in his early years. Yeats was the son (and brother) of a painter. Lady Gregory was an aristocrat.

O'Neill was an actor's son. He attended Princeton, but left after a year. Hellman was steeped in the theatre from an early age, and attended New York and Columbia Universities. Williams and Miller both graduated from university. Miller was, like Ibsen, the son of a man who suffered financial ruin.

Does it help to spend one's early days near a country's theatre capital? Jonson was born near London; Marlowe and Shakespeare were not. Corneille came from Normandy. Bjørnson was born in Kvikne, and Ibsen in Skeine. Chekhov's father's business was in southern Russia. Yeats and O'Casey were Dubliners, but Synge came from a village near Dublin, and Lady Gregory from Galway. O'Neill and Miller were born in New York, but Hellman was born in New Orleans. Williams was born in Mississippi and grew up in St. Louis.

What threads can we draw from this conglomeration? First, medical and religious training do not seem to be a barrier to becoming a playwright. A university education does not seem to hurt, but neither does not having a degree. For those with a university education, dramatic studies do not seem to offer much more advantage than law, medicine, or anything else.

A surprising number of the world's great playwrights excelled in other fields. Sophocles was a general and today's equivalent of minister of finance. Sheridan was a remarkably independent member of Parliament. Goethe excelled at nearly everything. Schiller is as well known as a philosopher as he is as a playwright. Marlowe was a spy, and Racine was a high-ranking government official.

People from the upper echelons seem to have worse odds than those who come up from the ranks. A playwright who hails from the provinces seems to have better luck than one born in the nation's drama capital. The strongest thread, however, is a background in theatre, either as part of a family tradition or from personal experience in acting, directing, or stage management. Many playwrights seem to have been noble souls, loved by all, but quite a few were real stinkers.

Literary skill, while important, does not seem to be worth much on its own. If it were, Wordsworth, Shelley, Keats and Byron would not have embarrassed themselves on stage in the 19th century.

One final note: playwriting does not seem to be good for your health. Sophocles lived to be 90, and wrote until the end, but most lived lives shortened by disease, alcohol, or in Marlowe's case, murder. O'Casey barely survived childhood; Synge hardly made it into adulthood. Goethe lived well into his eighties, but nearly died as a young man of a severe lung infection. Brecht died well before his 60th birthday. Suicide claimed German playwright Heinrich von Kleist and British playwright Sarah Kane (*Grave*).

3

Early Manitoba

> "There is a spot on this continent which travellers do not visit and from which civilization seems in a measure shut out. Deserts, almost trackless, divide it on all sides from the habitation of cultivated men; no railroads, or steamers, or telegraph wires, or lines of stages make their way tither; to reach it, or, once there, to escape from it, is an exploit of which one may almost boast. Receiving no impressions from without, it reflects none. It sends forth neither newspapers nor books. Yet Red River Settlement contains a population of 6000 souls, eleven places of public worship, a citadel of formidable strength, several large two-storey stone houses with modern conveniences, and an imposing body of mounted police. There is more than one good library there, and several good cellars; a man may dine there according to Soyer, dance the latest Cellarius polka redowa with ladies of any shade of colour from the pure bronze to the mere white, and discuss the principles of human society and the theory of popular governments as learnedly as the thing can be done at Washington or Cincinnati."
>
> —Account in an American magazine, 1856[6]

Since art is a reflection of and a reaction to its surroundings, a brief description of the forces that shaped Manitoba society is in order.

As the preceding quotation illustrates, Manitoba reflects a curious combination of remote rusticity and highly cultured engagement. More than a decade before Manitoba became a province, and before it even had a newspaper, it was a sophisticated settlement numbering in the thousands, with a taste for the finer things in life. As the brief description of a ball points out, it embraced ethnic tolerance at a level that would make most great capitals of the time seem provincial, and shames the province's later history. Reading accounts of the settlement from the mid-19th century make it sound like a veritable Eden. While a closer examination of events reveals a dark side to life here at that time, it was a remarkably calm and civilized place.

Equally remarkable is how tragically often outside influences have disrupted what was an enviable society.

The First Arrivals: Following the Glaciers

Human population came to what is now Manitoba relatively late in terms of world history. The first inhabitants almost certainly arrived as the shores of the prehistoric Lake Agassiz receded at the end of the Ice Age, about 12,000 years ago.

Throughout the 11,000 years or so before the first Europeans arrived, Manitoba was the scene of several migrations. The Cree arrived here first, and other groups, such as Mandan and a branch of Arapaho, came and went. The Ojibway and Assiniboine arrived shortly before the Europeans. At times more than one group would occupy the same territory, a precursor of the multiculturalism of which Manitobans are so proud today.

In *Aboriginal Migrations: A History of the Movements in Southern Manitoba,* Leo Pettipas describes how these groups shared and modified each other's customs and technology. We know that a highly complex culture existed, one that left behind architectural evidence, and in the case of the Ojibway, written scrolls, called Midewiwin scrolls. The birch bark scrolls gave cultural and medicinal instruction to later generations. Each summer these groups had large ceremonial gatherings not too dissimilar to the gatherings in Greece that spawned theatre as we know it today. These gatherings took place in a great lodge.

The sun dance was another ceremonial gathering that spread throughout the Midwest. It involved erecting a pole, which the group would decorate. The sun dancer would be attached to the pole and dance around it for days, as part of a vision quest or personal dedication. He would be the main participant, but the rest of the gathering would dance around him in a non-stop ceremony that took days and included fasting. It was a unifying social event with religious significance, much like the Festival Dionysia in Greece was.

The rich Ojibway storytelling tradition tells us much of what we know today about their history. In *Chippewa Customs*, Frances

Densmore describes their storytelling customs, which she collected from 1905–25.[7] (The Chippewa in Minnesota are the group called the Ojibway or Saulteaux in Canada.)

Old women were the expert storytellers: "One old woman used to act out her stories, running around the fire and acting while she talked." People requesting a story would accompany the request with a gift.

Stories fell into three broad categories:

1. "First Earth" stories (such as the turtle legend)
2. Adventures of Winabojo, a master of life, whose adventures taught wisdom and proper conduct
3. "Fairy" stories

Storytelling had a dramatic element, a unique aesthetic, and was a respected craft that people were willing to pay for. It was not only casual entertainment, a way to pass long winter's nights, but an art form. Its practitioners sought to enlighten their audience and broaden their outlook on life, in the same tradition as Sophocles, Shakespeare, Ibsen and Molière.

What is not clear from this account, coming as it did 40–50 years after European-style drama came to the area, is how much European theatre influenced the storyteller in the book.

We do know that rituals such as the Sun Dance spread throughout tribes in the Great Plains. It is not a wild assumption, therefore, that a Chippewa woman could have seen a European-style play. Like other artists the world over, she could have incorporated elements that she thought would please her audience and expand her artistic expression. On the other hand, it is just as likely that the dramatic storytelling Densmore describes represents an independent theatrical tradition.

Of course, once Europeans made contact, much of the traditional life changed or disappeared. At first this was an accidental outcome of contact, much like the cultural changes that occurred as different First Nations peoples migrated in and out of what was to become Manitoba. Later, this cultural displacement became an official part of government policy, motivated by a mixture of wrong-headed paternalism and outright racism.

Whatever the motivations, two outcomes are undeniable. The first is that the First Nations suffered an unconscionable loss of culture that came very close to genocide. The second is that their culture had no influence until very recently on mainstream Manitoba life. The survival of portions of First Nations' traditional culture and art from the brink of extinction is a testament to the power of the human spirit. As we shall see later, it is also one ingredient in the mix that might soon become a great theatre movement in Manitoba.

The Europeans Arrive: Let's Make a Deal

The first Europeans to discover what was to become Manitoba found it, in the time-honoured tradition of discovery, when they were looking for something else.

In this case, explorers looking for a northern passage to the Orient so they could compete with Spain for spices found instead the northern shores of Manitoba. Although the first explorers did not meet any First Nations people, they eventually made contact and discovered a profitable trade in furs. They intended first to finance their spice trade exploration with this trade, and later pursued it as an end in itself.

Exploration that started as a result of a trade war with Spain over spices soon became a trade war with France over furs. This war occasionally became bloody, but in Manitoba the Europeans generally fought among themselves with little involvement from the native peoples. (The First Nations also occasionally fought each other for the right to trade with the strange men who sailed in big, stinking boats to trade for furs.)

The fall of New France in 1763 meant an end to military hostilities, but the fur war proceeded apace. Traders from Montreal pressed westward along the canoe route to trade for the same furs that the Hudson's Bay Company shipped out over the ocean.[8]

The fur trade rivalry probably explains why the First Nations peoples in Manitoba fared better than corresponding peoples did in other parts of the Americas. The Europeans here did not (initially at least) want their land, their natural resources, or their souls. They wanted instead to trade in a commodity that the average European did not want to stick around to gather: furs. To harvest furs meant living rough in one of the most inhospitable climates on Earth. Much better, therefore, was to establish trading relations with someone who lived there. With two groups, the English and the French, competing for the same furs, the First Nations peoples' bargaining position was stronger than that of their counterparts elsewhere in the Americas.

The harsh and unpredictable climate also contributed to neighbourly relations. The Europeans were a long way from home with a slender and unreliable support line. They relied much more on their neighbours than did, say, the first arrivals in Newfoundland.

Settlement in the European sense came late to Manitoba. While the first ships touched land early in the seventeenth century, settlement did not start until 200 years later. Since men posted to the Northwest signed up for lengthy terms (seven years or longer), they developed a new custom: intermarriage. (First Nations women traditionally married outside their home community.) The Hudson's Bay company men, largely made up of Orkadians, and the primarily French voyageurs of the Northwest company took up with First Nations women.

Sometimes the marriages were enduring, and sometimes men with a weaker sense of honour would desert their Manitoba families when the time came to go home to Great Britain.

Regardless of the outcome of these unions, the result was a large mixed-blood population, or, more properly, two populations. The term "Métis" came to apply to descendants of French-speaking fur traders, and "half-breed" to descendants of English-speaking traders, although the terms were often applied interchangeably.

These two groups settled in different areas and lived slightly different lives. The English- (or Gaelic-) speaking mixed bloods often had a chance to go to the British Isles for education. Sometimes this separation from their native soil was beneficial, and often it was not, but it meant that they assimilated more with the European than the French-speaking mixed-blood population.

The Métis occasionally traveled East to Quebec, but more often their European influence came from the church, which sent people out to them. Not until 1858 did the church send three promising young Métis men to Quebec for a university education.

While relations between the European, mixed-blood, and aboriginal inhabitants was not perfect, the Beothucks and Aztecs would happily have changed places with the Cree, Saulteaux, and Assiniboine. Trade with the Europeans brought changes to their lives, but the Europeans' interest was, if not benevolent, at least the collegial one of trade with a partner instead of the flinty-eyed interest of the conqueror. Besides, the various First Nations exchanged customs and rituals in their ebb and flow across the prairies. The European influence was but one in an evolutionary stream.

In the beginning, the English settled on the shores of Hudson's Bay and waited for First Nations traders to come to them, and a French law forbade its Quebec citizens from wintering in the territory. This situation probably did much to preserve traditional life on the plains. The overwintering law stood until 1768, more than 100 years after first contact. (Naturally enterprising or independent young men flouted the law, especially if legal or other entanglements would make going home awkward.) The Hudson's Bay Company did not travel much inland until dwindling profits caused by the rival company forced them.

One negative effect of European contact was that the competition among First Nations for trade heated up inter-tribal wars. While war cannot be a positive effect of European contact, it is nevertheless remarkable that First Nations people would go to battle for the right to deal with Europeans.

Real trouble between Europeans and First Nations did not start until Lord Selkirk, who had gained controlling interest in the Hudson's Bay Company, decided to settle tenant farmers whom the clearances had uprooted in Scotland and Ireland. Selkirk's motive was only partly magnanimous. He hoped also to gain a competitive advantage over the North West Company by establishing an indigenous supply line.

Things did not work out as he had so carefully planned. Both the rival company and his own employees viewed the settlement with the same suspicion with which frontier people viewed settlers across the continent. They saw their way of life threatened; they feared the coming of agriculture would destroy the fur trade; and the North West Company had well-founded grounds for suspecting an ulterior motive. Escalating their distrust was the ethnic factor. The French-speaking population had largely aligned itself with the North West Company.

This animosity boiled over into an armed confrontation in 1816, at Seven Oaks. Governor Semple mismanaged a confrontation with Cuthbert Grant's Métis hunting party, resulting in a massacre of the settlers. At least 20 of the 25 settlers died, compared to at most one Métis. It would be more than 50 years before another European would be stupid enough to challenge the Métis militarily.

Eventually the rival companies merged, and after enduring tribulations of biblical proportions, the settlement prospered. The idyllic community described in the 1856 magazine article contained at least five groups:

1. First Nations people
2. Métis (mixed-blood descendants of French-speaking fathers and aboriginal mothers)

3. Mixed-blood descendants of English-speaking fathers
4. Selkirk settlers
5. Company men and their families, either active or retired.

While these groups were distinct in many ways, they shared one important factor: mutual dependence. The rigours of the climate and the limited population meant that the whole community had to protect each other's well-being. The groups were distinct, much like the inhabitants of a beehive, where the worker, drone, and queen bees all have their place and function.

One might wonder why the intellectually sophisticated, cohesive, cultured and well-read community the 1856 journalist wrote about had not yet developed a theatre in the European sense. The trials and triumphs of the previous 100 years or so had provided the sort of stories and characters Shakespeare, Sophocles, and Molière thrived on.

Several factors explain this. For one thing, most of the populace was nomadic for a large part of the year. The settlement became a virtual ghost town during the hunting season.

Another factor was that the vast majority of the settled population were French-speaking Roman Catholic until well after Manitoba became a province in 1870. The Catholic Church in Quebec forbade Theatre in 1694 after a planned production of *Tartuffe*. Occasionally afterwards an amateur production would happen, such as a French-language *Tartuffe* a British army garrison put on in 1774, but the church effectively discouraged live theatre until the 1860s.[9] Theatre was not something a devout French-speaking Catholic would support, and every visitor to the territory remarked on Métis piety.

Of the English-speaking population, many were Scots Presbyterian. This denomination strongly discouraged theatre at home, and there is little reason to believe that Scots emigrated to Red River so they could be free to create theatre. Many Company men came from the Orkney Islands and other thinly populated areas, rather than the fleshpots of London.

The Protestant Company men were equally devoted to their church, and complained often that the HBC did not send them a pastor of their faith.

Besides, even a relatively secular person would not have seen theatre as a desirable import commodity. Even in London, theatre had acquired a disreputable air almost as strong as during the early days, when actors held a place a scant notch above prostitutes and thieves.

Respectability did not return to the theatres until people such as Phelps and the Bancrofts started their theatres in the latter part of the 19th century.

Everything Was Fine Until You Came: Here Come the Canadians

Eventually the outside world intruded on Assiniboia, as the area came to be known. Ox carts established an ear-piercingly loud supply line with Minnesota. In 1859 riverboats began plying the Red River from St. Paul, Minnesota. A mechanized route to the area then became possible, by rail to Minnesota, and by riverboat from there to the Red River settlement. A newspaper (such as it was) started up the same year.

As the colonies to the East began speaking of forming one federation, interest in the Northwest grew. People started coming to Assiniboia from Ontario, the United States, and farther afield. It became an explosive mix.

The newcomers did not have the same attitude to First Nations as earlier arrivals had. While both groups came to the Northwest in hopes of striking it rich, the first European arrivals based their strategy on trade that required friendly relations with the existing population. These early venturers saw the land as a means to an end, and occupied only as much of it as they needed to set up and supply trading posts. They paid at least perfunctory attention to the title the existing inhabitants had to the land, and made at least a show of bargaining in good faith.

This was not as strongly true for the second wave of adventurers. For one thing, they saw the land as an end in itself. They foresaw a great agricultural boom, with industry to follow close behind it. The current way of life, and the people who led it, were an obstacle to this form of progress, and therefore not worthy of much consideration.

A further source of tension was that claims to land by all existing tenants were shaky at best. The Hudson's Bay Company, the titular owner, had for some years shown dwindling interest in governing and managing the territory. Negotiations to sell its interest in the land dragged on in London and Ottawa. No one knew for sure if local people would have any claim on land that some of them had occupied for generations. Land treaties with First Nations people were vague (and are still in dispute over 125 years later).

The local Company officials did not know what their share would be from the proceeds of the land sale. The other inhabitants naturally looked to them for some indication of the future, and found none. Worse, the most senior Company official in Assiniboia, William McTavish, was dying of tuberculosis.

The fabric that had held society together in Assiniboia had begun to rend. The pace of life increased. Independent merchants established businesses, one of which was the George Hotel mentioned earlier. Everyone knew that big changes were afoot, but not everyone welcomed them.

The French-speaking population, which made up the vast majority, did not hold an advantageous position. The buffalo hunt that had been its economic backbone was dwindling. New forms of transportation meant diminished reliance on pemmican, and besides, the bison population was falling fast. Those who made a living driving ox carts or rowing York boats had a new competitor, the steamboat. Jobs on these vessels were few for the Red River inhabitants. The fur trade would still be part of the economy, as it is today in Manitoba, but it would no longer dominate.

The priests saw a modernist, Protestant population boom coming, and they feared for the souls of the people they tended. Their 1858 experiment had disappointing results: none of the three men sent East returned with a degree. Attempts to persuade young Quebecois to settle in Assinniboia had disappointing results. Whether their fears for the future were well grounded is a subject for debate, but the priests cultivated in their flock a distrust of the way of life that seemed about to descend on them.

As the 1860s drew to a close, no one in the territories knew what the future political map of Manitoba would be: territory, province, self-governing British colony, part of the United States, or independent (Métis) nation. All outcomes seemed possible.

Some men pretended to know. One was John Christian Shultz, the recognized leader of the Canada Party. He owned a store and claimed to have a medical degree, although no evidence of this exists. He did acquire the *Nor' Wester*, and used it to promote the tiny Canada Party's interests. He let people believe that when Assiniboia joined Confederation, he would be the one who would settle land claims and award land to those he felt deserved it, regardless of who occupied it now. The Canadian government did little to dispel this impression when emissaries accepted Shultz's hospitality during visits to the territory.

When the British parliament cemented the transfer, therefore, they created a power vacuum. The Métis and French, under Louis Riel's leadership and with the priests' backing, declared that Canada did not have jurisdiction yet. They formed a provisional government, which they invited the English-speaking part of the population to join.

This approach did not receive overwhelming support. The long-term residents did not want to appear seditious. The tiny Canadian party, which stood to profit most from joining Confederation, wanted no part of what it considered a treasonous act committed by "miserable half-breeds."

Because of their overwhelming military advantage, the Métis set up a de facto government and arrested people who resisted, which did nothing to placate the unruly Canada Party. Still, they formed a functioning authority, and when Donald Smith came to negotiate a transfer to Canada, a representative body was elected to draw up terms and a bill of rights. For a time it seemed as if an orderly transfer would happen, the main sticking point being the Métis leaders' desire for an amnesty.

Shultz and his followers, in the meantime, continued to be a disruptive element, earning the enmity not only of the French-speaking constituency, but many English-speaking settlers as well, including the diarist Begg.

Despite great effort by people of goodwill, such as McDermot, Father Richot and A.G.B. Bannatyne, the unsteady peace at Red River eventually resulted in bloodshed. Three people, including a rabid Orangeman named Thomas Scott, died. One died at the hands of the Canada Party, and two at the hands of the Métis. (The family of the other English-speaking victim pleaded for peace, as the death was clearly a case of mistaken self-defense.)

Scott's death brought anti-French, anti-Catholic bigotry down on Red River in full force. Shultz escaped to Ontario and started a propaganda war that made a martyr of Scott and a villain of Riel in Protestant Ontario. Soon a military expedition, under Colonel Garnet Wolseley, marched west to "restore order."

The military force invaded Red River just ahead of the newly appointed Lieutenant-Governor, with the sound from Louis Riel's fleeing horse still echoing in the streets. Ignoring the provisional government, Wolseley installed Donald Smith (who traveled with him) as the civilian government. (Lieutenant-Governor Archibald arrived a few days later.) A promised amnesty never happened. Instead, mob justice prevailed, resulting in the death of at least one more Métis. While before 1869 Red River clothed itself in a many-threaded fabric, force of arms changed the province almost overnight into pure British wool.

In his journal of 1869–70, Begg speaks of Red River as "our country," a common sentiment of the time, for both English- and French-speakers. In contrast, in Margaret McWilliams' 1926 book, *Manitoba Milestones*, she describes the post-World War I recovery in Manitoba as "the most exhilarating of all the tales which Manitoba has yet written on the Pages of British history." In less than a lifetime, Manitobans' self image had shrunk from nationhood to colony. Its cultural outlook diminished even more.

The "amateur theatricals" that, in Begg's words, were "given to admiring crowds of settlers" in his book, *Ten Years In Winnipeg*, were banned under martial law. In time, these theatre groups might have spawned a Manitoba theatre that rivaled indigenous theatre elsewhere. Instead, in 1870, the Ontario Rifles opened the Theatre Royal. Garrison theatre, with its bold British stamp, came to Manitoba.

This was the least of the original inhabitants' worries. Families that had toiled to break land and establish a home would return from the buffalo hunt or the wagon trail to find an English-speaking Canadian family had usurped their property and moved into their house. Worse, the Métis would find they had no useful legal recourse. Many families fled to Saskatchewan and Alberta. (Eventually Métis families received scrip for their land, but many of these titles went for a song to unscrupulous dealers.)

French-speaking Manitobans were not the only ones to resent Canadian carpet-baggers. In 1881, William Wallace, a British settler, wrote of his Canadian neighbours:

> They as a class are very undesirable society. A good-going Yankee is a pleasure compared to them. They are about the greediest, least thankful, unenthusiastic lot I can imagine. Their ignorance of everything but surroundings is awful, and renders intercourse wearisome and unentertaining. Boors and clodhoppers is exactly the term they deserve.... Into the house they will march

> without asking your leave; no matter whether Sunday or Saturday, they will take an unabashed inventory of everything, spit all around and talk commonplace.[10]

No wonder the priests who ministered to the Métis were apprehensive about the effect Ontario settlers would have on their charges' behaviour.

Soon the bilingual legislature (illegally) became uniligual, and that legislature (illegally, again) banned French from schools. Manitoba's character changed permanently.

But we're getting ahead of the story. The migration to Manitoba from 1870 to roughly 1885 had a distinct character. The character of the migration had the side effect of dictating the nature of artistic expression for decades to come.

Manitoba life became stolidly British. In 1870, when Manitoba joined Confederation, the great majority of the population was Métis. By 1880 they were a minority, and in 1885–86, over three-quarters of the population was of British origin. This was not an influx of settlement like that seen a few decades later, when dispossessed people arrived in the famous "sheepskin coats" to settle and make a new life.

This migration had an imperial motive: as Doug Owram, Thomas Cross and others have pointed out in writings about this migration, the idea was to "build up a nation on the British plan."[11] As Owram said in *Promise of Eden*, "The British Empire was thought to represent man's highest achievement in the development of governmental and social institutions. The Northwest, promising great economic wealth, seemed to give Canada a unique opportunity to implant firmly those noble institutions in a rising world power."

Victorian Britons never suffered from a surfeit of humility. Indeed, many sincerely believed they represented the epitome of civilization.[12]

In other words, excellence would not define itself based on the local expression of local experience, but by drawing its models from the Imperial (British) paradigm. What came from Britain would, by definition, be the ultimate, and what developed locally would be deemed worthy only in the extent to which it followed the mother country's example.

This is not the climate in which a national theatre (or any national art) will flourish.

And Now, Back to Our Regularly Scheduled Subject

Looking at early Manitoba history, we can now easily understand why a great national theatre did not emerge in the 1860s.

The settlement may have had someone with the potential to be a great playwright; reading the journals and other letters that came out of the time shows that they had no shortage of people who could write well, in both English and French. As we have seen, it had the beginnings of a theatre community. The productions used a local script at least once, and it was a local hit. Given time, it's possible that something great could have emerged. Unfortunately, local aspirations withered once Wolseley's troops arrived. The community split along ethnic and religious lines. Garrison theatre replaced indigenous theatre.

The settlement had a second handicap: the population was too small and too far from other centres for its theatre to spread quickly. The railroad was more than a decade away. America was not interested in importing culture, and the rest of Canada held the local population in contempt. Britain believed itself to be the fountain of all good things, a feeling shared in Canada, and increasingly, as time went on, in Manitoba.

4

Post-Confederation Manitoba:
Boom to Bust and Back Again

> "I have had a most successful meeting at Winnipeg. Fancy 20 years ago there were only a few mud huts—tents: and last night a magnificent audience of men in evening dress & ladies half out of it, filled a fine opera house, and we took $1,150 at the door.... Winnipeg has a wonderful future before it. At the back of the town there is a large wheat field 980 miles long and 230 broad.... I called the town 'Great Britain's Breadspot'; at which they purred. They are furiously British and a visit to them is most exhilarating."
>
> –Winston Churchill, in a letter to his mother, 1901

All was not gloom in Manitoba after the conquest, however. The new settlers brought with them a sense of optimism and enterprise. Everyone knew a railroad was coming, and with it prosperity.

For the first ten years after Confederation, many people made fortunes. Shultz received thousands in "Rebellion losses." Donald Smith profited handsomely from the land transfer from the HBC to Canada, and negotiated title to Silver Heights. Land prices shot up. Greed, of course, produced many unwanted effects.

People who sense a quick fortune are seldom patient. Greed often brings out the worst in people, and Manitoba is no exception. In 1873 a mob tarred and feathered Dr. C.N. Bird, the Speaker of the Manitoba legislature. The perpetrators were never identified. (The proposed terms of incorporation for the city of Winnipeg angered many leading businessmen, who feared that the proposed taxation measures would place too heavy a burden on them. A watered-down version passed in 1874.) On another occasion, the Attorney General had to use his revolver to defend himself from an angry mob.

Later a mob burned Lieutenant-Governor Archibald in effigy. During the first national election, in 1872, riots broke out. Poll boxes were burglarized, the police chief was wounded, and the militia had to restore order. The insurrection of 1869–70 was tame in comparison. How ironic that the stated purpose of the Wolseley expedition was to "restore order" to the settlement.

In 1874, Winnipeg elected F.E. Cornish as its first mayor. The electorate, numbering 308, mysteriously cast 562 votes for him. Later the same year an angry crowd gathered, demanding to know why the city awarded the sewer contract to the highest bidder. The first police chief, John S. Ingram, found himself on the wrong side of the first crime crackdown. In July 1875, his two constables caught him in a raid at a brothel. He paid an $8 fine and resigned the next week.

Speculators grabbed choice land and left it undeveloped, leaving farm development scattered, and forcing many to settle on substandard land. For a while it looked as if the railway would go through Selkirk, as surveyors recommended. Instead, Winnipeg's promise to build a bridge and exempt the railway from municipal taxes in perpetuity changed the plan, preserving Winnipeg as a commercial centre (and its real estate values for speculators).

People who paid between 20 and 75 cents an acre for land early in the decade were by 1879 demanding $3 to $10. In 1882, John Taylor bought 38 acres in St. John at $1200 per acre. Similar land price booms took place in Emerson, Dominion City, Crystal City, and other emerging communities.

The point of this catalogue of misdemeanours is to show that the optimism of the times came more from people who could manipulate the system to their benefit than it did from a widespread civic pride in accomplishment. Winnipeg in the late 19th century was not so much a place where people thought anything was possible as it was a place where people with influence could make anything happen (or prevent it).

Nor was every new arrival a scoundrel. Adams Archibald, the first Lieutenant-Governor, was a man of extraordinary tact, ability, and character. He deserves a much more honoured place in Manitoba history than that accorded to him. His determination to be fair to all sides ensured that the transfer to the new order occurred with minimal bloodshed. (It also resulted in a shortened term of office when he accepted help from a Métis force, led by Riel, to help defend the province from an anticipated Fenian raid.)

Countless anonymous people arrived, settled, went to church, raised their children and died, leaving the province at least minutely better as a result of their efforts. These quiet heroes built the roads, bridges, schools and hospitals. They tilled the fields, sang in church choirs, and took meals to the sick and the elderly. W. L. Morton says in *Manitoba—A History*: "The provincial society which had taken form in Manitoba by 1887 had in fact little time for arts and letters; it was preoccupied with its own growth and its own urgent future." As we shall see, music and theatre played a larger part in society than Morton estimated.

Money flowed freely, and people wanted diversions. Soon the city boasted larger (but still very dangerous) performance spaces. Splendid homes sprang up. In 1876 the Winnipeg Literary and Dramatic club formed. (Sadly, as with many such organizations, the spark died when its founders, Mr. and Mrs. Brokovski, returned East.) The University of Manitoba started turning out graduates. Occasionally local scripts made the stage.

In 1870, Winnipeg had 276 inhabitants. By 1880, the total was 8,000. Saloons outnumbered churches. A recent arrival, Captain Goodridge, called Main Street "the roughest and rudest of its size and influence in the world." Churches across Canada prayed for Winnipeg and Barrie, acknowledged as the two most wicked places in the Dominion. Eugene Benson and L.W. Connoly report in *English Canadian Theatre* that the Reverend J.B. Silcox had a sermon published in the *Winnipeg Daily Times*, February 19, 1883. He said theatre "has sinned against morality and decency" that "the devil and hell had been let loose." "Within the last few years," the sermon says, "there were scenes on the boards that would cause even the Sodomites to blush and stop their ears for shame." Silcox probably directed his diatribe at the so-called variety theatres, establishments that used "theatre" as a way to attract patrons into their bars. Today's rough equivalent would be bars that offer strippers at noon with reduced meal prices. The slang term for this modern-day attraction is "dinner theatre." Regardless of Silcox's specific target, all theatres would have felt the effect of his scorn.

Not everyone was a sinner, however; Captain Goodridge said that the area around what is now Headingly had "a very distinctive group…including graduates of English universities; and people of sufficient means to live the life of the English country gentleman."

Rapid expansion put a severe load on the provincial treasury, and in 1881 Manitoba's boundaries expanded east and west to its present borders, and north to the 53rd parallel.

For a while, it seemed as if the bubble would last forever. Then, in 1882, the floods came. Land that was "worth" more than it is today was suddenly under water. The bubble burst. Thousands, many small-timers, faced financial ruin. For three years drought and early frosts ruined crops. People who a few years earlier thought themselves destined to be millionaires struggled just to make a living.

Hard living conditions and robber baron railway practices brought the farming population to near revolt. In *My Dear Maggie,* William Wallace tells his sister a revolt is imminent, but a few months later, he and his neighbours forgot their anger in patriotic fervour caused by the 1885 rebellion. The rebellion, while disastrous for Riel and the Métis, made a fortune for profiteers, saved the CPR and made the railway a unifying metaphor for Canada.

Unfortunately, the 1885 rebellion did not bring prosperity to a depressed province. The rapid expansion brought about by land and railway speculation did not result in the infrastructure the fledgling province needed. Choice land still lay dormant, diluting the tax base and placing a burden on school divisions. Monopolistic freight rates hampered agricultural and business development. The flood of British-born and Canadian immigration became a trickle.

In 1887, the provincial government under John Norquay fell. This is a turning point in Manitoba history. As Morton says, "The fall of Norquay's government...ended completely the old Red River era in Manitoba politics." Norquay, a man of outstanding character and ability, was Manitoba's first (and thus far the only) premier of mixed European and First Nations ancestry. He fought to keep party politics out of the legislature and struggled to maintain the established dual representation of French- and English-speaking communities.

By 1887 immigration had made this position untenable. In the ensuing election, the old order elected five members, and the new 35. It "marked the triumph of Ontario over Quebec in Manitoba." As Morton says, "Manitoba was to be predominantly a new, western Ontario." It would be British in outlook, Protestant in religion, and distrustful of anyone who was not.

This is not to say that the only arrivals to Manitoba at this time were English-speaking Victorians. Two waves of immigrants were to make a lasting impression on the province and contribute some of its most exemplary citizens.

Natural disaster at home created a New Iceland on the west shore of Lake Winnipeg, and persecution brought thousands of Mennonites from the steppes of Europe to create Manitoba's grain belt. The Mennonites brought with them the knowledge of how to convert the Prairies into Canada's bread basket, and the Icelanders opened up the Interlake and brought progressive ideas.

These two groups did not integrate quickly into Manitoba's cultural fabric, however. For a while, the stretch of land the Icelanders settled was the self-governing Republic of New Iceland. Religion, language, and cultural intolerance (and the new settlers' spirit of independence) kept these people (and others) out of the mainstream for a long time.

The period between the land boom collapse of 1882 and 1896 was quiet. The province slowly recovered from its growing pains and established the infrastructure it needed to sustain its population. Part of this time of social recovery was a natural result of expansion, and part was due to a world-wide depression.

The survey of world theatre history presented earlier suggests that this might have been a time to expect a vibrant theatre to emerge. The population had endured a period of turmoil, a new consciousness had emerged, and the province had assumed a state of maturity.

Two factors prevented this. One was the provincial attitude that prevailed at the time. Culture and artistic expression did not come from the colonies; the Empire sent it to them. A second factor was that artistic life, and specifically the world of letters, had not kept pace. Morton says of this period, "There was no equal to Ross' or Hargrave's historical writing...that had the literary charm and factual content of their work."

Theatre, of course, continued, and Winnipeg even saw original scripts: in 1880 a touring company performed local playwright Frank I. Clarke's *Hymen's Harvest*. In 1885 the Princess Theatre hosted two plays by Captain George Broughall about his experiences in the 1885 Northwest Rebellion. The first of these was *The 90th on Active Service* and the second was *The Tearful And Tragical Tale Of The Tricky Troubadour.* These plays do not seem to have had the "legs" to make it in other centres, perhaps for the reasons explained above.

Theatre of a sort enjoyed a brief period of prosperity as a result of the land bubble bursting. Carol Budnick describes the brief and colourful history of "variety theatre."[13] This was a kind of rough-and-tumble vaudeville designed to entertain the many single young men attracted to the burgeoning city. Six houses bloomed and withered almost as quickly as they appeared, some after only a few months: the Britannia Music Hall, housed in the Whelan House Hotel; the Board of Trade Varieties, part of the hotel bearing the same name; the Athletic Academy, the Théâtre Comique, the Royal Theatre, and the Victoria Theatre. The variety theatres all had names that lent an air of refinement. The Royal, besides its regal connotations, recalled an earlier theatre building. Two others assumed regal names, one used French, and the other borrowed its name from the hotel that housed it. It appears that the city fathers did not (officially, at least) support the idea, and the theatres aroused resentment from the beginning.

As the real estate boom petered out, Winnipeg's drinking establishments found themselves overrepresented on the city's commercial landscape. Variety theatres, like strippers, wet T-shirt competitions and video lottery terminals a century later, offered a way to attract a profitable level of business to a slumping drinking industry. Since men outnumbered women by a factor of almost 1.4 to one in 1881 Winnipeg, these theatres also offered their patrons the opportunity to "socialize" with the opposite sex. The theatres would have a "wine room" or "green room," where patrons could meet performers, who in turn would earn a 20 percent commission on wine sales. These theatres existed alongside legitimate theatres such as the Princess.

Even with the increased sales the variety shows produced, the concept does not seem to have created large profit margins. The Athletic Academy closed after a few months in business in 1882, when one partner left town with the evening's receipts.

No enterprise likes to sacrifice an evening's profits to crime, but a healthy business can survive it (unless, of course, the person who made off with the receipts had been helping himself to an unfair share all along). Clearly the entertainment in itself was not a big enough draw to be self-sustaining. The prices were low: the standard ticket price was 25 cents for the pit and 50 cents for better seating (and social privileges). The Britannia charged no admission fee, relying on liquor sales alone to make the venture work. Dan Rogers, the proprietor of the Royal Theatre, closed it after a little more than three months when he could not obtain a liquor licence. This theatre represented a major investment, since Rogers had converted the old court house at 494–500 Main Street into a 600-seat theatre with a gallery and private boxes.

The province introduced liquor licenses in part to limit the proliferation of variety houses, which the city viewed as a source of bad publicity that would restrict immigration and investment. The proprietors themselves scarcely viewed their offerings as high art. The Royal Theatre advertised its March 1884 show with the disclaimer, "No tiresome Dramas, no time killing first parts." Most reviewers ignored their programs. According to Budnick, only *Winnipeg Siftings* and the *Winnipeg Daily Times* seemed sympathetic in their reviews. Although leading citizens often attended, reviewers did not mention them by name for fear of causing embarrassment.

The editor of the *Manitoba Free Press,* C.F. Luxton, urged Winnipeggers to take the law into their own hands if the authorities refused to rid the community of what he considered to be a major corrupter of youth. The Théâtre Comique seems to hold the dubious honour of being the most lax of the theatres. A wide spectrum of forces joined the battle to close the variety theatres. Besides the obvious ones such as clergy and temperance groups, the hotel and saloon owners asked Council to suppress the theatres. *Winnipeg Siftings* pointed out that half of the city's aldermen were directly involved in the liquor trade, and complaints from major customers would probably have found a sympathetic ear.

Stewart Mulvey proposed the first city bylaw aimed at the variety theatres. Besides banning wine rooms and green rooms where patrons could meet performers and share a drink, he sought to establish standards of decency. That clause gives some clues as to what might have taken place at these theatres (or what the alderman thought people would believe took place, and would feel sufficiently shocked about to support the bylaw). It banned people less than seven years of age from indecent exposure of their bodies, or to "make any signs or overtures suggestive of lewd, lascivious, of licentious conduct, or to an invitation to the commission of such acts." This behaviour was proscribed for both women and men in women's clothes, which indicates either that drag acts were sometimes part of the entertainment, or that the alderman was trying to cover all eventualities. One alderman objected that the legitimate theatre in town, the Princess, would not be allowed to perform Shakespeare under those conditions.

The bill received third reading in May of 1884, but by then the bailiff had seized Richard Farrell's Théâtre Comique, and Dan Rogers had closed the Royal. The city therefore had no one to prosecute, but Rogers soon tested its patience. Laxity in liquor law enforcement encouraged Rogers to open the Victoria in November 1884 at the former Standard Opera house at 630 Main Street. One might ask why the Standard Opera House, a legitimate theatre, would be available to Rogers for his Victoria Theatre.

The answer tells a good deal about the effect that the variety theatres had on public attitudes to the theatre. Richard Farrell had earlier launched the Théâtre Comique, the most notorious variety theatre. His motives for operating the theatre must have been alloyed by a love for something other than a quick profit, because when the new liquor laws came on the horizon, he chose to open the Opera House instead of a mere saloon. The house had a capacity of 1,100, greater than that of the present-day Manitoba Theatre Centre. He planned to hire a resident stock company. It opened on April 30, 1884, with a production of *The Streets of New York*. His advertising strove to create the impression that he had turned a new leaf: he banned smoking and drinking, and said it was a "strictly family resort where nothing but legitimate attractions will be produced." As the saying goes, people stayed away in droves, and the theatre closed after three weeks. By November, therefore, when Rogers was casting about for a new venue, the Standard Opera House was vacant.

The Board of Trade Hotel opened its theatre in December of 1884. The two surviving variety theatres, the Board of Trade and the Théâtre Comique, found themselves facing charges in January of 1885. The theatres got off on a technicality: charges had been pressed before the law was signed and sealed, and a spirited defence got the charges dismissed.

Council minted a new by-law, and Rogers' theatre eventually sank beneath the weight of over 100 charges. Winnipeg's first theatre boom ended. Only the Princess, a legitimate theatre from the beginning, survived.

Publications promoting Winnipeg as a wholesome and profitable place to set up a home or a business could now tout the Princess as an example of refined culture. They could also boast that Winnipeg no longer had that disreputable cousin, the variety theatre, in its midst. As we shall see, though, theatre retained its unsavoury reputation for a while after the variety houses left town.

This fallow period in Manitoba's economic and cultural history contains one more noteworthy event: the Manitoba Schools Question, which lasted from 1889 until the Compromise of 1897. Legislation that removed French from schools, the legislature and the courts provoked strong opposition, international attention, and the end of the Conservative government in Ottawa. It further marginalized the French-speaking population that had seen its numbers swamped by the influx of Ontario and British immigration.

The furor that accompanied the Manitoba Schools Question had the unforeseen side effect of making the area famous at a time when crops (and prices) were improving, and freight rates were declining. Long-standing but largely futile efforts to attract immigrants began to pay off, eventually resulting in a flood of new arrivals. They fueled a new economic boom that was to last until just before the First World War.

One of the great mass migrations in human history began. People flooded to the Canadian West from Ukraine, the American West, and all points in between. In ten years Manitoba's population rose from 150,000 to 350,000.

Unlike the previous boom, this one sustained itself, and the province's character changed once more. To the predominantly Anglo population was added a mixture of other European cultures. Only racist immigration laws stopped the mixture from becoming even more exotic. It is estimated that three Chinese railway workers died for every kilometre of track laid through the mountains. A sacrifice of this order merits some consideration, if not gratitude, but instead a $500 head tax all but prevented Asian immigration.

Like the previous boom, the groups of new arrivals included many people with artistic ability and ambitions. Unfortunately, the theatre seen in Manitoba at this time, like the new settlers, came from "away."

5

Manitoba Theatre's "Golden Age": The Touring Companies

"The cabs driving up and disgorging their passengers. A man with his beard turned white as Santa Claus's with hoar frost. A dowager teetering across the perilous passage from curb to door, her chiffon scarf streaming out stiffly horizontal, her pearl dog-collar cold as ice cubes about her neck. And all the people coming along the street. The people pushing and staggering against the gale with their heads lowered and twisted, trying to avoid the pellets of snow, fine, dry, and sharp as sand, that the wind whirled into funnels and flung stinging across their faces. They came in with their brows and lashes white with rime, their cheeks pinched and pitted from the cold, and their lips so rigid from it that they could hardly speak until they got into the warm foyer.

"Why on earth, you might wonder, would anyone on a night like this move a step outside his warm house? And yet it was just such a night that made you realize the magic of the theatre, for if you watched the crowd you could see that it wasn't the heat of the foyer alone that brought mobility and smiles into their cold-stiffened faces. They had that special look—expectant, almost reckless—of travelers bound for adventure."

—from Ruth Harvey's *Curtain Time*,
the story of her parents' theatre, the Walker

Manitoba's second population and economic boom coincided with the great age of the touring stars, straddling the end of the 19th century and the beginning of the 20th. This period in theatre history saw celebrated actors leave their native stages to tour the world with a small company of supporting actors, sometimes supplemented by the best local talent in the places they visited. Sarah Bernhardt of France,

Henry Irving and Ellen Terry of Britain, the Booths from the United States and others all crisscrossed the globe to admiring audiences. When Winnipeg became a thriving metropolis with facilities of sufficient size and rail connections of sufficient comfort, it became a stop on the touring circuit.

Of course, history is not as cut and dried as all that. Touring to North America was common as early as the 18th century. Some adventurous touring companies even strayed to Manitoba as early as the 1870s. A *Manitoba Free Press* report states that Cool Burgess was the first professional actor to visit Winnipeg, on July 24, 1877. He performed a three-night run at the City Hall Theatre. Companies visited Winnipeg sporadically from then on, with varying degrees of success.

Early Touring Companies

J.J. Hargrave tells the story of an itinerant magician and ventriloquist named Professor Sands, who may have been the first such touring performer to come to Red River. In 1868 he leased the Courtroom for three nights, and impressed his audiences profoundly, especially when he appeared to catch a ball fired from the formidable James McKay's pistol in his teeth. Hargrave goes on to report that "a large portion of the time occupied by the entertainment was spent in listening to the cautions of the professor against the practice of gambling, especially in unknown society.... His remarks of this nature were illustrated by very clever tricks with cards, and magic box and ball, showing how delusive is the evidence of eyesight when imposed upon by expert adepts in legerdemain." He also gave classes, and told all assembled that "his sole object in the present trip was to recruit his health and raise funds for the completion of a little cottage in St. Cloud where he hoped to end his life."

Sadly, the settlers of Red River later learned that the professor, in a scene worthy of Saki or Mark Twain, had ignored his own advice, and instead had invested part of the profits from his trip in strong rum, and lost the rest by gambling with the soldiers at Fort Abercrombie and Fort Totten.

Hargrave's claim on behalf of Professor Sands as the first touring entertainment seems contradicted by a fragmentary newspaper account. The *Nor'Wester* of January 19, 1868, tantalizingly reports the second performance of the Montana Minstrels since the last issue. (Extant earlier editions do not report on the first.)

Ontario's Bob Marks traveled with a magician to Winnipeg and other spots on the Red River in 1870. He eventually formed a touring theatre company with his four brothers (The Marks Brothers), playing mostly melodramas and comedies to smaller towns in the touring circuit. The Marks Brothers knew what their audiences liked and wanted, and delivered the goods well enough to entertain rural audiences for several decades, folding in the early 1920s.

Speaking of magic acts, E. Ross Stewart also mentions magic acts in his *The History of Prairie Theatre.* The first reference is in Donald Ross' correspondence of 1833. He describes a magician called Magnus McGregor, who also juggled. And according to William Healy's 1923 *Women of Red River,* the always-enterprising Andrew McDermot charged one buffalo sinew for people to see a buffalo hunter called Desjarlais perform magic in the 1840s. The performance space was McDermot's kitchen.

The hardships the first circus to reach Red River experienced illustrate the rigours of the road for early touring companies. On June 20, 1878, Dr. Hagar's Paris Circus arrived by steamboat. The troupe had been touring the northern states, amusing lumberjacks and railway workers with acrobats, clowns, and a sideshow. The circus received favourable press, and things went well until June 28, when Dick Oglesby's "Troubadours, Bell-ringers, and Comic Concert Company" arrived and rented the city hall theatre across the street. Competition for the entertainment dollar was fierce, and the circus company performers' plight was worsened by the circus' manager, Dr. Hagar's son-in-law Dwyer, whose sticky fingers often visited the till.

Two prominent Winnipeg businessmen advanced the company enough money to pay some bills and allow the performers their first pay since the tour began. In gratitude, they offered the city a benefit performance, with the proceeds to go towards the Winnipeg General Hospital. The donation received was so small the hospital returned it to the troupe, believing that the circus needed it more than they did.

By this time the company was in really bad shape. No one would extend the circus credit, so a group of citizens mounted a concert for *their* benefit. The hope was to raise enough money to pay their passage out of town, and thus avoid having them on the city's charity rolls. A large sum was raised, but Dwyer absconded with it, leaving behind unpaid bills, a wife and children.

Their luck seemed to change when two liverymen in Fargo advanced them the funds to travel to Grand Forks. The flatboat journey was arduous. They ate complimentary salt fish and crackers, and drank water from the Red. Houses in Grand Forks were so good they returned to Winnipeg, confident they could relieve their debts. Unfortunately, this was not to be. Other creditors Dwyer had abandoned arrived, leaving them destitute again.

Once again the city came to their aid with a concert, this time raising only enough money to give the 15 remaining performers four dollars each. Dr. Hagar sold what he could to settle accounts. Some performers arranged to work their way home, staying only long enough so that the young contortionist, who was seriously ill, could recover enough to travel. A few stayed in Manitoba. One became a prominent citizen in Emerson. The clown, Dick Burden, became one of Winnipeg's most memorable characters, famous for practical jokes and kindness to children. He operated Winnipeg's first Turkish bath, at the Clarendon Hotel.

Of course, touring companies need somewhere to play, and ideally somewhere nearby to go to for the next gig. Brandon and Portage la Prairie had both become prosperous, smaller versions of Winnipeg's success, and farther west, Calgary, Edmonton, Lethbridge, Regina and Saskatoon had sprung up. An American company could leapfrog up to Winnipeg from Fargo and Grand Forks, tour the Prairie cities, and then head south into Montana. Companies from Europe could take the train to Fort William and Port Arthur (later to become Thunder Bay), Rat Portage (later Kenora) and then Winnipeg and beyond.

Once in Winnipeg, traveling companies had a variety of venues. Besides City Hall, with its seating capacity of 500, there was the Red River Hall. After it closed in 1870, a few short-lived theatre buildings took its place. In the 1870s, a number of houses, small by today's standards, but with capacity almost equal to Winnipeg's population at the time, opened. Garrison theatres used the Theatre Royal and a renovated boathouse at Lower Fort Garry. The Ontario Rifles performance at Theatre Royal in 1870 was the first performance that had an admission charge. Unfortunately the Theatre did not survive the Rifles' departure in 1871. Eventually it became a livery stable.

Local amateurs opened the Manitoba Hall on January 3, 1872. This hall later took on the more grandiloquent name The Opera House. The first performance there was the Manitoba Variety Club's *Box and Cox* and a melodrama called *Robert Macair.*

In 1875 a theatre group took over a rundown building that had been a Mennonite hotel, and revived the Theatre Royal name. Because it had a mud floor, they advertised it as fireproof. After opening with a temperance play, the group expanded its repertoire. They became more ambitious artistically, doing such plays as Boucicault's *The Colleen Bawn*.

The Winnipeg Literary and Dramatic Society opened the Dufferin Theatre in 1877. When Cool Burgess came to Winnipeg in 1877, therefore, it was to a place where theatre had become part of daily life.

The Pembina Branch rail line opened in December of 1878. A rail connection meant that touring companies could comfortably travel to Winnipeg, in a fraction of the time that other means of transportation would require. Touring to Winnipeg therefore became economical.

Carol Budnick writes in *Theatre on the Frontier: Winnipeg in the 1880s,* an article in the spring 1983 edition of *Theatre History in Canada*, that two businessmen built the Princess to capitalize on the touring companies that started to make their way west with the railroad. D. Cowan and T. B. Rutledge put up the 1,376-seat theatre in a few months over the winter of 1882–83. It looked grand on the outside, but, as Budnick says, the building "was not much better than most frontier theatres, which most often tended to be flimsy wooden firetraps."

The seating capacity, more than double that of City Hall, meant that touring companies who previously found Winnipeg uneconomical could now consider returning. Initial visits by Frederic Bryton and E. A. McDowall had paid off well, but in 1882 both lost money playing in a converted skating rink called the Musical Pavilion. Later in the year, lack of a suitable building caused Bryton to cancel ambitious plans to establish a resident stock company and bring touring companies.

When the Princess opened in 1883, the owners took pains to create an aura of respectability about it. At the formal opening, John Bell, an MLA, read a poem that expressed the wish for the theatre to stay on the "pleasant path of virtue's ways." The Hess Opera Company opened the Princess Opera House as part of their western tour. This was not to be another variety theatre, no sir. One week later, Thomas Keene appeared to present great scenes from Shakespeare.

The local papers strove to educate audiences in proper decorum, advising men to keep their hats off, and not to dangle their feet over the balcony. Patrons were not to arrive late from intermission, or to smoke during a performance, a practice both rude and dangerous.

Prostitutes, however, posed a thorny problem. The owners seemed reluctant to ban them altogether, either through a sense of egalitarianism, the need for their cash at the box office, or to serve their patrons' needs. Various solutions to this problem came and went, but the prostitutes, it seems, stayed.

The Princess soon became successful enough to attract investment interest. In the summer of 1883 a consortium called the Northwest Opera House Company announced plans to take over the Princess and set up touring in other Manitoba centres. It offered 200 shares at $500 each to raise the $100,000 needed.

Eventually all members of the consortium but Charles Sharp faded from the scene. He stayed on until 1888, by which time he set up Frank G. Campbell, Bryton's former stage manager, as the star of the resident stock company. The Campbell Company meant that the theatre could stay open most of the time, and when touring companies arrived, the company toured around the populated areas outside Winnipeg.

The company seems to have enjoyed a warm reception, and developed a reputation for good scenic effects. For *The Colleen Bawn* they flooded the Princess stage with 2,000 cubic feet of water.

Broughall's burlesques of the Riel Rebellion took place at the Princess. Unfortunately, it burned down in 1892 during a production of *Uncle Tom's Cabin*, a touring staple of the time.

The Victoria Hall opened in 1882 (later to become the Bijou). A theatre named the Grand opened in 1896, but it burned down the next year.

The Walkers: The Big Time Comes to Winnipeg

When theatre impresario C.P. Walker came to Winnipeg in 1897 to scope out the city, it was at the urging of his friend, James J. Hill. Hill promised Walker, "It's going to be another Chicago." At the time Chicago was becoming the booming transportation and processing centre that Carl Sandberg was to celebrate in *Chicago* as a "city with lifted head singing so proud to be alive." The same virile energy seemed to flow through Winnipeg.

In *Curtain Time,* Walker's daughter, Ruth Harvey, describes the first theatre her father leased: "It was a small old-fashioned building that very occasionally housed some entertainment—a lecture, a concert, or an amateur show got up in sheer desperation by the amusement-hungry people of the mushrooming town." Her patronizing tone might annoy today's reader (and would probably have infuriated the local amateurs if they had read it), but it shows that Winnipeg's performing arts scene had a vacuum. Walker saw potential. Like a baker who visits a town that does not have fresh bread, he realized there was money to be made. As Ruth Harvey says, "Winnipeg was full of people who had come from cities where they had gone to plays, to concerts, to the opera." The same was true of other growing cities in the Canadian West.

The Walkers were more than entrepreneurs, though. They were true visionaries. They operated their theatre circuit as much out of a love for the form as for the profits they hoped to make. They did not just open up a theatre, book shows, advertise them, and pocket the receipts. Often they would bring a symphony or other large-scale production to Winnipeg knowing it would cost them money, out of a sense that their audience deserved the experience. They realized that the performing arts would flourish in the Prairies if the right people took the right steps.

The Walkers were the right people. C. P. (Corliss Powers) Walker (1853–1942) was a descendant of New England clergymen and schoolteachers. He arrived in Rochester, Minnesota at an early age, where his father preached and ran an academy for boys. Apprenticed to a printer, Walker soon moved from making up advertisements for theatrical events to booking halls and finally owning them. He proved to be a capable businessman, and soon he had his own circuit, the Red River Valley Theatre Circuit. Ruth Harvey reports that he interlaced his books and ledgers with scraps of poetry and other literary excerpts he liked: a highbrow 19th-century version of the *Chicken Soup for the Soul* date book.

Harriet Walker (née Harriet Anderson) (1865–1943) had been a successful actor and light opera star before marrying. She performed with the Union Square Company, and while on tour met Walker. The contacts she made while performing beside such great stars as Lillian Russell became invaluable when trying to persuade New York companies to perform in what they considered to be a desolate outpost of civilization. (As one reluctant New York tour manager is reputed to have said, "How do you get there? By dogsled? What do they play in? An igloo?) While she performed rarely after marrying, she became a pillar of Winnipeg's cultural scene, directing and teaching amateur performers, reviewing, and being a general theatre patron.

Their first venue in Winnipeg was the rented Bijou theatre. They renovated it and renamed it the Winnipeg Theatre and Opera House, but it soon became inadequate for their ambitions. They wanted to book bigger shows with more technical requirements than the Bijou could handle, and they wanted to bring the best that the theatre world had to offer to their adopted home. To do this required a house big enough to make touring these shows economical.

The golden age hit its peak after C.P. Walker and his wife Harriet opened the Walker Theatre in 1907. Built with the help of architect Howard Colton Stone, at a cost of $330,000, it offered every modern convenience. The design considered actors' needs, because Harriet Walker had been one. The ventilating system was like the one then just recently installed in the Library of Congress. The stage was 70 feet high, and the theatre seated 1,798. Steel trusses held up the balconies and avoided the obscured sightlines that columns would have created. Built in the Edwardian style, it nevertheless used Canadian motifs in its decorations and designs. The opening night production, *Madam Butterfly*, starred a Canadian performer, Florence Easton.

At the opening, the Lieutenant-Governor, Sir Daniel McMillan, said, "I can say of this theatre what cannot be said of any enterprise in this city: that this is the only institution that is in advance of the development and growth of the city. A theatre of which we may be proud and which would be a credit to any city in the world."

Winnipeg During the Golden Age

What was the city Daniel McMillan described like early in the 20th century?

From 1901 to 1911, the population more than tripled, from 42,000 to 136,000. The value of manufacturing increased from $1.7 million in 1881 to approximately $50 million in 1913. The city had become a transportation hub. William E. Curtis wrote in the *Chicago Herald* in 1911: "All roads lead to Winnipeg.... It is destined to become one of the greatest distributing commercial centres of the continent." Sixty million bushels of wheat and a million cattle flowed through Winnipeg each year at the turn of the 20th century. The city's electric streetcars carried two million passengers annually.

By building their theatre in 1907, the Walkers caught the wave at its crest. As then-premier Rodmond Roblin said at the theatre's opening: "It will be a monument not only to the far-sightedness and confidence of Mr. Walker but this theatre, devoted to art and music, is, in the growth of our city, a grand climax of good for the people."

A new legislature also went up during this period, and, like the Walker, it was (and remains) an architectural treasure. Unlike the Walker, a political and legal scandal accompanied the legislature's construction. Historian W.L. Morton writes of the "sordid corruption of Manitoba politics revealed" in the construction of the province's seat of government.

The Conservative government of Rodmond Roblin finally had to resign, and a later inquiry proved corruption, perjury and faulty construction processes. According to Morton, among the discoveries were that "there had been a conspiracy to obtain election funds from 'extras' in the contract…the contractors had been overpaid to the amount of $892,098.10, and that 'large sums' of money had been paid by the contractor to Dr. R.M. Simpson, president of the Provincial Conservative Association." Roblin and three cabinet ministers were arrested on charges of conspiracy to defraud the Crown. A trial ended in a hung jury. (In 1917 Sir Rodmond Roblin was discharged of criminal charges due to ill health. He lived another 20 years.)

On a smaller scale, Winnipeg at this time had adopted a policy of "segregated vice." Prostitutes from other cities flocked to Winnipeg to work in the 100 brothels that existed in 1909. (Beginning in the 1880s, theatres obliged their patrons' fragile sensibilities by offering prostitutes segregated seating areas.)

The immigration flood continued until the First World War, with the Prairies receiving people from all over Europe, particularly Eastern Europe. In 1911, Winnipeg had the highest foreign-born population of any city in Canada, and the most Germans and Jews. Many of these new Canadians were accustomed to seeing theatre and other performing arts at home, and the Walkers often brought performers from Europe to capitalize on this.

Unfortunately, few of these "foreign" settlers turned their talents towards the theatre. Ruth Harvey writes about an exceptionally talented seamstress whom her mother wanted to help become established as a costumer. Her family had other ideas, though, and married her off at seventeen in exchange for a quarter-section of land.

Winnipeg was not just a haven for shifty businessmen, prostitutes and downtrodden immigrants. In 1913 the poet Rupert Brooke visited the city, and expressed a hope that the Walkers and others would have been sure to echo:

"[O]ne can't help finding a tiny hope that Winnipeg, that city of buildings...may yet come to something... That hope [of material success] is sure to be fulfilled. But the other timid prayer, that something different, something more worth having, may come out of Winnipeg exists..."

(Brooke was not the only literary figure to visit and speak in Winnipeg. Mark Twain, Rudyard Kipling, and Winston Churchill also stopped by in these bustling times.)

Other observers concurred with Brooke's assessment of Winnipeg's artistic potential. In the May, 1908 issue of *The Canadian Magazine*, Frederick Robson contrasts the lack of interest in Shakespeare's works among educated Ontarians, "while they are taken up with eagerness by the farmers of the West."

Winnipeg's reputation for radical politics also owes a debt to the Walker Theatre. In 1912 the famous suffragette, Nellie McClung, debated Premier Roblin on women's suffrage at the theatre. In 1914, McClung played a female version of Roblin in *The Women's Parliament,* a satirical farce in which women debated the question of allowing men to vote, throwing some of Roblin's paternalistic lines back at him to great effect. Harriet Walker and her daughter Ruth also performed. The performance earned a profit, which went to the Political Equality League, an organization devoted to advancing women's issues. *The Women's Parliament* is perhaps the most famous and influential play ever to be written and performed in Winnipeg. Many historians list this event as a turning point in the suffrage movement.

McClung was not the only member of this movement with a flair for drama. A colleague, Lillian Beynon Thomas, was an accomplished playwright who moved to New York, eventually returning to Winnipeg in 1923.

While Winnipeg and the surrounding prairies took on a more cosmopolitan population during the boom years before the war, the power base did not shift at all. A glance at the names involved in the Legislature Scandal (accused and accusers) proves this: Roblin, Horwood, Kelly, Coldwell, MacDonald, Hudson, Johnston, Norris, Howden, Simpson, Montague. People who reached the highest levels were almost inevitably of British ancestry. Immigrants were welcomed as consumers and low-level employees, but not into the parlours of the best houses. While Nellie McClung worked tirelessly for women's rights, she meant only *some* women. During World War I she proposed that only the wives and sisters of soldiers of British heritage be allowed to vote. (Her rationale was that allowing British women the vote would dilute the "alien" vote.)

Fear of enemy aliens was almost hysterical at this time. McClung, for all her energy in defending women's rights, nevertheless supported the War Measures Act. Under this act, 8,579 people who had emigrated to Canada from parts of the Austro-Hungarian Empire were interned in concentration camps. Another 80,000 had to register as "Enemy Aliens" and report to authorities on a regular basis. They lost the right to vote from 1917 until 1923. The vast majority of these people were Ukrainians who had fled this empire.

Although this was harsh treatment of people who had come to Canada with honourable intentions, it benefited Canadians and Canadian industry. The internees provided a low-cost labour force that developed Banff National Park, steel mills in Ontario and Nova Scotia, mines in British Columbia, Ontario, and Nova Scotia, and logging in northern Ontario and Quebec. The program proved so profitable that it continued for two years after the armistice.

(As a side note, the camps found a use during World War II, when the War Measures Act stripped 22,000 Japanese-Canadians of their rights. The Canadian government apologized to Japanese-Canadians and paid compensation in 1988. No apology or compensation has yet been offered to World War I detainees.)

The Winnipeg Falcons show how thorough British xenophobia was at that time. Winnipeg early became a hockey hotbed, winning the Stanley Cup twice around the turn of the 20th century. When a group of young men of Icelandic descent formed a team, however, they discovered that no other existing team would play them or allow them into their league. They had to form their own league of players of Scandinavian descent. Then they had to appeal to the Canadian Amateur Hockey Association for the right to compete against the Winnipeg Hockey League for the Allen Cup, and with it the right to represent Canada in the 1920 Olympic games. Their Olympic gold medal made them national heroes, and the team star, Frank Frederickson, later played in the NHL. We know about the Falcons and Frederickson because they successfully overcame the discrimination that existed. We do not know how many other talented people the attitudes of the day buried in obscurity.

The Manitoba power base saw the British as ideal, and anything else, even if homegrown, as inherently inferior. In a thousand ways, it sought to ensure the British ideal remained Manitoba's defining character. The Métis culture that once dominated Manitoba life had become a trace element. First Nations people were trapped on reserves that could not sustain themselves economically. For over a century (from 1879 until 1986) their children were consigned to genocidal residential schools.

This does not mean that the elites were ashamed of their home turf. Like Torontonians of the 1990s, they sought to prove Winnipeg was a world-class city and saw proof of this in the number of acclaimed stars they could attract here. Buffalo Bill's Wild West show would do as well as opera singer Ernestine Schumann-Heinck to prove this.

It is equally true that the elites saw Manitoba as *their* turf. While from time to time events such as the Legislature Scandal would cause embarrassment and even imprisonment, these events did nothing to alter the essential power structure. Those who questioned or challenged the existing power structure paid a price.

Lewis St. George Stubbs was an idealistic judge. When, in his capacity as a police commissioner, he criticized the uneven application of the prohibition laws, he became very unpopular with the city's power structure. A teetotaler, he criticized his fellow judges for imposing fines when the law clearly called for prison sentences. He claimed that the railway hotels, the Fort Garry and Royal Alexandra, escaped serious punishment, while "second- and third-rate hotels are hardly as lucky." The manager of the Fort Garry sent a lawyer to Stubbs to demand a retraction. Stubbs produced a photograph of a party held at the hotel with beer bottles on every table, and the matter dropped...for a while.

Later Stubbs became embroiled in a controversy over the probate of the will of Alexander MacDonald, a wealthy citizen. Stubbs had reason to believe that the first will forwarded was a fraudulent attempt to thwart the deceased's wishes for the bulk of the estate to go towards a charity in his name. He refused to grant probate and asked the legislature to rule on the validity of an earlier will that lacked the required two signatures.

When the case was removed from his court, Stubbs published a pamphlet called the *MacDonald Will Case* at his own expense, and booked the Walker Theatre for a public meeting, at an agreed fee of

$150. Lawyers representing the estate got wind of this, and offered Walker $250 to keep the theatre dark.

Walker refused to go back on his agreement with Stubbs. On February 13, 1930, Stubbs addressed a sold-out house: "Mr. Walker, apparently, is one of the few men of this city who had anything to do with this case, who had not the wits scared out of him by the two million dollars in issue, backed up by a battery of big-gun lawyers. That is how we came to have the theatre tonight, and that is how Mr. Walker lost $250 easy money."

This would not be the last time the Walkers would make a business decision at odds with the establishment's wishes. Clearly considerations other than money figured into the Walkers' judgment. What is less clear is how their willingness to take a stand in favour of the underdog affected the theatre's declining fortunes.

Over the years, leading performers such as Ethyl Barrymore, Maxine Elliott, Mrs. Campbell and of course Lillian Russell played the Walker, many for return engagements. The local public justified the Walkers' faith. For example, E. Ross Stewart reports in *The History of Prairie Theatre* that one week's gate for John Martin-Harvey's *Oedipus* was $6,090 in Chicago, and $11,500 in Winnipeg. (Martin-Harvey received a knighthood for "his pioneer efforts in the wilds of Western Canada." During one week in Winnipeg, besides performing, he addressed four different groups.)

As mentioned before, the Walkers were not just theatre entrepreneurs. Harriet directed local amateurs and taught at the University of Manitoba. She replied to correspondence from smaller centres asking for advice on plays for their amateur productions. Often she sent books from her personal collection, as well as wigs, safety pins and other items she thought the companies would find useful. Letters containing detailed advice often accompanied these packages. When her copies of plays became too worn out to use, she replaced them with newer ones.

One cannot underestimate her influence on theatre development in western Canada. When people sent her their plays, she responded with detailed criticism, and often sent the more promising ones to local amateur groups or to New York. Ibsen's arrival on the Prairies caused more than Charles Handscomb's famous scornful review of *Ghosts* in the March 10, 1904 *Free Press*. A flurry of new plays also arrived on Harriet's correspondence table. The Prairies apparently had an affinity for Ibsen.

It is instructive to pause here and reflect on the attitude implied in Harriet Walker's treatment of local playwrights. Certainly she encouraged them, and they were lucky to have someone so well versed in the theatre willing to comment intelligently on their work. Her recommendation would have opened doors for them, both among local amateur groups and potentially in New York, the theatre capital of North America.

The highest praise would not result in a professional performance at the Walker, though. For the Walkers, plays came from somewhere else. As they saw it, their audience wanted to see either the classics they had read in school or grown up seeing in their native land, or the latest hits from the east coast or abroad. Second, the star actors who came to Winnipeg brought with them plays that had become their vehicles. They chose from their repertoire plays that past popular and critical acclaim proved to show them at advantage. Touring was a cash cow, and performing an unknown script would have exposed them to a risk they did not want to take.

Also, one must remember that the Walkers were not Manitoba born. They were both Americans, who, although they became proud Winnipeg boosters, did not come to Winnipeg until well into their adult years. One cannot blame them, therefore, for not recognizing or searching for a prairie dramatic voice.

The only way for a local play to reach an audience in Winnipeg, therefore, was for local actors to perform it. Local actors gained access to Winnipeg's main stage in one of two ways: either in an amateur production, or (as once happened to Ruth Harvey) as a bit player in a professional production, usually in a juvenile role.

For a local play to have a professional debut here would have required it to play here with imported actors supplemented with the best amateurs Winnipeg had to offer. It would not have been cheap. Then it would have had to tour to recoup the development costs. The conservative money at the time thought that bringing the world's best to Winnipeg was a dodgy venture; reversing the flow would have seemed like absolute madness. This position, although doubtless irksome to aspiring playwrights and stultifying to theatre development in Winnipeg and elsewhere, nevertheless had some justification. Why would an audience accustomed to seeing name stars performing famous plays turn out in numbers large enough to defray travel costs if the bill was an unknown play with unknown actors? The answer probably is that they wouldn't, but they would turn out in great numbers to see local plays of a different sort, as we shall see.

It is unfortunate that the outpouring of interest in theatre and other performing arts did not produce a professional theatre with a local outlook. While in retrospect the time seems to have been ripe, the community at large obviously did not see the potential. It seemed to be perfectly happy with the theatre opportunities offered at the time. Perhaps a dramatic genius might have found an audience if the climate for playwrights had been better; we shall never know. The Walkers, who were the dominant figures in the theatre scene, did not make finding a local dramatic voice a priority, and that probably sealed the fate of local playwrights. The Walkers' cosmopolitan outlook, while it might have stultified local voices, nevertheless made a huge contribution towards Manitoba's performing arts heritage.

Other Touring Companies and Houses: "Something for Everyone"

The Walker was not the only big theatre house in town during this period. The 1907 *Blue Book*, published by *Henderson's Directory*, lists the Winnipeg Theatre (home to the Winnipeg Stock Company), the Bijou Theatre, and Manitoba Hall. The Pantages (opened 1914) and Orpheum also played to the public. By the 1920s, there were six houses hosting professional theatre. In contrast, today, if you count occasional productions at the Centennial Concert Hall, the Walker, and summer productions at Rainbow Stage, Winnipeg has eight professional theatre venues, while the city's population has doubled.

The enduring landmark of this period (besides the Walker) is the Pantages Theatre. It still hosts theatre and other performances. When it opened, it was part of a chain that Greek-born American Alexander Pantages founded across North America, using profits he made in the Klondike gold rush.

In many ways, Pantages was the opposite of C.P. Walker. Although he could speak six languages (his friends say he spoke English as badly as the rest) he couldn't read much more than his name. What he lacked in formal education he more than made up for in business sense and power of observation.

He arrived in the Klondike nearly penniless, but with knowledge of the world gained through associating with the rougher elements of society throughout his life. He soon learned that, while it was possible to make a fortune extracting gold from the ground, it was faster, safer, and more profitable to extract gold from sourdoughs.

Working as a bartender, he learned that a bar that offered entertainment attracted more customers than a bar that just offered booze. He persuaded the owner to set up as a theatre, and soon learned the tricks of the trade.

He started his entertainment empire in the Nome gold rush, buying out a theatre in financial trouble and charging $12.50 a head for admission. Since he lacked the capital to buy the theatre himself, he persuaded the entertainers to lend him the money. Although he prospered, his backers had to wait for their investment to pay off. One of the people he bilked was Klondike Kate.

By 1902 the gold rush had petered out, so he moved to Seattle. He set up a small theatre with some movies and a projector, and hired a vaudeville act. The admission was ten cents, and he moved the audience through the set program as quickly as he could, running the silent films so fast the patrons could scarcely make out what was happening. Unlike Walker, he had no ambition to elevate his audiences' sensibilities. "Give them what they want," or the slightly less mercenary "something for everyone" would have been his mission statement. The lowest common denominator was where the money was.

Vaudeville was a cutthroat business, but Pantages' life experience and flexible scruples served him well. He flourished. His main rival, the Considine circuit, often met his acts at the train station with bribes to entice them to perform in their houses. Pantages would send delivery vans instead, and hold the company's props and costumes until they agreed to play at his house.

His skill in sharp business practice met its match in Winnipeg, however. His practice was to set up his buildings on the city's main street, but Winnipeg bamboozled him into buying a lot on Market Street, one lot off Main.

Pantages discerned the impending death of vaudeville (and the 1929 crash) before most others, and sold his chain to Radio Keith Orpheum in 1929 for $24 million. He retired to Los Angeles and his daughter married John Considine Jr., his chief rival's son.

The Pantages was the first reinforced concrete vaudeville house of its size in North America. It became the Playhouse in 1923. Sold for taxes in the 1930s, it became city property and regained its former name, the Pantages.

Other buildings occasionally hosted touring stars. In Sarah Bernhardt's first appearance in Winnipeg in 1906, she performed *Camille* in a rink. During her western tour in 1913, she gave two performances in French. In all she made three western tours, sometimes as part of a vaudeville program. Even at almost seventy years of age, she thrilled audiences.

Canada's Contribution to the Touring Era: Manitoba as Gateway to the West

While touring companies were mainly American and British back then, Canada did have some homegrown professional companies. As mentioned before, the Marks Brothers had a long and happy career in the small centres. Ida van Courtland and her husband Alfred Tavernier formed the Tavernier Dramatic Company. The company sometimes toured as far west as Winnipeg in the late 19th century, touring smaller centres with comedies and melodramas in the Marks Brothers tradition.

Harold Nelson was a little different. He was dedicated to bringing fine theatre to the people. He had acted and taught elocution in Toronto before establishing his first company at Winnipeg's Grand Theatre in 1898. His first attempt failed. When he returned to Toronto, he wrote *The Tribune* drama critic, Charles Wheeler, "What a long, bitter season it was for me, and I am glad it is all over, even if it left me such a poorer man."

Nelson eventually formed a business arrangement with C.P. Walker. He returned to Winnipeg in 1902, and by 1904 Walker was managing Nelson's small company as it toured Shakespeare and other classics throughout the West. Although he ran a shoestring operation, Nelson had a very high reputation. In 1904 Nelson told the *Edmonton Bulletin* that he wanted his theatre to take its "rightful place as a refining and elevating instead of a blunting and degrading influence."

Unfortunately, not enough patrons shared his lofty aims, and by 1906 Walker ended the relationship. By this time Walker was marshaling his resources to build his great theatre building, and he probably needed to maximize his cash flow.

The Nelson Company adhered to the highest standards, both artistically and in their personal conduct. They had a large repertoire of classics, mainly tragedies (something the newspapers of the day sometimes complained about), and introduced melodramas only towards the end. This move was most probably dictated by pressing finances.

From 1902 until his last tour in 1910, Harold Nelson did much to raise the standard of performance seen in the Prairies, and was a living example to Canadians that top rank professional theatre did not have to come from outside their borders. Unfortunately, history does not give Nelson the recognition he deserves. Standard general Manitoba history references do not mention him, despite his heroic efforts to advance theatre in the Prairies.

Some Winnipeg artists did use their experience on home stages to launch careers in "the big time." The Winnipeg Kiddies was a vaudeville act that toured North America. Ann Bronaugh left Winnipeg's Permanent Players to become the original Rose in the Broadway hit *Abie's Irish Rose*. Evelyn Morris, as Judith Evelyn, starred on Broadway in *Angel Street* and opposite Jose Ferrer in *The Shrink*. Another Winnipegger might have risen to even greater heights. Charlie Chaplin was in Winnipeg in 1913 when he decided to accept a telegrammed offer to make silent movies. He offered a young reporter named Ted Dafoe the opportunity to tag along, but Dafoe chose to stay in journalism instead.

Winnipeg made other small contributions to theatre lore. Fatty Arbuckle, one of the first big Hollywood stars, started his entertainment career here in 1905, as a bouncer at the Unique Theatre. The 18-year-old also seems to have had janitorial duties and to have slept there. He narrated one-reelers and ad-libbed during pauses. This time on stage seems to have inspired him to greater things, because he left later that year and soon became the star of Paramount Studios.

Jack Benny reports that it was in Winnipeg that he first learned about Stephen Leacock (from Groucho Marx, who called Leacock the funniest man alive).[14] Bob Hope allegedly played his first game of golf here. (When he first came to Winnipeg, it was as a tap-dancer named Leslie Townes Hope.) Deanna Durbin, a major star of 1930s and '40s musicals, left Winnipeg shortly after her birth.

Although touring dominated the theatre scene, this does not mean that theatre lovers were unaware of the local void it created. As the great British actor Sir Henry Irving said to a reporter during a visit early in the 20th century, "Someday you will crown it [Canada] with a national drama; that's what you need next, a Canadian drama." It would be a while coming.

6

Passing the Torch:

The Fall of Touring and the Rise of Amateur Theatre

"Although Canada built splendid theatres, and had audiences eager to fill them, Canadian playwrights, performers and designers were given little scope to exercise their art in their own land."

—From *English Canadian Theatre*
by Eugene Benson and L.W. Conoly,
Oxford University Press, 1987

The touring era effectively ended in Winnipeg in 1936, when the Walkers gave up their theatre for back taxes. As Ruth Harvey writes, touring lasted longer in Winnipeg than elsewhere, because they could bring acts over from Europe when American companies ceased touring.

Touring died due to a number of causes, but probably the most prominent was the surge in movie popularity that accompanied talkies. Movie houses invested a lot of money in building an infrastructure, often buying theatre buildings and converting them to cinemas. Since they viewed vaudeville and other live entertainment as competition, Famous Players banned live performances from all its cinemas. This meant that touring companies had fewer and fewer places to perform, effectively cutting their supply lines.

When touring became uneconomical, no artistic infrastructure remained at the professional level. Some sporadic professional activity remained, but in the main theatre lovers had to rely on amateur companies to satisfy their habit.

The Little Theatre Movement: Making the Very Best of It

This is not to say that amateur theatre did not exist at a high level during the golden age. As we have seen, the Walkers spent a great deal of their personal time supporting amateur theatre. Even before the Walkers, settlers started amateur theatre groups as soon as—and sometimes before—they had established the necessities of life in their community.

Thanks to such stalwarts as Harriet Walker and Lady Tupper, Winnipeg and Manitoba were in better shape than most parts of Canada when touring died. Besides, Winnipeg still had resident professional theatre: the John Holden Players and the Permanent Players.

The Remains of Professional Theatre

The John Holden Players played summer stock in Muskoka, Ontario during the cottage season, and entertained Winnipeg in the winter. This arrangement gave the actors a steady income, and satisfied the needs of two audiences. They were therefore a kind of hybrid of the touring company and the resident professional company. It probably also explains why this was the only professional company in Canada to survive the 1930s.

The actors were from outside Manitoba, although the company sometimes hired other local actors, such as Joe Zuken of the activist New Theatre group. The company included some revered Canadian actors, such as Dora Mavor Moore, William Needles, Robert Christie, Austin Willis, and Jane Mallett.

The John Holden Players used the Dominion Theatre. When the Richardsons rented the building to them, it forced the Winnipeg Little Theatre to move, an event that many people blamed for the company's disappearance from the scene between 1936 and 1948. The Holden Players placed an emphasis on speed rather than artistic exploration in the rehearsal process, but Holden can be forgiven for his stress on economy. He spent his life savings establishing the company, and bankruptcy killed it. Strange as it may seem, when the John Holden Players folded in 1940, Canada had no professional theatre until the Stratford Festival opened in 1953.

Another stock company, the Permanent Players, boasted a North American record for continuous existence in one building, the Winnipeg Theatre. They performed there from 1897 until 1918, 21 years. The theatre burned down in 1926.

From Faraway Places: Theatre of Diversity

History, of course, does not always arrange itself neatly for us to chronicle it. Amateur theatre began and reached a high level before the Walker Theatre opened, and it flourished after the Walker closed. For people living outside Winnipeg, the amateur groups often produced the only theatre they would see.

The people who arrived in Winnipeg from all over Europe often set up their own theatres. Yiddish theatre existed in Winnipeg from the turn of the 20th century. At one point Yiddish theatre groups used the Queen's Theatre. The National Federation Hall hosted the Winnipeg Ukrainian Theatre. In 1927, Winnipeg had three Icelandic theatre companies. Since many Ukrainians settled in farm country, they often set up theatre companies in church basements. A plaque outside the church in Cook's Creek attests to early Ukrainian theatre activity. The Ukrainian community constructed a log theatre in Shornecliffe in the 1920s.

Mennonite theatre has a long history that started with the mass immigration in the 1920s. The Mennonites who fled Russia during and after the Bolshevik revolution were well educated and prosperous. By the 1930s they were producing theatre in church basements. Winnipeg's Mennonite Theatre Company, incorporated in 1972, is a direct descendant of this activity.

Eaton's employees founded the very popular Masquers Club. This club represented Manitoba at the national drama festival several times, winning the first competition. Churches often sponsored drama clubs.

Lady Tupper, daughter-in-law to former Prime Minister Charles Tupper, founded an umbrella group in 1934 called the Winnipeg Players Guild. She hoped it would "draw together the outstanding talent among our 'new Canadians' many of whom, among the French, Ukrainian, Scandinavian, Hungarian and Polish populace, are doing work to be found in no other city in Canada." The Guild sponsored some productions and helped to coordinate activities, but in the long run its achievements fell short of its lofty goals, and eventually it died. The guild did not vanish without a trace, however; Esse Ljungh, a Swedish immigrant, established himself as a fine amateur actor and later became a CBC drama executive. (Lady Tupper would later enjoy greater success when she helped found the Royal Winnipeg Ballet.)

Perhaps Winnipeg's most successful non-English theatre company, though, is La Cercle Molière. Founded in 1925, as a means of preserving

French in Manitoba, it remains as Canada's oldest professional theatre company.

In 1931, the Manitoba Drama League formed, with 90 member companies. They hosted a festival sponsored by the *Winnipeg Free Press*, and John Russell wrote a weekly column on their activities.

The Winnipeg Little Theatre: A Bridge to the Future

Of equal importance in Manitoba's theatre history is the Winnipeg Little Theatre, which was originally called the Community Players of Winnipeg. In *The History of Prairie Theatre,* E. Ross Stewart writes of the Winnipeg Little Theatre: "At its peak in the 1930s its productions were of a professional standard." He goes on to say that the Winnipeg Little Theatre became the model for other theatres across Canada.

Active between 1921 and 1937, and then from 1948 until it merged with Theatre 77 to form the Manitoba Theatre Centre, it was a leading force in Manitoba drama. The Winnipeg Little Theatre's founders were two young lawyers, Alan Crawley and Harry Green. Their objectives are interesting in that they sought to develop the entire repertoire of dramatic arts. This was not a timid group. One objective was:

> To lay the foundation for such a Canadian Theatre as will offer to Canadian playwrights the possibility of national recognition, and to Canadian players the possibility of acquiring and practising their art in their own country, and under the direction and control of their own countrymen.[15]

Unlike some other groups with high-flown ideals, they managed in large part to live up to their aspirations. From 1921 until 1937, they produced 18 locally written plays, representing about 10 percent of their playbill for that period. Lillian Beynon Thomas's *Among the Maples,* produced in 1931–2, was the first full-length Canadian play performed as a regular attraction. Harry Green also wrote popular comedies and filled a great many other roles for the theatre. His one-act play, *Au Salon du Coiffure,* was so popular it had three productions, April 12 and 15, 1935, and January 9–11, 1936 and again in April 1936.

The Little Theatre operated out of the 340-seat Winnipeg Little Theatre after its first season. The group toiled to convert the abandoned movie house at the corner of Selkirk and Main into a venue that would meet its demanding standards. The Little Theatre also offered workshops and tryout nights. In 1930 the theatre hired John Craig, a professional engineer and respected amateur theatre artist, as its first full-time professional director. He became the first great Winnipeg director. On his death, Winnipeg Little Theatre founding member Hilda Hesson said, "The loss of John Craig as a director is a loss to the city as a whole, to the province, and to dramatic work throughout the West."[16]

The Winnipeg Little Theatre, as noted before, became a model for other amateur groups across the country. It gained a reputation for excellence in all aspects of theatre, acting, writing, set and costume design. Noted actors were Tommy Tweed (later to gain fame as Daddy Johnson on CBC Radio's *Jake and the Kid* series), George Waight, and Esse Ljungh. W.O. Mitchell appeared in at least one Winnipeg Little Theatre production.[17]

Ljungh arrived in Canada in 1924 after studying drama in his native Sweden. After working at farming for a few years, he arrived in Winnipeg in 1927 to edit the *Swedish Canada News*. By 1934 he was acting in Winnipeg Little Theatre shows and attracting attention for his skill, particularly in comedic roles. Ljungh was slated to star in *Hamlet* when the Little Theatre started its eleven-year exile. A respected expert in drama, he served as a Dominion Drama Festival (DDF) adjudicator and went on to become a respected radio producer.

By 1933 its theatre was not adequate for its growing popularity, so the company moved back into the Dominion Theatre. This move allowed more people to see its work, but it also eventually closed the theatre. When the John Holden Players took over the theatre, the Winnipeg Little Theatre had to move once again, first to the Playhouse and then to the Orpheum. It folded at the end of the 1937 season.

Another Lost Opportunity: Theatre Loses Out to Empire

The period between the 1920s and the Second World War is another time when a Manitoba theatre might have emerged. Winnipeg had a few splendid theatre buildings and several smaller venues. It had a core of local amateurs who had had the benefit of expert training and exposure to the best theatre the world could offer.

In Nellie McClung, the Beynon sisters and others, they had talented writers. Sister Mary Agnes, Canada's most published playwright, wrote approximately 50 plays between 1914 and 1927. In Charles

Handscomb of *The Free Press*, Ernest Beaufort of *The Telegram*, and Charles Wheeler of *The Tribune*, they had intelligent, honest critics who loved their beat. They also had the final, crucial ingredient, one often overlooked in assessing a centre's potential for great theatre. They had an intelligent, experienced audience.

Why did Manitoba not produce a great theatre at this time? Two explanations come to mind. One might be called a spoiled audience. As Tannis Prendergast of the Winnipeg Little Theatre wrote in *Food For Thought,* the Walkers had helped to create "A theatre-minded public which would not be satisfied for long with the new substitute for its accustomed entertainment." That new substitute was, of course, amateur theatre.

This audience attitude would have been a double-edged sword. On one hand, it would spur amateurs to attempt a professional standard in their work. On the other, it would have dampened their enthusiasm for new work. It is one thing to bring an existing script that another company (or century's worth of companies) has honed to perfection on the stage. It is quite another feat to work with a playwright to develop a performance-ready script. Not many professional companies are up to that challenge. It takes a director skilled in dramaturgy, a patient and generous cast, and a mature, cooperative playwright. To expect this of an amateur company is probably asking too much.

The second explanation for Manitoba theatre's failure to break through to a larger world is more complex: the Dominion Drama Festival, and its predecessor, the Earl Grey Musical and Dramatic competition.

Theatre Like the Mother Country Used to Make: The Dominion Drama Festival

Founded as a means of encouraging Canadian drama development, the two national drama festivals did do that, but in a constrained manner, as we shall see.

At the start of the 20th century, Canada's Governors General were British aristocrats. (Canada did not have a native-born Governor General until Vincent Massey in 1952.) Often these men wanted to leave a permanent memorial to their stay in Canada. For this reason, we have hockey's Stanley Cup and Lady Byng trophy, and football's Grey Cup.

As one might expect with British aristocrats as sponsors, these festivals attracted the cream of Canadian society. The plays reflected that stratum of society, and the performers almost all belonged to it. As Earl Grey said,

> It is because I regard the British Empire as the most potent instrument that has ever been fashioned for spreading the blessings of equal rights of Imperial Justice, of Christian Service and true chivalry that I regard it as the greatest privilege allowed to any man to proclaim himself a British citizen...

Winnipeg did very well at the initial festivals, winning twice in the five years the festivals lasted. (Harriet Walker directed one of these.) As people somewhat removed from the centre of Canadian society, however, they committed a faux pas at the first Earl Grey festival. Somehow they got the idea that an original script would be the best way to proceed. (This could also have been a version of pioneer resourcefulness. The rules limited length to from 60 to 90 minutes. One obvious way to guarantee playing time would be to create the script.)

In any case, Major Devine sketched out a plot for *The Release of Allan Danvers* over a plate of devilled kidneys at Mariaggi's. With the help of Ernest Beaufort of *The Telegram* and Wilson Blue of the *Free Press*, he fleshed out a script. It won the first prize. (Beaufort also earned special praise for his acting, as did a Miss Crawley.)

Betty Lee writes in *Love and Whisky,* a history of the DDF, that participation in both festivals very much depended on being part of the social register. She quotes Dora Mavor Moore as saying of the 1911 festival, held in Winnipeg: "Social acceptance was apparently quite as important as good diction."

Of the prevailing attitude at the time, she writes, "Performances of suitable plays by ladies and gentlemen who were not hell-bent on commercial gain were tolerated and even encouraged—provided the group had background." Speaking of entrants, she writes, "It seems that either blue-blood entries alone bothered to apply, or the committee wielded a sharp hatchet. Dora Mavor Moore insists that the hatcheting of socially unacceptable groups was fierce."

For all its blue-blood leanings, neither this festival nor the one that followed it spared the knife when it came to adjudication. One Earl Grey judge, in assessing the London, Ontario entry, said that it would have won first prize if the lead actor had not been so weak, and if the supporting cast did not have several actors who seemed more suited to the lead role.

Unfortunately, the festival died when Earl Grey returned to England. His successor, the Duke of Connaught, who was also Queen Victoria's son, was apparently not much of a drama fan.

A New Earl, a New Festival

In 1931, as the Earl of Bessborough was preparing to travel to Canada to assume his vice-regal post, he reportedly wished that "there is plenty of theatre there." The reply he received was, "Abandon any such hope, Milord. Theatre in Canada is dead."

The Earl would have nothing of that. By 1931 the British aristocracy was used to getting what it wanted, and if Canada did not have theatre, it would bloody well have to get some. Of course, theatre was not completely dead in 1931, but the body was pretty anemic.

Amateur groups across the nation performed regularly, and radio dramas reached people who couldn't attend a live performance. Still, in 1922 future Governor General Vincent Massey estimated that Canadian drama comprised little more than a dozen published Canadian plays. All the earnest rehearsing, set painting and performing across the nation had failed to produce many works publishers felt worthy of preservation. On the other hand, it may have been that the amateurs were keen to do their minor bit to preserve the British way by honouring the playwrights from the old sod. Or it may have been a bit of both.

Bessborough hoped to change that. "I should like to see as a normal part of life in this country, dramatic performance taking place of plays by Canadian authors...performed by Canadian players." In his opinion, "The spirit of a nation, if it is to find full expression, must include a national drama." His vehicle for bringing that expression forward was to be the Dominion Drama Festival. Lady Tupper was part of the committee that organized the first festival.

At the first festival, Bessborough's wish seemed on its way to fulfillment. Winnipeg's entry, using an original script (Lillian Beynon Thomas's *Jim Barber's Spite Fence),* tied for first place. Adjudicator Lawrence Mason, drama critic for *The Globe*, commented on "a special, rather independent feeling which prevails in Winnipeg."

Still, the idea of fostering a national drama through a national festival for amateurs met with skepticism. In the April 1933 *Saturday Night* magazine, B.K. Sandwell wrote, "It may be doubted whether a Canadian drama can ever be developed on a purely amateur basis." He also cast doubt on Bessborough's picture of drama as a rallying point for a nation's psyche: "A Canadian drama whose sole impelling motive is a rather self-conscious patriotism is not likely to get very far."

Whatever the merits of the DDF as a cradle for Canadian drama might have been, in practice it had several fatal flaws.

The first of these was a short-sighted brain trust which just couldn't see beyond the present moment. French Quebec lobbied tirelessly to host the conference in Montreal. To the organizers, however, the time was never right: what if attendance fell? It took a full 28 years for the festival to rise to the challenge and allow what was then Canada's most populous city to be the host. The result was a resounding financial success. Unfortunately, by that time the festival's best years were behind it.

Similar fears prevented the DDF from embracing Canadian playwrights wholeheartedly. Not until 1967 did the festival feature all Canadian plays, and it did not repeat the experiment. These two breaks with tradition did not happen until the DDF found itself metaphorically backed to a wall. Had the festival embraced both the French and writing communities at the outset, Bessborough may have proved to be a prophet.

A second problem was the DDF's regal association. From the start it was an upper-crust organization, but unfortunately it never grew beyond that outlook. An apocryphal story has one glassy-eyed attendee at the closing gala grumping that "this would be a fine organization if it weren't for all those plays."

The DDF not only ignored the exciting social theatre that arose in the 1930s, it took active steps to keep it out of the festival. In the tradition of groups practising exclusion, each year it invented reasons why these companies couldn't attend. When the Theatre of Action finally qualified for the final, its members did not receive invitations to the ball, the crowning event. When they complained, invitations hastily arrived, with an explanation that it was "an oversight." Curiously, *Love and Whisky* does not mention Theatre of Action.

The DDF's conservative nature also affected its aesthetics. Occasionally, exciting new scripts would create a splash. This might have inspired other groups to take a chance on new scripts or new forms. Unfortunately, the other groups were not inspired; instead they admired the pioneer's courage and went back to the safe, old scripts. The adjudicators knew these scripts, how to respond to them. The groups knew the correct (classical) interpretations. This was the tried-and-true way to the podium.

Finally, the DDF perpetuated the British ideal, and because the festival was for many years the premier drama event of the year, this meant diminished opportunities for other events to receive attention.

Despite this rather lengthy catalogue of sins, the DDF accomplished many good things. It raised drama's profile at a time when the art form desperately needed it. It gave many artists a path to recognition and professional work. Kate Reid, John Colicos, Lorne Greene, William Hutt, Wayne and Shuster, and William Needles went from the festival to careers as respected professionals. Gratien Gelinas, John Herbert, Gwen Pharis Ringwood, Gabrielle Roy and Mazo De La Roche flexed their playwriting muscles there.

Manitoba owes a special debt to the DDF. La Cercle Molière won repeatedly at the festival. Without that avenue for national recognition, it is doubtful that it would have earned the level of respect it deserves. From Gabrielle Roy to Claude Dorge, Franco-Manitobans have proved that they can write with the very best, and that great drama does not always come from large communities.

The Chautauqua Movement: The Touring Era Goes Small

The Chautauqua movement grew out of a New York Methodist summer school for Sunday school teachers in the 1880s. Chautauquas were traveling tent shows that offered communities entertainment, education, and an opportunity to do some fundraising. They were a kind of clean-cut vaudeville, with spiritual and educational growth as the prime motives, instead of profit, as was the case for vaudeville.

A community that booked a Chautauqua had to guarantee the fee up front. It would also provide volunteer labour to raise the tent, and help promote the show. At the end, it would split the profits, if any. Chautauquas would arrive and depart with military precision, staying for a few days to a week, and booking next year's show before they left.

A typical Chautauqua would have lectures by famous or controversial people, variety acts and plays. The afternoon would have a children's puppet show or other such play, while the evening's production would be an innocuous comedy. E. Ross Stewart reports in *The History of Prairie Theatre* that in the prairies the lectures were the most popular part of the program.

While some sources date Chautauquas on the Prairies from 1917, when J.M. Ericson and his wife Nola set up their operation, Arthur Ford's memoir *As the World Wags On* suggests Chautauquas arrived earlier than that. Ford attended Grace Methodist when J.S. Woodsworth was assistant pastor. The church had a Young Men's Club that wanted to host a series of Chautauquas, but at the time only American speakers were available.

The group approached Mr. Ford, who organized a series of four lectures: in Winnipeg, Brandon, Regina and Saskatoon. This event took place during Laurier's term as prime minister, which ended in 1911. At a Conservative dinner in Foster's honour during the Winnipeg stop, Sir Rodmond Roblin coined the phrase "Tin Pot Navy" to describe the Liberal naval policy. Since the naval debate took place in 1910, it seems likely that Chautauquas came to Manitoba in that year (if not earlier, since Ford indicates that the Young Men's Club already had some experience).

Ford chose a prominent Conservative and former MP, Sir George Foster, as his headliner. It is hard to know if Ford's motives were entirely driven by a desire to help the Young Men's Club. He writes that "Sir George at that time...had been under a cloud owing to the insurance investigation under which his name was involved." As a reporter for the Conservative *Winnipeg Telegram,* perhaps he thought he could kill two birds with one stone and rehabilitate a loyal MP's career.

Ford's choice of Foster was not entirely political, however; he was a Sir John A. Macdonald protegé. One day while walking to a session of Parliament, Sir John A. heard a magnificent speaking voice coming out of a temperance meeting. He told an aide to find out who the speaker was and get him into politics. Temperance man or no, Sir John A. wanted George Foster on his team.

Ford reports that "the series may have been a success, but I was lucky to break even, and I abandoned any idea of being an impresario." Once the Chautauqua movement took hold, however, it spread rapidly across the Prairies. The series eventually made stops in 600 towns from coast to coast.

While the Chautauquas emphasized wholesome entertainment, and while most, if not all, plays were old chestnuts, they played an important role in theatre development. No doubt the series inspired aspiring local theatre artists to test their skills and to found amateur groups. Ryley, Alberta, a town with a population of 241, raised enough money to build a community hall. The companies often used professional actors (although the low wages meant these actors were usually young people just starting out or university students). At least one, Judith Evelyn, went on to star on Broadway.

By 1935 the Chautauqua movement had died, victim to the Dust Bowl, radio, movies, and improved transportation that allowed people from small towns to travel greater distances for entertainment.

7

Political Theatre in the Early 20th Century:

The Fighting Days

"There was the 'Little' theatre, but it was la-di-da stuff. It was pretty sterile drawing room comedy. The average person didn't relate to it..."

—Former New Theatre member, Communist, school trustee and City Councillor Joe Zuken, quoted in Toby Gordon Ryan's *Stage Left*

As we have seen, from the arrival of Colonel Garnet Wolseley in 1870 Manitoba gradually became a place where wealth and proper (British) heritage were the sources of power. In many ways, Manitoba in the early days resembled the stereotypical banana republic. The poor lived in squalour. Public works lagged because the elites refused to pay the necessary taxes and also because speculators snapped up much of the best land. The legal system often seemed to have little to do with the law.

The police were so overworked that it is not surprising crime often overwhelmed them. In 1907 only 90 police officers served a city of 115,000—at a time when Winnipeg had the reputation of being the wickedest city in the Dominion. (In 1999, with a population of 660,000, Winnipeg had 1,203 police officers: almost four times as many, per capita.) Not surprisingly, prostitution and other vices abounded. A low point came in 1914 when the Winnipeg police arrested John Krafchenko for murdering a bank manager during a robbery in Plum Coulee. Krafchenko's lawyer persuaded a police officer to allow a gun and a rope in to the prisoner, which he used to escape. The constable faced seven years in prison and died in a mishap there a few months later. Meanwhile, the lawyer received only three years, and the bar reinstated him after he served his sentence.

That does not mean that everyone in the province accepted the status quo meekly. Clashes with authority were frequent and often bloody. And like any place where corruption and abuse of power are rife, Manitoba attracted idealistic reformers.

Missionaries, forward-thinking members of the middle classes, and new arrivals who had enjoyed more humane government in their homelands strove to alter the existing power structure and improve the lot of desperately poor slum dwellers. It was heavy going.

Perhaps the best example of the effect idealists such as J.S. Woodsworth had was The Peoples' Forum, an offshoot of the All Peoples' Mission. (Woodsworth would later found the Co-operative Commonwealth Federation, the NDP's forerunner.) A former Methodist minister, Woodsworth saw a role for the church beyond simply dispensing charity. He wanted churches to help non-British citizens integrate into their new community. This was part of the so-called Social Gospel.

This was not the imperialist become-British-because-British-is-best school, however. Woodsworth and others set up their programs to help desperately poor people improve their lives. The Peoples' Forum operated out of the Grand Theatre at the corner of Main Street and Jarvis. On Sunday afternoons people could attend free lectures on subjects such as civics, home economics, birth control, socialism, art, history, and current events. Often the lectures were illustrated to make them clearer to people with limited English. In the evening various ethnic communities would perform the music and dances of their homeland.

The Mission and Forum did foreign-born people three great services: it gave them vital survival skills, it provided an opportunity to take pride in and share their heritage with a larger community, and it united disparate groups into a self-supporting whole. The model soon spread to other large cities in Canada.

A side benefit that was to have a profound and lasting effect on Manitoba's public life is that the Forums and Missions allowed talented foreign-born people a place of prominence. Leaders emerged from their "home" communities to play a larger role in public affairs, with a solid understanding of their new home that the Forums had given them, and a network of contacts among their fellow new Canadians.

Women's Suffrage: Where Feminism and Theatre Met

Partly because of late-19th century attitudes to women, and partly because of Icelandic immigration to Manitoba, women's suffrage became the rallying point for reform elements in the province. (Icelandic women enjoyed full political and property rights in their homeland and were reluctant to accept disenfranchisement in Manitoba.) And as in many social causes before and after, theatre played a large and public part.

Women's suffrage spawned the first national theatre movement in Canadian history: the mock parliament. Kym Bird describes the history of this little-known aspect of our theatrical past.[18] The first mock parliament took place at Winnipeg's Bijou Theatre on February 9, 1893, under the auspices of the Women's Christian Temperance Union (WCTU). The chief organizer was Mrs. Annie J. McClung, future mother-in-law to Nellie McClung. Nellie had been boarding at the McClung residence since 1890, so she must have been aware of this mock parliament. Apparently 20 members of the provincial legislature attended.

This mock parliament inspired at least 11 others, according to Bird. Four were in Manitoba, six in Ontario, and two in British Columbia, making the mock parliaments a truly national phenomenon. Bird also cites evidence that two more parliaments may have taken place in Manitoba following the Bijou one, and possibly another in Alberta.

These parliaments were highly popular affairs, usually taking place in the largest venue in the host city, and usually selling out. Reviews were overwhelmingly positive. Their financial success went a long way towards securing the vote for women.

From a dramaturgical point of view, these plays followed a set path of role reversal. Other political issues rose out of the debates before the main event, which would be men petitioning for the vote from a female legislature. The women would point out to the men the weaknesses of their sex, which made them unsuited for the responsibility of voting. The vote invariably went against the petitioners. Evidence suggests that the plays were collective creations. Another noteworthy aspect of the mock parliaments is that the Canadian version emerged before either the British or American ones. This seems to be the one instance in our theatre history where Canada exported an aesthetic to the dominant cultures.

The most famous of these parliaments, and probably the most successful from a monetary and artistic point of view, was the Political Equality League's performance at the Walker in 1914. This was Lillian Beynon Thomas' suggestion, and one of McClung's great moments.

The Political Equality League was the most potent force for reform in the early days. Founded in 1912 by prominent middle-class women and men, it boasted some of the province's most intelligent and articulate citizens: Nellie McClung, Francis and Marion Beynon, the Walkers, Frederick Dixon, A. Vernon Thomas, Dr. Amelia Yeomans, and Cora Hind. Many worked for local newspapers and magazines. Their nemesis was the premier of the day, Rodmond Roblin.

Roblin was a powerful speaker of the old school, with a commanding presence. A former cheese buyer and Carman grain dealer with a farm of his own, he owed much of his popularity to the farm vote. He could justly claim that he knew most farmers in the province by name.

He was not as conversant with urban issues, however, and seems to have been somewhat naive in the political aspects of his job. (McClung once hoodwinked him into touring some of the more notorious sweatshops.) A contemporary, Arthur Ford, who was the legislative reporter for *The Telegram*, wrote in his memoir, *As the World Wags On*, that Roblin was more sinned against than sinning. Regardless, the suffrage movement saw Roblin as the main obstacle to their goals, which included Prohibition, minimum wage laws, and political and property rights for women.

When a meeting with Roblin failed, McClung and others, outraged at his imperious and patronizing manner, wrote and staged a satire called *The Women's Parliament*. The play took place in an imaginary situation where men did not have the vote. McClung, as Roblin, used many of his best lines against him:

> I must congratulate the members of this delegation on their splendid appearance. Any civilization which can produce as splendid a type of manhood as my friend, Mr. Skinner, should not be interfered with....
>
> If all men were as intelligent and as good as Mr. Skinner and his worthy though misguided followers we might consider this matter, but they are not. Seven-eighths of the police court offenders are men, and only one-third of the church membership. You ask me to enfranchise these....

> O no, man is made for something higher and better than voting. Men were made to support families. What is home without a bank account? The man who pays the grocer rules the world. In this agricultural province, the man's place is the farm. Shall I call man away from the useful plow and harrow to talk loud on street corners about things which do not concern him! Politics unsettle men, and unsettled men means unsettled bills—broken furniture, and broken vows—and divorce… When you ask for the vote you are asking me to break up peaceful, happy homes—to wreck innocent lives….[19]

Probably no other mock parliament had more dramatic resources at its disposal than this one did. In Harriet Walker they had a seasoned professional whose husband owned the theatre. In McClung they had a gifted writer and platform performer. Lillian Thomas was to become a very successful playwright, so they had all the ingredients they needed to structure an effective evening of theatre. McClung reports in *Stream Runs Fast* that they mounted the play a second time in Winnipeg and took it to Brandon for a third performance. The proceeds from these three performances funded the rest of the campaign for votes in Manitoba.

The event has a celebrated place in Manitoba history, but one must remember that Roblin won the 1914 election. (He claimed that all the short-haired women and long-haired men were against him.) Only the Legislature Scandal allowed the pro-suffrage Norris to assume power and enfranchise women in 1916. Although *The Women's Parliament* achieved its result only after a two-year delay, it nevertheless played a direct role in achieving the vote for women, because of both its rhetorical and financial contribution to the cause. Manitoba was the first province to enact women's suffrage. It is one of the rare events in Canadian history where theatre directly affected events. The tradition revived in the 1970s when The Nellie McClung Players started, presenting theatre with a feminist view.

Some evidence of other local feminist playwriting exists. Kate Simpson Hayes (1856–1945) had a number of plays produced in Winnipeg (and Regina). Her Winnipeg plays were *Divorce for $50,* which played in the early 1890s, and *The Duplicate* (also called *The Bargain Husband)* that played in Fort Garry Park in 1897. From the titles, we can deduce an early feminist aesthetic.

As a side note, the provincial archives contain photographic evidence of a less savoury theatre tradition during this period. A 1915 photo shows the suffragettes in blackface for a minstrel show, with a banner reading "Votes for Women" in the background. Whites posing as blacks in minstrel shows for comic effect was an accepted form of entertainment back then, but it does not play well today. Before we condemn them for racism, however, it would be wise to know what the context was. Perhaps the event was a joint effort to attain suffrage and create better conditions for blacks in society.

The Political Equality League had many writers with a provincial—and sometimes national—voice. Lillian Beynon Thomas edited the Women's page of *The Free Press*. Her sister Frances edited the Women's page of the *Grain Growers' Guide*. Cora Hind was a respected agriculture expert who, like McClung, was a popular speaker all over the Prairies. We must remember, though, that the daily papers of the day all had an Imperial outlook, regardless of political loyalty.

On the topic of political loyalty, the papers of the day would make *The National Post* during Conrad Black's ownership seem neutral. Alfred Ford writes in his memoir that *The Telegram* editor once swore a blue streak at someone who wrote a headline that read something like "Laurier cheered by his followers." The editor shouted at the hapless copy editor, "Don't you know that no Grit is ever cheered in *The Telegram*?"

The Political Equality League might have had an even greater influence, and its members might even have duplicated the Abbey Theatre's success in Ireland. Sadly, outside events revealed fatal divisions within the group. The First World War divided the League. Some members opposed the war as an Imperialist conflict outside the concern of ordinary citizens, while others rallied around the flag. McClung, with a son overseas, belonged to this second group. During the war, she fought for disenfranchisement of "foreign" women.

The British patriot element of this movement was to prove more powerful than the reform element. Frederick Dixon was an outspoken pacifist. When A. Vernon Thomas, a *Free Press* reporter and fellow League member, shook Dixon's hand after a pacifist speech in 1917, it cost Thomas his job. He and his wife Lillian Beynon Thomas spent the rest of the war in virtual exile in New York, not returning until 1923.

The 1919 Strike: Theatre Splits Along Class Lines

The League could not survive the tensions the war created. Maternal feminists such as McClung went their way, and the more radical Equal

Rights feminists became part of the next great social movement in the province. Their allies would be the working class and some disenchanted soldiers who returned from the war.

When the First World War ended, the result could hardly be called peace. In the first place, many soldiers found themselves assigned to ancillary conflicts, such as those in Palestine and Russia, where the White Army attempted a counter-revolution against the Bolsheviks. This was a particularly brutal conflict involving savage reprisals and counter-reprisals as territory changed hands. Secondly, soldiers who had signed up in an orgy of idealistic patriotism found themselves in the trenches, with hideously incompetent aristocrats commanding them to die by the tens of thousands attacking impregnable machine gun posts. Canada lost more people to the First World War than it did to the Second: more in fact, than in all other conflicts combined.

Political influence resulted in Canadian troops using the Ross rifle, a sharpshooter's weapon that jammed when used in muddy conditions or for rapid fire. Unfortunately, it rained a lot in the trenches and rapid fire was the only way a trench soldier could hope to stay alive during the mass suicide of an assault. Many died futilely, trying to unjam the rifles. It took a cabinet order to scrap the rifles, by which time over 300,000 men had received the useless weapons, and unknown numbers had paid for unscrupulous and incompetent management with their lives.

This war had a profound social effect. Those who came of age during the conflict expressed a spirit of rootless, neurotic disillusionment. Gertrude Stein named these people the Lost Generation, apparently after a conversation with Ernest Hemingway, a leading spokesman of these people. Hemingway, Fitzgerald, Callaghan and others struck a chord with soldiers who went home promising themselves that social conditions would be different, that they would never again allow themselves to be manipulated by powerful elites into a useless conflict. Unfortunately, many of them returned to learn that they had traded the horror of trench warfare for the misery of unemployment. Irwin Shaw's *Bury the Dead,* a powerful one-act play adapted from Austrian playwright Hans Chlumberg's *Miracle at Verdun,* captures this feeling of betrayal and impotent anger.

Men who had given up four years of their youth (and sometimes more) came home to learn that others had grown rich exploiting the conflict for whatever they could gain.

A second trend weakened their bargaining position with employers. Scientific management, a theory propounded at the turn of the 20th century by Frederick W. Taylor and eagerly applied by Henry Ford and others, was rapidly making the skilled tradesman extinct. (It should be noted here that Henry Ford, unlike some of his contemporaries, understood that if you were going to apply scientific management to mass production, the masses had to be in a position to buy the products of their labour. Workers on his revolutionary Model T assembly line earned the highest wages in the automotive industry. Although he later applied some of the worst union-busting tactics, his motives came more from a sense of betrayal and paternalism than exploitation.)

The most visible effect of scientific management was the assembly line. Taylor's specialization of labour theory meant that experts would study jobs to minute levels and reduce them to component parts. They could then automate many aspects with jigs and fixtures, and a machinist's job could shrink to tightening a few bolts. Charlie Chaplin in *Modern Times* satirized this trend.

This automation of production vastly reduced costs and improved quality. Working people could now afford machines and tools that previously belonged only in wealthy households. The automobile went from being a toy for the rich to being an almost universal means of transportation. The downside was that a skilled worker could no longer command a strong place at the bargaining table. An employer could say, "If you don't like it here, there's hundreds of stiffs outside who could take your job in a minute," and it would have been true.[20] J.M. Bumsted reports in *The Winnipeg General Strike of 1919* that in Winnipeg from 1916 to 1919 the labour work force doubled in size. Early in the 20th century, Winnipeg was a major manufacturing centre. The Ford Motor Company manufactured automobiles here until 1940.

The One Big Union movement came out of recognition that workers could not achieve their aims if they allowed employers to play one group off against the others. This more militant, socialist group quickly supplanted the Trades and Labour Congress of Canada as the dominant labour organization in western Canada and northern Ontario.

The employers justifiably feared the power this united labour movement might wield. Added to this rational fear was an irrational fear of foreign elements fueled by the war effort, and the not-quite-so-irrational fear of Bolshevism. The business community consistently blamed "enemy aliens" as instigators of the growing labour unrest, although most leaders had British heritage. Workers standing up for fair wages and safe working conditions were branded as traitors to the Imperial cause overseas. When soldiers returned in droves after the war, looking for scarce jobs, tensions reached a boiling point.

On May 1, 1919, metal workers at three separate firms went on strike. The management of these firms refused to bargain simultaneously. The building trades struck the same day, setting up the ideal conditions to test the One Big Union idea. The unions referred their cases to the Trades and Labour Council of Winnipeg. More than 11,000 members supported a sympathy strike, and only 524 (less than five percent) voted against. Of the 94 unions, 93 voted to strike.

Although the police union voted to strike, they remained on duty until June 10. At this time the Police Chief called each officer into his office individually. He asked the officer either to leave the union and sign an oath of allegiance to the police force and the city or to face immediate dismissal. Of the 274 officers, only 22 signed the oath. This must have given the city government quite a chill.

Its reaction was swift. It asked Chief MacPherson to take a leave of absence (presumably for having his bluff called so badly), and when he refused, he lost his job. The deputy chief, Chris H. Newton, replaced him. (In 1934, Newton followed the tradition of Winnipeg's first chief. A fist fight after a traffic accident resulted in assault charges. The public outcry forced him to retire before he was fired.)

No one in Canada had ever seen a strike like this before, and none has happened since. The city shut down tighter than it ever did for any natural disaster, be it a flood or blizzard. All three daily papers stopped delivery. The Strike Committee took control of telephone and telegraph lines. Bakeries, dairies, and streetcars all ceased operation. There was no garbage removal or mail delivery. Over a third of the city's population was on strike.

This was clearly a situation that could not last long. The Strike Committee, surprised by both the effect its strike had had on the city and the elites' stubbornness, mobilized to minimize the adverse effects on the poor and to maintain solidarity. It held mass daily meetings at Victoria Park and published daily *Strike Bulletins*. It issued permits for essential services like milk delivery. Small businesses began displaying permit cards that read "Permitted by authority of the Strike Committee." It became the de facto government, something the established authority could not be expected to take lying down.

Its response was something called the Citizens' Committee of 1000, a silly name when one considers that 30,000 workers supported the strike. Still, the Committee had money and power behind it. It hired 1800 special constables to replace the 252 police the City Council had fired. Some of the same strikebreaking thuggery that occurred across North America happened in Winnipeg as a result. Battle lines were drawn.

Despite the Strike Committee's overwhelmingly Anglo-Saxon leadership, the elites painted this event as a further example of foreign agitation. John Dafoe, legendary editor of the *Free Press,* said that authorities should "clean the aliens out of this community and ship them back to their happy homes in Europe which vomited them forth a decade ago."

From May 15 until June 28, the strike held. Then two events broke the movement.

One cannot imagine a federal government seeing what was then the nation's third-largest city paralyzed, and doing nothing. Unfortunately for the strikers, the government of the day was the worst possible one for their situation. The Union Government in Ottawa that Conservative Sir Robert Borden led had started to disintegrate. It knew it needed to take a strong stand on a major issue to survive. With the strike spreading across Canada, the party knew what that issue was.

Borden sent his key man, Interior Minister and acting Justice Minister Arthur Meighen, to Winnipeg with Senator Gideon Robertson, the Minister of Labour. Meighen was a ruthlessly intelligent man who many claim was the best orator ever to speak in the House of Commons. (He also became Manitoba's only citizen ever to hold office as Prime Minister.) Meighen and Robertson met with the Citizens' Committee of 1000, but refused to meet with the Strike Committee. Their goal was obviously not to find a peaceful solution. They wanted to show the masses who was boss.

The federal government ordered public servants to return to work immediately or face dismissal. Parliament amended the Immigration Act so that immigrants could be deported, and broadened the Criminal Code's definition of revolution. The next step was to give the Mounties special authority to start what Meighen considered to be the necessary deportations.

On June 16, six Anglo-Saxon and four "foreign" strike leaders were arrested. This was the first fatal event of the strike: arresting the leaders. The second happened the same day. Workers gathered in what was at first a peaceful protest against the arrests. The mayor read the Riot Act, the authorities lost control of the situation, and Mounties fired into the crowd. One "foreigner" died on the spot, and a second later died of gangrene. Mounties arrested 31 rioters. On July 1, raids across the country resulted in more arrests of "known agitators" and "radical organizations."

The way the government dealt with those arrested illustrates the temper of the times. Anglo-Saxons received jury trials. "Foreigners" were to receive deportation hearings before a Board of Inquiry. Of the non-Anglo-Saxons arrested June 16, only one was deported. Those arrested on June 21 did not receive even a deportation hearing. Magistrate Hugh John Macdonald (Sir John A. Macdonald's son) sent them to an internment camp in Kapuskasing. Despite angry protests at this treatment, authorities sent these men away and later secretly deported them.

The One Big Union movement died, but the 1919 strike left a lasting impression. Some strike leaders became local heroes that their admirers voted repeatedly to office, at the federal, provincial, and municipal level. Winnipeg's North End became a powerful constituency.

The other side of the ledger is long. Distrust of non-Anglo-Saxons ran deep with the ruling class. Racist policies lasted a long time. The Winter Club and Victoria Beach banned Jews for decades. The faculty of medicine had a quota on Jews and women. People with Slavic last names often anglicized them in the hope of gaining entrance into government and other jobs. It would be 50 years before the province would elect a left-leaning party to the government side of the legislature.

Still, one cannot merely accuse the elites of the day of hysteria over Bolshevism. The Russian Revolution was Europe's bloodiest civil strife since France's Reign of Terror over a century before. Later events in Stalinist Russia proved that more than just the ruling classes had something to fear in Bolshevism. That the strike was not a Bolshevik uprising in the making would not have been clear to the rulers of the day, or to the ordinary citizen, for that matter.

Another outcome of the strike is the effect it has had on the provincial psyche. It is part of our collective consciousness, and as such has passed into our literature and other arts. Ann Henry's *Lulu Street* was the first (and for another 25 years, the only) locally written play to appear on MTC's main stage. Jack Gray's *Striker Sniderman* had a 1970 production at the St. Lawrence Centre in Toronto. Margaret Sweatman's *Fox* gained acclaim as a novel and later appeared on PTE's stage as a play. William Harrar's *Bolshie Bash* is a humorous one-man play that has had two Winnipeg Fringe Festival productions. The Manitoba Federation of Labour commissioned Rick McNair to write *Labour on Trial,* a one-man play that has had many sponsored productions.

The strike also galvanized leftist and workers' groups across the country. Any attempt to crush a movement creates martyrs, and martyrs help to sustain a movement.

Unfortunately, the strike caused a fatal split in the city's progressive element. Nellie McClung's sympathies were clearly with the ruling class, as the following quotation illustrates:

> Every newspaper except [the strikers'] own was suppressed, water pressure was reduced to 30 pounds, for this was enough to bring it to the one-storey buildings, and *The Western Labour News* stated that it was in one-storey buildings that the "workers" live, the inference being that it did not matter whether the other people lived or not.

McClung may not have known that in 1919 many working class people in Winnipeg had to carry water to their houses from a communal pump. Requiring more affluent people to carry their water upstairs was, relatively speaking, less of a hardship, and hardly life-threatening.

On the other side were J.S. Woodsworth (who later bragged about being arrested for sedition after quoting from the prophet Isaiah), the Beynon sisters, Frederick Dixon and his wife, Winona Flett. Since the progressive element contained the literary leaders of the day, the split meant that theatre did not have a cohesive group to draw from for scripts.

If You Can't Beat Them in the Streets, Rock Them in the Aisles: Theatre of Action

In *Stage Left,* Toby Gordon Ryan describes how labour groups across the country formed theatre and arts groups for the dual purpose of education and keeping unemployed people busy. Progressive arts groups sprang up. A new theatre, called Theatre of Action, developed. Much of it was agit-prop, agitation-propaganda theatre with a simple, didactic message.

Toby Ryan helped found Winnipeg's Progressive Arts Club. It called its theatre The New Theatre. A member, Fred Narvey, describes what it did as "theatre with a social context." Unfortunately, it did not create its own works, but its standard was very high. Narvey says that the *Free Press* respected it and gave it positive reviews. It won a DDF first prize in English in 1939 when Albert Maltz directed the troupe in *The Rehearsal* at the festival in London, Ontario.

Not everyone approved of the New Theatre, however; in 1934 the city banned its performance of *Eight Men Speak,* by Oscar Ryan, E. Cecil-Smith, Frank Love and Mildred Goldberg. When the Walker Theatre refused to cancel the contract it held with the New Theatre, the Walkers had their licence revoked. *(Eight Men Speak* is a play about eight men arrested for being Communists and about the attempted murder of their leader, Tim Buck. It had a tumultuous opening night in Toronto, selling 1500 tickets. The next night's performance was banned. Although Cecil-Smith mentions in his foreword to the printed edition that parts of the play had productions six times "and never once has the government dared to prosecute the producers or actors," the play did not have another full production until 1982.)

Joe Zuken reports in *Stage Left* that Deputy Police Chief MacIvor called him in and asked to see the script before he would allow a performance. Zuken refused, and a political firestorm started, with *Free Press* editorials on the side of the theatre group, and a demonstration at Old Market Square protesting the ban. The group later performed excerpts at labour halls and other events.

These labour theatre groups had a hard time qualifying for the Dominion Drama Festival. They did not get much respect in the literary press, either. In the October 1934 issue of *Canadian Forum,* E. Cecil-Smith, co-author of *Eight Men Speak,* complains about what he believed to be false hopes resting on the newly formed DDF.[21] He demanded that what he called Workers' Theatre receive its due.

> Here is the new Canadian Dramatic movement in very truth. A drama rooted in the lives and struggles of the toilers of Canada's shops, mines, farms, and slave-camps. Plays written in the heat of life by the same workers.... Life to these Canadians

is too serious to worry about polite bedroom scandals, or the ridiculous cavortings of a flat-footed detective in pursuit of *The Black Ace.*"[22]

Workers' Theatre used chanting, direct address and other aspects of Brechtian theatre, and innovations in the use of props and lighting. It was shoestring theatre (Cecil-Smith writes of packing six actors and one suitcase into a roadster for a tour. The suitcase contained the costumes and props for seven plays.)

The Winnipeg New Theatre group grew out of the Progressive Arts Club. It contained many young people who would later rise to prominence. Besides Zuken, the company had future cabinet minister Saul Cherniak, George Werier, who later became a professional actor, and Max Goldin, a guiding light during the glory days of the Canadian Authors' Association's Manitoba Branch. Bob Orchard, its director for many productions, had travelled to Russia, where he met Meyerhold and saw the Moscow Art Theatre. He later taught at the University of Calgary, which became the first university in Canada to offer a fine arts degree in drama.

While Winnipeg's New Theatre did not write its own plays, it made ambitious choices: *The Rehearsal, Volpone*, and *Waiting at Madrid*. Narvey says of those days, "We were young and enthusiastic. We tried to follow Stanislavsky. *An Actor Prepares* was our Bible."

Narvey is quoted in *Stage Left* on the motivations that drove the New Theatre: "It was a terrible time of crisis and this was one way of expressing our frustration, our indignation and our disgust with living conditions at the time. This is what brought most of us into the progressive theatre movement." Narvey reports that although he worked a twelve-hour day, he never missed a rehearsal and always found time to study his lines. "The beauty of it was its spirit," he says. "It all came from the heart."

Ryan quotes Max Goldin about the Progressive Arts Club: "The Progressive Arts Club really became an oasis from the terrible load of the Depression and the feeling of not being wanted—of being excess baggage in the world."

During a performance of *Waiting at Madrid* at the Walker Theatre, Narvey made a contribution to local theatre lore. His character had to shoot a fascist, but when the time came, the revolver they borrowed from the police department (loaded with blanks) would not fire. Narvey, in the best theatrical tradition, improvised. He ran across the stage and bonked the other actor on the head with the revolver. *The Tribune*'s reviewer, Cooper, wrote, "Hats off to Fred Narvey for quick thinking."

Workers' Theatre formed an early example of what could be called a national theatre movement, and like the mock parliament movement before it, sprang from ambitions other than a pure love for drama. Much of their material came out of their daily lives, and the groups formed a loose network across the country. Fred Narvey tells the story of when Vancouver's Theatre of Action stopped in Winnipeg on its way to perform *Waiting for Lefty* at the Dominion Drama Festival. It did a one-night performance in Winnipeg to help offset the costs of the trans-Canada trip. This must have been a powerful night of theatre. "I was a plant in the audience," Fred recalls, "and when I shouted a woman almost fainted."

Despite promising achievements, Workers' Theatre did not spawn a national theatre. Many reasons exist for this: the movement had a chronic lack of funds, many people in the movement saw theatre as a means to an end rather than an end in itself, the authorities frowned on and often censored the movement, and the outside world intruded on Canadian life.

Hostility and outright censorship by the authorities played a large part in limiting Workers' Theatre. Key people in the left attracted RCMP surveillance. If an economic revolution had taken place here, as happened in Russia and elsewhere, the actors and playwrights might have had a place of honour in our culture. Instead they are a footnote.

The second external factor, and probably the more important one, was the start of World War II. Canada found itself mobilized in a worldwide conflict, and social theatre gave way to light entertainment aimed at bolstering armed service morale.

Changes in the Wind: The American Cultural Invasion

The golden age of radio in the 1930s and the arrival of sound in movies made a profound impact on people's lives. By purchasing a radio, a family could enjoy the leading entertainers of the day without leaving home. Burns and Allen, Jack Benny, and the Lux Theater, to name a few, became part of a family's daily life. A person with a good radio could pull in Chicago and points beyond on a clear prairie night. The world began to shrink and expand at the same time, as people gained greater access to outside information.

For the first time in history, the common people had news, drama, comedy, and music at their fingertips, subject only to programming and their receiver's ability to pull in a signal. This was the beginning of home-based electronic entertainment. In the 1930s, a city street would often hold a group singalong on a summer night. Gradually those community-based forms of entertainment gave way, as families shared piped-in entertainment alone.

The impact of movies was no less important. For less than a dollar, a family of four could attend the latest blockbuster movie. When colour came to movies in the late 1930s, the average person could enjoy a spectacle previous generations would have had a hard time imagining. The glamour of movies came at a time when most peoples' lives were glum, especially on the Prairies. The Great Depression and the Dust Bowl (ten years of drought) made life a struggle. What a pleasure, then, to spend a few cents and see *The Wizard of Oz* or the Marx Brothers, or countless B movies.

Thanks to a monster Hollywood publicity machine, radio and movie stars became bigger than life. Publicity magazines and gossip columnists churned out thousands of pages celebrating and exploring the entertainers who helped people forget their worries for a while.

While the British element still dominated Manitoba life (Manitobans turned out in droves to welcome the King and Queen during their 1939 visit), gradually an American consciousness invaded the prairie mindset. Boys drew their ideals from The Lone Ranger, Gene Autrey, and The Shadow. Young men sought to emulate Humphrey Bogart, Jimmy Stewart or John Wayne. Female role models were Shirley Temple and Judy Garland, and, as women became older, Katharine Hepburn or perhaps Loretta Young. Our mythology came from *Gone with the Wind* or *Mr. Smith Goes to Washington*. Later Davy Crockett and Annette Funicello would be cultural icons.

The entertainment scene was not devoid of Canadian examples. W. O. Mitchell's excellent *Jake and the Kid* had a huge following, as did *The Happy Gang* and *Wayne and Shuster*. Local stations such as CKY presented radio drama, often of a very high quality. Esse Ljungh was a leading figure in this venture, and later at the CBC.

Thanks to the CBC, Canada had a national radio presence that gave Canadians excellent entertainment from coast to coast. Still, the stars and stripes predominated, and continue to dominate our consciousness. The prohibitive cost of producing live competition for what almost amounted to free top-drawer entertainment did a lot to keep professional theatre off Canadian stages until after World War II.

8

The Universities: Where Revolution Begins

"The delicate thing about the university is that it has a mixed character, that it is suspended between its position in the external world, with all its corruption and evils and cruelties, and the splendid world of our imagination."

—Richard Hofstadter,
Professor of American History, Columbia University

Universities historically have been centres of revolutionary activity, whether political, artistic, or scientific. That was the role society expected of universities: to develop new ideas in the arts and sciences, and inculcate them into the upcoming generation of professionals. If these young people were diligent and lucky, they would take these new ideas to the outside world and use them to make useful and rewarding lives for themselves.

For that reason, theatre in the universities has had a very lively past. Theatre has tended to attract the most adventurous students, and often university campuses were the only places where the audience of the day could see groundbreaking theatre. They also have a very interesting history of struggles with internal politics, the other area where universities traditionally excel (and still do today).

Theatre Goes to University

Drama got its start in Manitoba university life as part of the Walkers' far-reaching efforts to stimulate interest in theatre. Harriet Walker had met university students through the Theatre Nights her theatre offered to university students. She helped form the University Players before the First World War. When war struck in 1914, Harriet Walker and the students conceived the idea of a student production as a fund-raiser for the war effort. They presented *The Bankrupt*, by Bjørnstjerne Bjørnson.[23] The play had a two-day run, the first for the general public, and the second for the military. The public supported the event with the same fervour with which they supported the war effort.

Out of that event grew the University Dramatic Society, the University Players' successor. Harriet Walker directed the first few productions, although after the first year the students used the Winnipeg Theatre. The Dramatic Society was very successful with audiences from the beginning. It attracted an audience outside the university community: 2000 people attended the 1918 production when the total university enrollment was only 1000. Even accounting for friends and family, that still leaves a good number of walk-ups.[24]

Harriet Walker was the first of several women to play a leading role in university theatre. Besides directing student productions, she used her persuasive powers to talk the university into offering a play-reading course in the 1917–18 academic year. Walker wanted the university to be a place where a student interested in theatre could develop. This was a departure from the original goal, which was to present plays for audience appreciation (and to fund the war effort). She also wanted students to take part in all aspects of theatre, from costuming and sets to writing plays. Her ambitious plans for the university did not all happen, but in 1919 she did succeed in introducing a one-act play festival, in which each faculty presented a play. In 1921 the university presented a student-written play, Peter Hoffer's *Five Thousand Dollars,* as part of its one-act play night. Another student she inspired was John Russell, who constructed sets while still an undergraduate. He later became a prominent city architect. He taught architecture at the university and had the Russell Architecture building named after him.

When one looks at Walker's level of commitment to the university, one wonders how she found time to do anything else, and yet she was also involved in the family theatre business, reviewing, and politics.

Harriet Walker retired as stage director in 1921, although she remained active with the Society.[25] Her replacement was the second woman to play an influential part in university drama, Rowena Brownstone. She had been Harriet Walker's star student, and she later became a key member of the Winnipeg Little Theatre. The 1923 production of *The Imaginary Invalid* she produced featured student F. D. Bradbrooke's *Jerry Makes it Fast* as a curtain-raiser.

By the late 1920s the university Dramatic Society faced internal competition from the Glee Club. This group produced professional-quality Gilbert and Sullivan at the Playhouse Theatre. They often imported professional leads and directors. This period also saw the Dramatic Society produce radio drama at CKY under Professor Perry, a tradition that has continued in various forms until the present day.

Nancy Pyper was the next woman to exert enormous influence on university theatre. She had trained and acted at Dublin's renowned Abbey Theatre and was a friend of George Bernard Shaw. She had signed photographs from numerous Irish theatre people on the walls of her house, including Synge, O'Casey, and Lady Gregory. Pyper's husband, C.B. Pyper, was a journalist who also wrote plays, including *Après la Guerre* in 1926 and *You Win if You Lose* in 1933.

Nancy Pyper took the helm of the Dramatic Society in 1929 and immediately made her presence felt. The first play she directed as Society director was Karl Capek's *R.U.R.* This was a challenging play in both ideas and form, and although it received praise in the *Free Press*, it apparently did not go down well with its audience, perhaps because of its socialist world view.[26]

The next production, *Pygmalion,* marked the first success for two actors who would later enjoy long and celebrated careers: Tommy Tweed and Evelyn Morris (who later changed her name to Judith Evelyn). W.O. Mitchell also took part in the Society at this time, which might help to explain why Tommy Tweed became a star of the *Jake and the Kid* radio series.[27]

Not all of Pyper's productions met with success. In 1930 the Phi Delta Epsilon sorority planned to stage Elmer Rice's *Street Scene.* It had to abandon those plans when a telegram threatening a lawsuit arrived hours before the production. (This was not Pyper's fault; correspondence requesting the rights had arrived between the time they became available and when a New York theatre manager bought exclusive rights.)[28]

In 1932, Pyper planned to present Herman Suderman's *The Joy of Living,* but the faculty banned the production on the grounds of its supposed "immorality and unsuitability." The Playhouse theatre manager booked it as an independent production and capitalized on the scandal.

In 1933 Pyper directed her husband's play, *Ambrosia,* as part on the one-act festival. The Engineering faculty performed it.

Judith Evelyn: A Star is Born

When Pyper left Winnipeg to become Artistic Director of Hart House in 1935, she took Judith Evelyn with her. Judith Evelyn was the first of many University of Manitoba graduates to make a name for themselves in the outside world of theatre. She created a sensation at the 1935 DDF, and left for England for further development. (She had earned both a Bachelor's and Master's degree in her final year at the University of Manitoba.)[29]

While in England, Evelyn read with interest a play called *Gaslight,* by Patrick Hamilton. The play stayed in her mind when she went back to North America in the early days of the Second World War. (Her ship sank in a U-boat attack and she had to tread water for several hours before her rescue.)

When she moved to Pasadena in search of a film career, she met a group of young actors who wanted to produce a play to gain attention for themselves. She suggested *Gaslight,* under its North American name, *Angel Street.* The group agreed and started rehearsing, but there was one major obstacle: as starving actors, they could not afford to pay royalties and rent a theatre.

Eventually they learned that the owner of a tiny theatre also wanted to do *Angel Street.* They approached him and told him they were ready to perform whenever the space was available. The result was an eight-day run in a theatre not much bigger than a large living room. On the eighth and final day the manager of a larger theatre saw the play, resulting in a much longer run. One day Vincent Price and his wife came to see the ambitious young company. Price knew this was the play he wanted to perform in New York. When he went there he persuaded a theatre owner to take a chance, not only on the obscure play, but on an unknown actor to play the lead opposite him. The owner was reluctant, but Price insisted he would not do the show without Evelyn. Perhaps in retaliation, the owner refused to print more than a few days' tickets, expecting the play to close soon after it opened.

He needn't have worried. *Life* magazine said of the 1941 production: "Broadway...produced only a single hit on a serious subject, this being a dark-horse melodrama called *Angel Street.*" Evelyn's performance created a sensation and won her the Delia Austrian medal for the most distinguished performance in New York. From then on her career was set. She had a long and prosperous career on Broadway and occasionally on film, although she later said the only movie she was proud of was *Rear Window.* (MTC produced *Gaslight* for the 1960–61 season, but did not use Judith Evelyn.)

Unfortunately, illness cut her life short. She returned to Winnipeg for Christmas in 1966, expressing in a *Winnipeg Tribune* interview the wish to perform at MTC. She died a few days later.[30]

Evelyn's career is interesting from a number of perspectives. For one, it proved that Manitoba could produce first-rank theatre artists. Her career also proves the value in making your own breaks. She found the play that made her career, found the first group to perform it, and found the space to perform it in. Most important, she made the most of her big break when it came. It is also interesting to speculate how her career might have developed if she had graduated 25 years later, when professional theatre returned to Winnipeg. Would she have stayed, and enjoyed a career here? Or would she have used MTC experience to gain employment at Stratford and elsewhere, as so many of those who came after her did? Most tantalizing of all, would she have become the artistic director who established Manitoba as the home of a great indigenous theatre? We of course will never know. We do know that a similarly gifted artist, Maggie Nagle, left Winnipeg in the 1990s.

Back to School

World War II was an eventful time for the University of Manitoba. It began to offer classes in dramatics to all students for the first time. Students took complete control of their festival for 1943. The university also began to offer adult education classes. Unfortunately, these classes ended after funding ran out in 1945. During this time Mercer McLeod led the Dramatic Society.[31]

The university began to collaborate with Gwen Pharis Ringwood, doing such a good job with *Still Stands the House* that she asked them to premiere her next play, *Dark Harvest.* Vic Cowie also began his illustrious career in this period. During this time the Society began to experience financial troubles, and since it was an arm of the student union, its budgets suffered.

Robert Jarman took the helm of the Dramatic Society after the war ended. This transplanted Englishman was also active in the Little Theatre. His first production, *The Male Animal,* starred Douglas Rain and was a critical and financial success. During Jarman's tenure the Society took on more artistically ambitious projects and established a reputation for excellence. Its 1948 production, *Meet John Doe,* went to the national DDF finals. Rain went on to become one of Canada's most respected actors. He spent four decades at Stratford and is the voice of HAL 9000 in the movies *2001: A Space Odyssey* and *2010.*

In 1949 Vic Cowie became the Society president. He emphasized artistically challenging work and more Canadian content. This position had its detractors, who felt that a popular play was needed to draw houses and pay for the Society's efforts. Cowie believed that almost any play could attract a decent house, given adequate publicity. Meanwhile the Glee Club changed its focus from Gilbert and Sullivan to Broadway hits. This was a popular move. Its revenues (and houses) must have caused some envy with the Society. It certainly did not help the Society when it applied to the student union for funding.

During the early '50s the Society faced a number of trials, culminating in the cancellation of its planned major production for 1952, Clifford Odet's *The Golden Boy.* Some cast members quit, and others were very lax about attending rehearsals. The Society staged the play the following year, but the houses were disappointing. This event is also interesting because two cast members in the second production were John Hirsch and Reg Skene.[32]

In 1953 Society president Al Desjardin led off his annual report with the statement, "The state of drama at the University of Manitoba is indeed a sorry one." He had a three-part suggestion for the following year:

1. The play be well known in Winnipeg.
2. The play be a comedy.
3. That it only entail a small or medium cast (under 15).

These were certainly not artistically bold steps. The following year the Society produced an eleven-person Broadway comedy, and the year after that, nothing.

In 1955–56, English professor George Broderson revived theatre with a plan to produce all of Shakespeare's plays. Broderson was a colourful character who seems to have loved theatre, alcohol, and cigars in almost equal measure, but who was nevertheless a charismatic teacher. The Society produced *Hamlet,* followed by what was probably the Canadian premiere of *Troilus and Cressida* in 1956. Perry Rosemond, who played Troilus, went on to a moderate career in Hollywood. Alvin Blye, who acted in *Julius Caesar,* also became a minor Hollywood figure. The university audiences grew tired of Shakespeare in 1966, before the cycle ran its course.[33]

Cowie returned to the University of Manitoba in the 1957–58 academic year after completing graduate studies in Toronto. Under Vic Cowie the Society undertook such challenging modern plays as Pirandello's *Six Characters in Search of an Author.*

The Society's Centennial project was a film rather than a play, *And No Birds Sing*, which Cowie wrote and directed. It was a critical and popular success, touring the Canadian and American campus circuit. The film received three nominations for Canadian film awards in 1969, and Michael Posner won Best Supporting Actor, although he never acted again.[34]

Unfortunately the film accidentally killed the Dramatic Society. The student union used the film as an excuse to cancel funding. The UMSU (University of Manitoba Students Union) Theatre Group replaced the Dramatic Society in 1970. Harold Dollin, Jeremy Gibson and Frederick Edell directed some very good productions in this period.

The next period of major change in university theatre came about ten years later. Two people, George Toles (who arrived in 1978) and Chris Johnson, who became the first professor specifically hired to teach theatre in 1979, revitalized theatre at the University of Manitoba, and made it the force it is today. The university theatre program began to turn out a growing number of people who would later make a mark for themselves in theatre and related fields. One example is the 1980 student-directed production, *After all is done and said.* Greg Klymkiw directed 15 sketches that he, Robert Nixon, Guy Maddin and Andrew Coyne (the right-wing columnist for the *National Post)* wrote. The fast-paced show was a hit.

Chris Johnson inspired Vic Cowie to once again become involved in university drama, both as a director and a performer (most notably as Fiers in *The Cherry Orchard).* Over the years the university added theatre courses to its curriculum, both on the performing and technical side. The performance program became broader and more varied as well. Johnson used ideas such as co-productions with the Irish Club (home of the acclaimed community theatre group, the Tara Players) and the local cable channel to finance productions, and turned the studio space into a small but workable theatre. (It got its present name when then-student Bruce Michalski named it the Black Hole Theatre, after the Black Hole of Calcutta.)

Although funding from UMSU continued to be a problem, the Theatre Group mounted a noon-hour theatre (the Lunch Bhagg) in

1984. (Bhagg stands for Black Hole Anarchist Theatre Group, with a silent second G for effect.)

Over the years, the University of Manitoba theatre department has contributed actors such as Anne Ross, Ross McMillan, Gord Tanner, and Sarah Constible to the local scene, and writers such as Ian Ross, Angus Kohm, and Gary Jarvis.

One University Becomes Three: Brandon University and the University of Winnipeg

In 1967 the University of Winnipeg and Brandon University received charters as separate degree-granting universities. From this point, the three universities pursued different educational goals and programs.

Although it is better known for its School of Music, Brandon offers a minor in theatre to its Fine Arts students. This program suffered during the funding cuts of the 1980s and '90s, but survives to this day with a varied program of academic, technical, and performance courses.

Shortly after the University of Winnipeg received its charter, it began graduating theatre students. It now offers both general and honours degrees in Theatre. In the beginning, the university's ambitions seem to have been a bit more modest. As Ross Stuart says in *The History of Prairie Theatre,* "[It] believes in teaching theatre as a means of exploring play texts rather than for the purpose of training professionals."

What might have been an accurate statement in 1984 is not completely true any more. For one thing, the university trains people in such technical aspects as lighting, stage management, and set design. The university also offers courses in playwriting, mime, voice, and stage fighting. In Rick Skene (Mimeworks founder) they have one of the most talented fight directors in the country. The university has also been lucky in other faculty members.

Alan Williams, a charismatic performer and writer, taught at the university in the 1980s. He was no less charismatic in the classroom. Besides being the first Open Door dramaturg at the Manitoba Association of Playwrights (MAP), he inspired the formation of the now-defunct Rude Players. Per Brask has given the department an intellectual underpinning, and has brought many modern ideas to the curriculum. Until he retired in the 1990s, Dennis Noble, a playwright with many plays and over a thousand productions to his name, gave students a sound background in dramatic structure (although his structured approach sometimes frustrated the more adventurous playwriting students). Tim Babcock, besides offering a solid technical program to students, has been the technical foundation of the Fringe Festival since its beginning.

The University of Winnipeg, like its big sister the University of Manitoba, has a growing list of graduates who have gone on to successful careers. Harry Nelken, Lora Schroeder, Chris Sigurdson, Rick and Jan Skene, Michelle Boulet, and many others regularly grace Manitoba stages (although not as frequently as they would like). Kelly Daniels graduated from the University of Winnipeg, went away to complete a master's degree, and now teaches at the University of Winnipeg. She and Rick Skene have completed the traditional cycle all good institutions experience, where star pupils return to teach future generations.

The two Winnipeg universities take differing approaches when teaching drama. The best illustration of this is the student presentations. The University of Manitoba charges admission. The fee is nominal, but it puts pressure on the Black Hole to break even. The traditional problems the theatre has had securing funds from UMSU probably account for this.

The University of Winnipeg presentations, on the other hand, are free to the public. They are part of the curriculum, and students' grades depend at least in part on their work in these productions. One University of Winnipeg professor explained this apparent lack of financial acumen in pedagogical terms. Because the productions are practicums for the students, he explained, the choice of material and casting depend on factors other than entertainment value. Students may get roles because they need to stretch themselves, not because the roles suit their abilities and current development. By not charging admission, therefore, the university absolves itself of the obligation to consider the audience in its presentations.

This reasoning is fine, as far as it goes. By inviting a public audience, however, the university claims a far more precious and rare resource than the nominal admission charge they might have levied. Each production takes up a finite portion of the audience's time. Audiences who attend the presentation, therefore, have already made a significant sacrifice with the knowledge that their presence helps future artists develop their potential.

The University of Manitoba is not so squeamish. Its presentations are just as artistically bold as the University of Winnipeg's, and by introducing the reality of budget constraints, it also educates its students in the harsh reality that even artists must find a way to pay the rent. The University of Manitoba also seems to have a slightly more favourable attitude to the career versus the aesthetic aspects of theatre. The University of Manitoba has for at least 10 years kept a detailed student database that professors can consult. This has helped Fringe producers and others find cast members from among the theatre students.

Both university programs succeed in developing people who reach a professional level of artistry, so perhaps the philosophical differences mentioned above are not as significant as they might at first seem.

Post-secondary Theatre Institutions Today

Where theatre once seemed a disreputable way to earn a living, today Manitoba universities all offer education in the theatre arts. Even the independent denominational colleges like Providence College offer drama training. Adults who want to develop artistically can also take evening classes at Prairie Theatre Exchange (PTE) and Manitoba Theatre for Young People (MTYP), and through various private teachers operating independently of any theatre.

Drama training has crept back into the high school curriculum. Grant Park High School, which a few years ago had almost no drama activity, is fund-raising for a performing arts building.

The wealth of choice for theatre training has caused at least one traditional avenue to close. The Summer Theatre School of Manitoba, an offshoot of the Association of Community Theatres, closed in the late 1990s when attendance dropped drastically at its annual residency-based training program in Portage La Prairie. This group gave community theatre enthusiasts and others professional-level training from people such as Nancy Drake, Anna Barry and Michael Burrell.

9

Post-War Prosperity:
Theatre in Canada Turns Professional

"The Canadian is often a baffled man because he feels different from his British kindred and his American neighbours, sharply refuses to be lumped together with either of them, yet cannot make plain his difference."
—J.B. Priestley,
in the introduction to *The Bodley Head Leacock*

Canada emerged from the war effort a changed nation. At the close of hostilities, Canada had the fourth-largest navy in the world. The war effort gave Canada a huge industrial base. While many factories in Europe disappeared under bombing attacks or behind the Iron Curtain, Canada and the United States had excess capacity after the war. Despite the ominous presence of the nuclear age, therefore, a spirit of optimism prevailed.

The nation did not repeat the mistakes it made dealing with returning veterans after World War I. Losses, although high, did not reach the tragic levels of the previous conflict. The government took steps to ensure that veterans came home to a support system. Many took advantage of free tuition and gained a university education, a goal that would have been impossible otherwise.

Young men and women who had spent six years under wartime and rationing came home and started families, the men often bringing home a spouse they had met abroad. The so-called baby boom started.

Added to the tide of returning veterans was a new stream of immigration. After a shameful lack of compassion during the Holocaust, in which tens of thousands of Jews died while hoping to escape to Canada, our doors opened to those displaced by war: the so-called "displaced persons," or DPs in crude slang. Many new arrivals made huge contributions to Canadian life. One of them, John Hirsch, helped renew professional theatre.

Thus while no nation can ever logically claim to have won a war, Canada emerged pretty well out of the conflict.

The Search for Identity

The nation had a sense of pride tinged slightly by jealousy over its role in the war. By any standard, Canada's contribution to the war was huge. Still, there was the sense that the world still viewed us as a British colony. In his memoirs, Lester Pearson writes about his frustration with American officials who suggested that Canada needed to hold up its end more, at a time when Canada had proportionally more people in uniform and resources committed to the effort than did the United States.

During the 1950s and early 1960s Canadian magazines and newspaper articles often seemed to assume an air of wounded self-esteem. When Harry Jerome, the world record holder in the 100-yard race, failed to take gold at the 1960 Olympics, some Canadians treated the result as an act of treason. Wags suggested that the national pastime was debating whether Canada had a national identity.

At the same time, Canadian artists in all genres began to express increased militancy at what they considered to be colonial attitudes to their work. In the October 29, 1955 edition of *Maclean's*, playwright, screenwriter and novelist Lionel Shapiro explained his success this way: "A long time ago, I decided that a writer born, bred and educated in Canada is not necessarily less skillful, less perceptive or less readable than a writer born in the United States, Britain, France, India or China. I decided that a Canadian has not only an equal chance but an equal right to jump out into the world forum and make a reputation and a livelihood as a writer."

Manitoba in the Post-War Years

Manitoba was a microcosm of the national experience. When war broke out, high unemployment and poor crops meant that the Prairies had more young men willing to enlist. At the same time, there was (and is) a sense that the national psyche did not appreciate the contributions made here.

After the trauma of the Dust Bowl, the Great Depression and war, bumper crops restored prosperity to Manitoba. With this prosperity came a change in Manitoba's predominant attitude, from one of cautious conservatism to a more outward-looking, adventurous spirit. It did not happen overnight, but in the 20 years after World War II, Manitoba went from being a place that imported the best artistic experiences from around the world and exported people to excel elsewhere, to the place that gave the world a top ballet company and the model for professional regional theatres.

The 1950s were a strange time. Social conformity lived side by side with great scientific advances and enormous changes in the way people lived their lives. Just about everybody went to church. An unmarried couple living together was a scandal. The men always wore white shirts and ties to formal occasions, while the women always wore hats and gloves. (Shopping downtown qualified as a formal occasion.) Shopping centres, television, and rock and roll were just three revolutionary changes that started to influence society during this time. Medical advances were astounding: antibiotics and new surgical techniques seemed to offer the possibility of eternal life. Later The Pill seemed to offer the possibility of eternal sex.

Manitoba emerged from the war in its traditionally cautious Anglo-Saxon mode. The province had had a coalition government under John Bracken during the war. This coalition included the members from all the parties except the Communist member, James Litterick, and the independent Lewis St. George Stubbs. (This was a particularly diverse coalition that contained the CCF and Social Credit parties.) In the post-war 1946 election, then-premier Garson ran on a coalition ticket, minus the CCF. The province was not ready for full democracy, it seemed.

First Nations citizens did not get the vote in Manitoba elections until 1952, and not in federal elections until 1960. Residential schools, founded in 1879 to integrate First Nations forcefully into mainstream life, caused broken lives instead for over a century. Aboriginals were punished for speaking their native language or trying to observe their customs.

Although there was a space race on, school curricula did not change much. As late as 1965, the grade 10 science text contained a sentence that read, "Unless you have been to a world's fair or a radio station, you have probably never seen a television set." The buildings that housed St. John's and Kelvin High Schools would have been condemned if they had been commercial buildings.

The teacher shortage that the baby boom created had unforeseen effects. The combination of low salaries compared to other provinces and the population bulge caused by the war meant that Manitoba faced a critical shortage of teachers for about 15 to 20 years.

Teacher shortages in Manitoba were a long-standing problem that the baby boom made intolerable. In the years before the war, a person could become a teacher with grade 11 standing and one year of training at Normal School.

During the baby boom, even these relaxed standards could not entice enough people into the classrooms. Elementary school classes often numbered in the forties, and high schools suffered from similar overcrowding. Incompetent teachers could stay in the profession as long as their transgressions were not outrageous.

Baby boom parents had often waited years to have their children, and therefore took an active and activist interest in them. The provincial government could not afford to ignore the problem. A shortage of skilled labour was the root problem, and it could not be solved merely by raising salaries. Training people takes time, so Manitoba began to recruit abroad.

Teachers came to Winnipeg from all over the English-speaking world, but one of the main sources of talent was South Africa. The apartheid regime both limited advancement opportunities for non-white citizens and made wanted criminals of those brave enough to protest. As a result, Manitoba received many highly talented, highly principled people into its teaching ranks. Sometimes a person who had barely escaped his homeland ahead of the hangman found himself teaching history to a mainly Caucasian, middle-class group of students. Teachers also came from other African countries, the Caribbean, Asia, and Great Britain.

This hiring strategy became possible in 1962, when Canada's destructively racist immigration policy changed to its present universal, nondiscriminatory one. (The previous policy listed country of origin by priority, giving first precedence to white British and American immigrants, and flowing downward from there. Northern Europeans held the middle ranks, followed by southern Europe, while the bottom of the order belonged to Asians, Gypsies, Jews and blacks.)

The most obvious effect of this immigration, other than reducing class sizes, was that students received a broader outlook on life than they would have had if their teachers had all been home-grown. They also saw their own culture from different eyes.[35]

Another effect of the influx of foreign-born teachers was that it helped to break the WASP superiority stereotype. Believing that blacks are intellectually inferior is more difficult after someone from Nigeria has taught you mathematics. Students who belonged to minorities found they had new role models, people from outside the WASP hegemony who held responsible, white-collar jobs. Another side effect was that Manitobans of Ukrainian and other central European heritage found that they had become part of the white majority, seemingly overnight.

Many foreign-born teachers had a different teaching style than some Manitoba-trained teachers. Quite often a foreign-born teacher would teach a subject in its broader context instead of as a means of passing an exam. (Until the 1970s, students had to pass province-wide examinations to gain entry to university. A lazy teacher would spend the year "teaching to the exam," which would encourage students to learn by rote.)

These are broad generalizations that obviously do not hold in all particular instances. Some Manitoba-born teachers gave their students a broad perspective (a history teacher at J.B. Mitchell school had actually canoed the fur trade route during his summer vacation, and could give a first-hand perspective) while some uninspiring people came from other lands to teach in our classrooms.

The overall effect that the teacher immigration had on Manitoba should not be underestimated, however. Almost any baby boomer nostalgia session will evoke at least one story about a teacher who came from afar to make a profound effect. For aspiring theatre artists, especially playwrights, the broader perspective foreign-born teachers brought was invaluable.

New Leaders with New Approaches

Gradually, however, society changed. People who had fought in a war did not want to come home to be treated like second-class citizens. Manpower shortages meant that the old, invisible barriers to promotion and advancement began to crumble. In 1956, Winnipeggers elected Steve Juba as their mayor. As J.M. Bumsted says in his *Dictionary of Manitoba Biography,* "His election symbolized the end of WASP domination of city politics."

Juba was many things, but stodgy was not one of them. A self-made millionaire, he drove around town in a bright yellow Cadillac, much to the chagrin of the more conservative elements, who thought the mayor should use more dignified transportation. Sometimes his flamboyance did not achieve the results he desired (his monorail idea never came to fruition) but on the whole his visionary attitude inspired Winnipeggers. He introduced the three-digit emergency numbers to North America, brought the Pan-Am games to Winnipeg, and boosted the city tirelessly. During his term of office (1956 to 1977), Winnipeg developed the Manitoba Theatre Centre, the Centennial Concert Hall, a new stadium, and a sense of pride in its diversity. Once the Ukrainian-heritage Juba opened the door, all ethnic groups saw their chance to charge through.

Although they did not see eye to eye politically, Duff Roblin complemented Juba's activist, progressive style when he became premier in 1958. Although he was a blue-blood Conservative, he took many steps to bring Manitoba up to date. In 1951 he led his party out of the coalition government. He became leader in 1954. Under his leadership, the provincial government embarked on an ambitious program of public works and renewal. His lasting monument is the Winnipeg Floodway.

In 1950, the Red River overflowed, causing the greatest mass evacuation in Canadian history. Over 200,000 people had to flee their homes. When he became Premier, Roblin started building a floodway. It became the source of mockery ("Duff's Ditch") but it proved its worth 17 times before 1997, the so-called Flood of the Century. The Roblin years were years of change in which both public works and social programs expanded. The conservative tradition of low taxes and little public expenditure evolved into a more activist, but still conservative, operating philosophy. On the national stage, John Diefenbaker swept into power on a platform of change.

Conditions for a national theatre were once again ripe. It nearly happened.

10

The Manitoba Theatre Centre: Manitoba's Great Contribution to World Theatre (Part One)

"The MTC under John Hirsch soon became the model for and an inspiration to similar regional theatres across Canada and the United States.... Although it has not been able to retain its initial pre-eminence, the MTC remains a major Canadian institution."

—James Aikens' entry
in the *Cambridge Guide to Theatre*

The Manitoba Theatre Centre has a mixed place in our theatre history. Before we discuss the MTC in depth, though, let's return to the post-war situation. This was a time when Canadian arts and letters began to emerge from its Anglo-Saxon roots to express itself in a purely Canadian way. This outpouring encompassed both popular culture (DDF alumni Wayne and Shuster's comedy team made more appearances on *The Ed Sullivan Show* than any other act) to capital "A" arts and letters. Northrop Frye's pioneering work in literary criticism, and Kelvin High School and University of Manitoba graduate Marshall McLuhan's work in communications theory showed that Canada could produce great thinkers. Writers such as Morley Callaghan and W.O. Mitchell had begun to interpret the Canadian experience to the world.

The Canada Council: Canada Gets Serious About the Arts

The Massey Commission, formally known as the Royal Commission on National Development in the Arts, convened in 1949 and wrote a report that resulted in the Canada Council in 1957. The

Commission drew a lot of public attention and debate. A major focus was the lack of what they called a National Theatre.

Theatre artists and lovers complained that a country as wealthy and developed as Canada was should have a professional theatre. Eventually the pieces began to come together. In 1953 professional theatre returned to Canada: in a tent in Stratford. Denounced as folly, the first Stratford Festival used director Tyrone Guthrie from Ireland, and designer Tanya Moiseiwitsch and actor Sir Alec Guinness from England to prove that professional theatre could again thrive in Canada.

On the heels of this success, people across Canada began to look for ways to make professional theatre work in their communities. In Winnipeg the right combination of people and infrastructure existed.

MTC: The Birth of a Notion

In 1957, John Hirsch, who came to Winnipeg as a refugee from Hungary, and Tom Hendry, an aspiring playwright born in Winnipeg and trained as an accountant, formed Theatre 77. Theatre 77 drew its name from its location, seventy-seven steps from Portage and Main. This semi-professional repertory company merged with the Winnipeg Little Theatre in 1958 to form the Manitoba Theatre Centre. It was a propitious time to form a theatre, because the Canada Council was looking for a theatre to fund, so it could fulfill the part of its mandate that called for a national theatre.

At a backyard party at Don Campbell's, two groups that could not accomplish what they wanted alone decided to join forces. For Hendry and Hirsch and their company, it meant more opportunities to be paid for what they loved to do best. For the Winnipeg Little Theatre, it meant more help in maintaining the Dominion Theatre, a building Kathleen Richardson had donated to them, but which was proving to be a mixed blessing because of the upkeep cost.

Theatre 77 had drawn 24,000 people in its inaugural season. Junior League-sponsored children's theatre had given the local acting community what Tom Hendry described as "the heady, if irretrievably corrupting experience of being paid for our endeavours." The Dominion Theatre offered to Manitoba theatre artists the concrete possibility of a livelihood.

The Winnipeg Little Theatre faced a dilemma that the merger with Theatre 77 offered to solve. They had lost their artistic director, Arthur Zigouras, to the CBC. Running the theatre had become more than an amateur group could handle. Hirsch had the solution, a theatre centre that would attract funding from the Canada Council. The Council was looking to fund a national theatre, and by establishing a professional theatre in Winnipeg, Hirsch felt that some money would come from that source.

When one reads the documents of the day, the artistic community's idea seems hopelessly idealistic, but it also helps to explain why professional theatre evolved the way it did in Canada. In the post-war years, there was a conviction that there was something called a Canadian identity. No one was quite sure what it was, but the idea was that if someone could express that idea clearly and passionately enough, it would become part of a movement towards national unity.

The Canada Council hoped to foster that movement. Today, when we witness countless premiers' conferences at which provincial leaders rail against that great evil in our land, Ottawa, and by implication the national presence in our lives, it is hard to believe that once there was a passionate movement dedicated to finding and expressing a national consciousness. The idea may seem quaint now, but in the 1940s and 1950s there was evidence to back up the conviction. CBC radio had produced a number of national treasures, among them W.O. Mitchell's *Jake and the Kid*. Wayne and Shuster's lowbrow brand of sketch comedy moved from radio to television, and conquered not only Canada, but all of North America. They were the only act that Ed Sullivan did not censor. Once Eartha Kitt, on finding out that her act had been cut by one song (and Tony Bennett's medley from four-and-one-half minutes to three) to accommodate an 18-minute Wayne and Shuster sketch, walked up to them in the wings and said, "Who *are* you guys?"[36] *Spring Thaw* toured the country every year to large crowds. It therefore would have seemed a natural progression to have a National Theatre develop plays that would subsequently tour the country, and in the process help to unite Canada.

In the late 1950s, the pieces seemed to be coming together. Stratford had developed a strong international reputation. They used international stars, to be sure, but Canadian actors such as Martha Henry, William Hutt and John Colicos proved they were more than able to share the stage with them. Radio drama proved that Canadians could write effective scripts. In 1945, the University of Saskatchewan in Saskatoon pioneered university drama training by founding the first university drama department in the British Commonwealth. Other universities followed suit.

If the Manitoba Theatre Centre had come into being with the idea of becoming a beachhead in the growing encroachment of professional theatre into Canadian life, that alone would have been a significant accomplishment. At the start, however, the Centre's ambition (and later accomplishment) was far greater. It created a new way of doing theatre that later theatres in Canada and the United States would copy.

A Manitoba Theatre Centre publication, *The First Twenty Years,* gives valuable insights into this period. Tom Hendry explains that John Hirsch had been reading about a theatre in Villerbanne, France. Roget Planchon had created a centre there that did much more than just produce plays. It involved the entire community, offering lectures and classes. The name, Manitoba Theatre Centre, was therefore no accident. They could have called it the Winnipeg Theatre Centre, but they wanted to involve the whole province. They could have called it the Manitoba Theatre, but they wanted to do more than just put on plays. They seemed to realize that if their dream were to become reality, it would take the whole province to support it.

Once Hendry and Hirsch sold the board of directors on the idea, the hard part started. As Hendry says, "I remember working our asses off to get enough publicity, enough promotion and so on to attract people to the theatre. Our problem was to expand a very tiny audience of about 1200 regulars into a big audience of at least 10,000 people so that we would have credibility."

As with many other great ventures, the Manitoba Theatre Centre happened because the right people came together at the right time in the right place. Winnipeg had a long history of supporting theatre, and a strong amateur tradition. The University of Manitoba had been producing student drama since 1914, quite often pushing the envelope of acceptable public standards. In the Dominion Theatre, there was a theatre building, which although decrepit, had not become a movie house or bowling alley. In John Hirsch, the theatre community had a charismatic leader, and in Hendry, they had Anglo-Saxon respectability.

The original MTC mandate had three parts:

1. Mainstage productions that would eventually attract an annual attendance of at least 150,000, combining a strong season ticket base with walk-up trade.

2. Touring productions that would travel throughout the province and eventually beyond.
3. An educational component that would develop in children and students a taste for theatre.

When one stops to examine this mandate, two things become apparent. The first is that this was a very ambitious blueprint. The people who conceived and subscribed to this mandate were anything but timid. One must remember that at the time, the two founding groups were struggling just to stay in operation. And yet, these people had the foresight to realize that if theatre was to thrive in Manitoba, it would need to have almost universal support. They aimed for an audience base that represented a one hundred-fold increase, to one-sixth of the province's population, and one-third of Winnipeg's. This would obviously not happen overnight.

The second significant part of this mandate is what it does not mention: it does not mention using local actors, directors, or playwrights. It does not mention developing a Manitoba theatre, just a Manitoba Theatre *Centre*. (In *The First Twenty Years,* Hendry says, "We viewed the Manitoba Theatre School as a school for an audience rather than a school for actors."). Perhaps using local talent was thought to be so obvious it did not need mention. Perhaps they decided just to specify the destination without prescribing the route. Regardless, any assessment of MTC's role in Manitoba's theatre history must in fairness consider that creating indigenous theatre art was not part of its original mandate.

Whatever the group objective was, we know that the individual artists saw MTC as an avenue to further their careers. John Hirsch of course applied his unique artistic vision to everything he directed, and went on to direct at Stratford and elsewhere. In *The First Twenty Years,* Tom Hendry confesses, "Initially, I wanted to work on starting the theatre so I could get out of it and write plays for it." (Ironically, while he has had many successes as a playwright elsewhere, his only success writing for MTC was a children's play.)

Any account of the early days at MTC carries the image of people on a mission, acting on and responding to the highest human motivations. The people who founded MTC and set it on its path virtually lived there, when they were not out in the community selling the concept.

They gave away over 5000 coupons to unions, service clubs, companies, and to anyone else they thought would come to a performance on a trial basis, trusting that one experience would lead to another. This type of selling has as much effect on the seller as it does on the customer, because with each free ticket comes a direct or tacit promise that the recipient will be glad they took a chance. This in turn puts subtle pressure on the company to do well. MTC became one of Canada's great success stories. Other cities, encouraged and inspired by MTC's example, followed their pattern with varying degrees of success.

History gives us countless examples that prove you do not create a thriving theatre just by throwing money, materials and people at it. It is to the credit of Hendry, Hirsch and the others involved in this venture that the Manitoba Theatre Centre went on to become the model that other regional theatres in Canada and elsewhere followed.

Great change comes at a cost, and MTC was no exception. People who used to get parts as a matter of course were unhappy to learn that they no longer had a place in the company, either through lack of ability or because they could not or would not commit the time necessary to rehearse a professional-quality production. As Hirsch says in *The First Twenty Years:* "The policy of the Manitoba Theatre Centre was that you must use the people you have but you must also bring people in, so that the people there can learn, in order to establish standards for the audience as well as for the actors." In later years, the first part of that policy would almost disappear.

The Dominion Theatre itself proved to be a decidedly mixed blessing. In the 1959–60 season the company had to move to the Beacon Theatre so that much-needed repairs to the Dominion could take place. As Hendry recalls, ticket sales dried up almost immediately. When they moved back to the Dominion, however, the company was stronger than ever, and launched its theatre school on Albert Street (and later, on Portage Avenue East, called Theatre Across the Street). The theatre also launched its first summer season, its first studio series, and its first provincial tour. While the theatre had not yet attracted 150,000 patrons, it had met the other two objectives in its mandate.

In that year (1960) the Canada Council awarded the theatre its first grant. MTC had arrived on the national scene, just two years after its launch. Hirsch sold the company both within Manitoba to potential patrons, and outside Manitoba to actors and directors. In the early 1960s, MTC became the home to many legendary productions and performances, such as Zoe Caldwell's in *Mother Courage and Her Children.* Winnipeg became a kind of Stratford West, a wintering spot for out-of-work Stratford actors. Manitoba also started sending actors from its stages outwards. Len Cariou got his start in Winnipeg, and MTC is also responsible for launching Heath Lamberts on the professional stage.

The Changing of the Guard: The Siege Begins

From its inaugural season until the 1964–65 season, a period of six years, MTC went from 63 performances and a budget of $63,700 to 240 performances and a $333,650 budget. Attendance approached the dreamed-of 150,000. In six short years, MTC had grown from being an unknown quantity on the local scene to a national presence, an exemplar for theatres throughout the continent.

MTC had also encountered two perilous events in any organization's life. The first comes after an organization realizes its initial goals. It then has two choices: it can consolidate, and hope to sustain its position, or it can look for new horizons.

To use an example from the world of commerce, a restaurant might have opened with the goal of paying off its investors in the first five years. Once it has done that, the proprietor could choose to serve the clientele at the present location with the goal of becoming a local institution. When it is debt-free, the restaurant might pay the owner a comfortable living as long as it is popular with the public and well managed. The second choice would be to expand the business by franchising, opening similar restaurants in other locations. The potential returns are higher, but so is the risk. Organizations typically go through this growing pain during their first six to eight years of existence.

The second peril point comes when the founders leave. Can those who replace them carry on? Eaton's and Massey Ferguson are but two examples of thriving businesses that withered and eventually died once their dynamic founders left. Tom Hendry left MTC in 1963, ending a very productive partnership. John Hirsch left in 1966.

People who replace inspirational figures face an almost impossible dilemma. If they attempt to emulate their predecessor, they risk betraying their own vision and personal strengths. If they choose to follow their own vision, they risk alienating the organization the former leader left behind, and being accused of betraying the founder's vision.

MTC was fortunate in the people who replaced both Hirsch and Hendry. One year after Hendry left, the legendary theatre manager William Wylie, husband to author Betty Jane Wylie, took over the financial and management reins. From 1964 until 1968, when he left to become general manager at Stratford, Wylie excelled at making sure the resources were there to pay for the artistic decisions that others made. He is credited with inventing the science of theatre management in Canada. Like Hendry, Wylie was a native Manitoban.

On the artistic side, Edward Gilbert proved to be a competent replacement for Hirsch. The Austrian-born Gilbert had trained at Oxford and worked with a number of prestigious British theatres, including the Royal Shakespeare company. He had worked at MTC before, and was Hirsch's choice as his successor. His British training and theatre aesthetic fit well with the predominant cultural attitudes the board and audience held at the time.

Gilbert inherited more than the normal problems a replacement for a popular charismatic leader would have faced. A partnership Hirsch had formed with Stratford had resulted in a disastrous run of *Nicholas Romanov,* putting a financial strain on the organization. He also faced another crisis point for any organization that associates itself with a specific location: the Dominion Theatre faced demolition. Despite these distractions, the 1966–67 season broke attendance records. A keystone production in that season was *Winnipeg Tribune* theatre critic Ann Henry's script *Lulu Street.* It was the first Manitoba script to reach the main stage.

Lulu Street came about because the I.O.D.E. (Imperial Order of the Daughters of the Empire) donated $10,000 to MTC to commission a script for centennial year. The play dealt with the 1919 strike. Henry had impeccable credentials to write it: besides being a talented writer with an eye for theatre, her father had been one of the platform speakers during the strike. (Her son is actor Donnelley Rhodes, who starred in the American comedy Soap and the Canadian adventure series *Danger Bay* and *Da Vinci's Inquest.*)

Treena Laird, who worked in the box office then, describes the audience *Lulu Street* drew: "I think a lot of our [*Lulu Street*] audience...were people that had never been in a theatre...They could relate to that and they came to see whether it was really what happened in 1919. A lot of them were older people and they knew Ann Henry. They probably never came to the theatre again."

That statement sums up the fear that theatres across Canada had about producing Canadian plays then: the theatres understood and could predict the reaction clientele would have for the imported theatre they usually produced. On the other hand, new plays were unknown waters with unpredictable undercurrents. Organizational behaviourists call this timid reaction to change "retreating to the familiar."

Still, *Lulu Street* might have been the play that launched MTC into its next phase of development. There was a national groundswell calling for new Canadian plays, and MTC had proved that it could survive the experience. Unfortunately, other events drained the theatre's creative and managerial resources.

In 1968, MTC lost the Dominion Theatre before it had a new home. It booked the Centennial Concert Hall as a stopgap. Its seating capacity dwarfed the Dominion. Costs mounted, and other disasters befell the theatre. MTC had to cancel a touring production of *Funny Girl* when a makeshift cast arrived one week before opening without having had any rehearsals. Gilbert left after one frustrating season at the Centennial Concert Hall. His replacement, Kurt Reis, lasted one year. His short tenure points out the choice MTC had made regarding its future course. Whether it was because of Hirsch's lingering aura, or whether it was a return to Manitoba's traditional conservative roots, MTC's board took a stance in favour of the status quo in everything except its choice of artistic directors.

Kurt Reis came to Winnipeg with impressive academic and professional credentials, but his determination to plot new directions ran into direct conflict with the board. The impossibility of presenting the type of work he wanted to do at the Concert Hall made his position untenable. As Reis himself says, "Perhaps I made more [mistakes] than anyone else because I didn't understand that I was in Winnipeg. I had never been in a small city and I'd recently come back from Europe determined to make the Manitoba Theatre Centre an international theatre."

Although the theatre accepted Hirsch's grand schemes, they rejected Ries'. Why? Reis gives part of the explanation himself. Hirsch, although born in Europe, had grown up in Winnipeg and had established himself there. He had a support base. That is not the whole story, however. Because of the loss of the Dominion, MTC's very future was in doubt. To the sober businessmen on the board, this would not have seemed an ideal time to take new directions. And yet, taking new directions was exactly what had made MTC successful in the first place.

MTC could have made the leap of faith to new ways of doing things, and with *Lulu Street* under its belt, Winnipeg could have become the cradle for new Canadian drama. Unfortunately, uncertainty caused by a real estate crisis clouded the issue, and MTC became a creative backwater. (Although popular belief holds that caution should apply when an organization faces troubled financial times, often the opposite is true. In the 1980s, when Chrysler faced almost certain bankruptcy, it revived its fortunes by launching two radical new concepts in automobiles: the K-car and the minivan.)

One positive step that occurred during the transition period was the opening of the Warehouse Theatre in 1969. This theatre became the home for all Manitoba plays MTC produced between *Lulu Street* in 1967 and when Maureen Hunter's *Transit of Venus* finally reconquered the main stage for Manitoba playwrights in 1992.

The MTC board's behaviour for the next 20 years or so is very curious. A number of artistic directors came and went. The otherwise cautious MTC board developed a habit of hiring artistic directors whose sensibilities ran exactly opposite to their (and often the audience's) tastes.

The next stormy relationship was with Keith Turnbull, who was only 23 at the time. (Imagine the uproar today if a major theatre were to hire an artistic director barely old enough to have finished university!) This does not seem to have been a rushed or whimsical decision, however; as former Administrative Director Gerry Eldred says, "Both Keith [Turnbull] and Kurt [Reis] came in and went through a series of interviews with a number of people and I think they both fairly clearly explained to the board the kind of plays they were interested in doing and how they would do them..." Perhaps the board thought they could find a Winnipeg version of Orson Welles. Perhaps they thought that Hirsch and Gilbert, who were still involved with MTC in limited capacities, could provide the mentoring these two young men would have needed.

The opening night at the new theatre, Brecht's *A Man's a Man,* was an artistic triumph. Hirsch directed a production that stunned the opening night crowd, a group that included "outsiders from eastern Canada and the States." As one of the actors, James Blendick says, "They hadn't seen really good genuine theatre in a long time other than in New York."

Then MTC did a rock musical, *Salvation*. Its *Hobson's Choice* toured to Vancouver as an emergency replacement. Certainly the theatre seems to have generated excitement during that time, but it also seems to have generated a lot of red ink. The board did not renew Turnbull's contract for the 1972–73 season.

What went wrong? Turnbull says: "What I wanted out of MTC is what I want out of any regional theatre in Canada. I want it to reflect to the people in that community something about their community, and then that can be their gift, their donation to the rest of the world." He describes the Shakespearean comedies, West End hits and "slightly revolutionary Bertolt Brechts now and then" as a "complete rejection of the validity of the lives of the...community."

The clue as to why this vision did not inspire confidence in the board lies in a statement he makes later in *The First Twenty Years:* "The age level of the audience dropped." Here we have a telltale clue. Audiences must renew themselves, or a theatre dies. At the same time, young people typically do not have the money to attend theatre regularly, unless the theatre discounts prices for them. Meanwhile, the plays and approaches to plays that appeal to young people are unlikely to fire the imagination of a typical board member.

A cryptic quote Edward Gilbert makes later on confirms that Turnbull's youth orientation had a negative effect on the balance books: "There is a certain line of credit and when it runs out, forget it." In an effort to restore the theatre's viability, the board persuaded Gilbert to return. Gilbert describes the situation as alarming: a large deficit and the first drop in attendance in the theatre's history. Hard decisions had to be made. Gilbert returned on the condition that Thomas Bohdanetsky join him as general manager. They closed the theatre school, and chose plays they knew would sell well. They wiped out the deficit. (By closing the school, they accidentally spawned their chief rival, but that's a story for another chapter.)

The New Home Becomes a Successful House

For the next few years, MTC was in a recovery mode. As Arif Hasnian says in *The First Twenty Years,* "When Eddie Gilbert came back, he assessed the situation very quickly, realized...that the theatre was not in good shape itself, that the audience was finding it hard to relate to the theatre.... He did solid productions and solid plays and moved the audience back to the theatre." Hasnian does not mention that Gilbert produced no Canadian plays in the first two years of his return, a time of growing attention to Canadian drama in other Canadian cities. In fact, Gilbert has been quoted as saying that he didn't think there was such a thing as a Canadian play.

A less charitable interpretation of this period was that MTC decided to play it safe, or as Hasnian says, "solid." At a time when playwrights were making their way onto main stages in Toronto, Calgary, and even Regina, MTC stuck to its practice of presenting Broadway hits and plays from the classic repertoire. Still, the fact stands that during Gilbert's second tenure the deficit disappeared. While the local community might have applauded this evidence of sound fiscal management, the theatre community in Manitoba and elsewhere in Canada put the Manitoba Theatre Centre at the top of its blacklist.

Canadian plays, if produced at all at MTC, found themselves in the low-budget Warehouse, with few exceptions. Canadian actors found it no less daunting to find work on the MTC stages. E. Ross Stewart in *The History of Prairie Theatre* quotes the 1974 Actors' Equity president Dan MacDonald as saying that MTC was "the most flagrant" offender of refusing to hire Canadian performers:

> They proudly told us that one-third of our cast last year were composed of non-Canadians. In one example, the production of *Hobson's Choice,* where you need British accents, and with so many British-born Canadian actors around, the Manitoba Theatre Centre hired nine of eleven members from the United States.

A generation later, some progress became evident. Instead of complaining that MTC did not hire Canadian actors, even when it was convenient, actors complained that MTC hired from Toronto almost regardless of the talent available locally. This trend began to dissipate slightly only in the later years of Steven Schipper's tenure.

Many people in the Canadian theatre community would have agreed that John Coulter's assessment of London's West End applied equally to Canada's regional theatres:

> What shocked me was the spectacle of a theatre doing supremely well what seemed to me to be supremely not worth doing. I thought of it as a theatre which had lost touch with life and reality, or which made false whatever touch it had for the sake of a flashy theatrical artifice reflecting the improbable manners and doings of worthless creatures without any roots in soil. (From *Theatre Arts Monthly,* July, 1938.)[37]

In its defense, one must consider that MTC had narrowly escaped a fiscal crisis that saw it close its theatre school in 1972. The board would have preferred Geoffrey Rush's formula in *Shakespeare in Love*

("You see: comedy, love, and a bit with a dog.") to the surging creativity evident in even the pedestrian Canadian plays that emerged during this period. MTC may have missed the great Canadian theatre train, but it kept the enterprise on the rails.

This conservatism did not arise in a vacuum. In Winnipeg and elsewhere, the Canadian centennial celebrations resulted in a number of arts facilities built to memorialize the event. The Canada Council and other bodies began to see the arts as a vehicle for job creation and employment. As Mark Czarnecki says of this period in an essay published in *Contemporary Canadian Theatre: New World Visions* in 1985, "Buildings and institutions represented visible and quantifiable capital investments which created jobs in construction, administration, technical production, even theatre acting—everything necessary for a vital theatre except the playwrights to create the works and directors of vision to interpret them." Manitoba, because its centennial fell in 1970, experienced a double shot of this building boom.

Then the bottom fell out. The Canada Council annual report of 1969–70 announced that austerity was at hand. Funding declined in constant dollars, with more companies sharing the limited pool of cash. The Council began to stress financial stability; deficit-ridden companies suffered under the Council's wintry gaze. As Czarnecki says, "The threat of reduced funding and increased reliance on box office only strengthened the intrinsic conservatism of the regionals' boards."

Speaking of boards, University of Winnipeg professor Douglas Arrell puts forward an interesting theory to explain why MTC did not embrace the flowering of Canadian playwriting that occurred across the country in the late '60s and early '70s. In "Paradigm Shifts at the Box Office," which appeared in the *Canadian Theatre Review* in 1991, he explains that the board members, audience, and artists that founded MTC would have had New Criticism inculcated in them during their education.

New Criticism is a literary theory in which all high art was subject to interpretation by critics, whom Arrell calls "high priests." It takes its name from an influential book of essays called *The New Criticism,* published by American poet and university professor John Crowe Ransom in 1941. Ransom advocated evaluating literature according to its structure and elements, regardless of its historical and geographical context. Art was seen to be above place and time, so works that dealt with local issues and places held a lower rank. New Criticism separated art from entertainment. A work was much more than its literal, obvious meaning. Interpreting and appreciating a work of art was therefore a difficult process requiring special expertise and education; one could not just go to a theatre or read a book and understand it at one go. Supporting and producing this High Art was a calling worthy of the enormous sacrifices involved.

MTC's founders and early audience and board members subscribed to this theory, and the theatre's work reflected it, with the necessary adjustments needed to maintain a respectable box office. This movement is antithetical to nationalist sentiments, however, so when literary trends changed, MTC was caught flat-footed.

The attack on New Criticism came from an unimpeachable Canadian source, at time when Canadian nationalism was at its height. Northrop Frye, the legendary Canadian literary theorist, was a savage critic of New Criticism. He considered it to be hopelessly subjective, an illusory way for elitists to justify their personal tastes. His *Anatomy of Criticism* in 1957 gained worldwide acclaim and became part of university curricula just as Canada entered its joyful centennial summer.

The Rise of Canadian Unity: Expo 67 and the Pearson Pennant

During this time, Canadian artistic nationalism was becoming more strident. Radio stations chafed under new regulations that required them to air a set percentage of Canadian content to keep their licences. The predicted death of Canadian radio did not happen. Instead, musicians like Anne Murray and The Guess Who found national and, later, international audiences. Playwrights and other theatre artists started calling for their place in the sun.

During this time, also, Canadian novelists and short story writers began to find their way onto school curricula. In Manitoba schools in the late 1960s, Roger Lemelin, Robertson Davies, Stephen Leacock and Margaret Laurence began to take their place beside Dickens, Hardy, Twain and Austen. A student would be as likely to study a Shaun Herron essay or a Morley Callaghan short story as one by G.K. Chesterton or Stephen Crane. Students learned that there was such a thing as Canadian art, and that Canadian art went beyond the Group of Seven print that many would have filed past in elementary school on their way to assemblies in the gym. The Canadian coins issued during the centennial year in 1967 featured Colville representations of Canadian animals.

This newfound sense of nationalism occasionally ran up against barriers. This is not surprising, since it was in part an official federal response to the Quiet Revolution taking place in Quebec. The thinking was that if Quebecois would not accept living in a Canada whose symbols and institutions rested on British models, they might accept purely Canadian replacements.

On May 17, 1964, Prime Minister Lester Pearson stood before "the steely eyes of a hostile audience" and told a national convention of the Royal Canadian Legion in Winnipeg that they would have a new flag. Each step to replace the imperial British face of our Canadian public institutions met with firm resistance in many quarters. The Royal Mail became Canada Post (or, more accurately and even more annoyingly, *Postes* Canada Post).

Pearson's attempts to Canadianize our public face had a double-edged effect. The flag issue alone revitalized the career of John Diefenbaker, Pearson's nemesis. Some Canadians, perhaps most, embraced the changes, but a very vocal faction opposed them. In response to this vocal opposition, many provinces where the resistance was strongest adopted provincial flags with a Union Jack in the upper right corner. Manitoba was one of these. (In 2001, a poll named the Manitoba flag the ugliest in North America, resulting in a newspaper contest to design a new one.)

As with many attempts to assert a new identity, some elements of this new Canadianism expressed and defined themselves in terms of what it was not. You could not call a writer a Canadian writer just because a Canadian doctor helped him or her to enter the world. Therefore, Canlit classes would carefully point out that while Stephen Leacock was very successful and influential as a humourist, his writing was not Canadian because Canada was not distinctly recognizable in his style. Meanwhile, the dense and morose Susanna Moodie qualified. A much lesser writer who had Canada oozing off every page would be held up as a better example. During this period, Canada meant nature, or at least a rural setting, as a backdrop.

In theatre, this tension played itself out in an unusual scenario. As Ronald Bryden says in his preface to *Whittaker's Theatre,* a book about renowned theatre critic Herbert Whittaker:

> This led him to some difficulties when the political mood of the 1960s shifted towards a militant and morally tinged Canadian nationalism, in passionate revolt against all foreign influences as subversive of Truly Northern culture, strong and free. Whittaker, as keenly committed as anyone to a genuinely Canadian theatre, found himself in occasional embarrassment when such a theatre began to emerge from a national shivaree of the Centennial celebrations of 1967. It took the form of a rash of 'alternative' theatres, dedicated to the production of Canadian plays. Most of what they were alternative to they declared loudly and combatively. They intended to provide an alternative to the mainstream supply of touring productions from Britain and United States; to glossy local mountings by Canadian subsidized theatres of imported plays and foreign classics; to alien accents, alien topics and alien performers on Canadian stages. What was seldom said aloud, almost never confronted squarely, was that the new theatres also stood for an alternative to professionalism in every sense in which Whittaker had spent his life understanding and valuing the word. They faced him with the old demand for moral-political criticism in a new form. To perform Canadian plays, all Canadian plays, was a moral act. The professionalism with which they were presented was therefore beside the moral point, and to criticize any lack of professionalism in their presentation an immoral act of disloyalty. One of the ways of stating this unequivocally in their production was to scorn any attempt at professionalism.[38]

Part of the problem was, with the lion's share of the population, Ontarians seemed to feel that the national consciousness was but a wider expression of their local consciousness. Elsewhere, the idea of national unity was partly expressed as a multi-faceted expression of distrust for Toronto, and its parliamentary branch office, Ottawa.

The newly minted Canadian theatre therefore faced numerous obstacles in Manitoba: one, it was untried. Nobody knew if an audience would grow with a taste for it. Two, its stance against traditional models offended the sensibilities of the elites who ran theatre and other cultural institutions in Manitoba. And three, since it arose in Toronto and other eastern Canadian centres, it had the stamp of evil.

Playwriting Becomes Political: The Gaspé Manifesto

Winnipeg was far from the only centre where playwrights had trouble reaching the large regional stages. In 1971, twelve playwrights and theatre professionals, including Tom Hendry, met in the Gaspé at the Canada Council's behest. These twelve issued what is now known as the Gaspé Manifesto. Even the Canada Council representative signed it. The far-reaching manifesto contained many points, but the first two are of key interest:

1. That the grant-giving bodies make it a policy that the theatres they support become Canadian in content.
2. That such theatres be required to achieve a fifty-percent Canadian content (one play in two) no later than January 1973, such content to apply in all areas of their season—main stage, studio, workshop, children's plays, and tours, etc.

It didn't happen. As mentioned earlier, MTC did not produce one Canadian play in 1973; its artistic director did not believe Canadian plays even existed. Other points dealt with granting policies, the need for agents, a union, greater use of plays from the other official language by both linguistic groups, and the need for copyright reform. Some of these ideas bore fruit, and others died. The major concrete outcome of this event was the eventual emergence of the Playwrights' Union of Canada.

Eventually, though, more Canadian plays appeared on Canadian stages. Some made a great impact: David E. Freeman's *Creeps* at the Tarragon in Toronto in 1971 (an earlier version had an off-Broadway production in 1963) and Sharon Pollock's *Walsh* at Theatre Calgary in 1973, for instance. By the late 1970s, almost every Canadian city had a celebrated playwright, except for Winnipeg. Don Rubin's celebrated essay, "Creeping Toward a Culture," first published in *York Theatre Journal*, Fall 1972, sums this up:

> Canadian writers are beginning to speak with their own voices and they're demanding that Canadians listen to them. No longer is the goal New York or London or Paris. The goal has become Toronto, Vancouver, Montreal, Halifax, Edmonton, Calgary, Regina Fredericton, Charlottetown and other cities East and West.

Fredericton and Regina merited mention, but not Winnipeg. The great alternative theatre movement had passed us by, at least for a while. When it did reach Winnipeg, as we shall see, another literary theory swamped it just as it began to make headway.

11

Rainbow Stage: The Pot of Gold in Manitoba's Theatre Sky

"...to present professional musical theatre to as large an audience as possible, [and] to ensure that the theatrical experience is kept within the reach of all socio-economic groups."

—Rainbow Stage's objective

Located in Kildonan Park in Winnipeg's North End, Rainbow Stage is Manitoba's forgotten theatre treasure—except for the tens of thousands of people who have attended performances there, and the hundreds of theatre artists who owe it at least part of their careers. In his *Winnipeg Book*, playwright and author Charles Wilkins calls it "certainly the only theatre in Canada where the smell of 6–12 [mosquito repellent] is stronger than that of greasepaint." Today, Shakespeare in the Ruins can challenge that claim, but at the same time, it owes a debt to Rainbow Stage for showing Manitobans that outdoor theatre can be an enjoyable experience.

Rainbow Stage's unlikely beginning was the 1950 flood that tore away the existing bandstand. Renowned music and theatre critic Frank Morriss, upon learning that the city would not have a venue for the outdoor band concerts that had graced Assiniboine and Kildonan Parks in the early post-war years, wrote a newspaper article suggesting that the city build a replacement bandstand. The superintendent of parks, Thomas R. Hodgson, was an avid music fan, so the campaign started. The architectural firm of Smith, Carter, Katelnikoff designed the 3000-seat facility. When someone at a planning meeting group observed that if lights were strung along the top curvature of the structure it would look like a rainbow, the theatre got its name.

On September 22, 1953, the stage had its inaugural concert, featuring Bill Walker, Len Andree, Eric Wilde, Maxine Ware, Cliff Gardner and Ethyl Lowe. Cliff Gardner became a regular performer once musical drama began to appear with *Brigadoon* in 1955.Winnipeg's beloved Evelyne Anderson performed in what was to be the first of many shows there.

For the next ten years, Rainbow Stage built an audience. It became part of John Hirsch's inspiration for founding the Manitoba Theatre Centre, by proving that people would appear in large numbers to see first-rate theatre. He directed a few early shows, which probably helped give him the confidence to launch MTC.

Over the years, Rainbow Stage has had numerous opportunities to die a dignified death, but each time its public support has been so strong that someone always came forward to revive it. The first such near-death experience happened in 1963. The company had a $42,000 deficit and seemed to lack direction. By this time it had grown from an amateur company to one that hired many professionals, with the accompanying price tag.

The company hired a New York producer named Michael McAloney. He promised to erase the debt in two years, but the methods he used worked against this goal. His flashy style also offended many. His strategy was to hire American stars to attract larger crowds. Perhaps with big-name stars this would have worked, but the people he hired were middle-name at best. In 1965, Rainbow Stage announced it was closing. It didn't.

Instead, board member Jack Shapira reopened the theatre in 1966. Shapira, a University of Manitoba graduate, knew his community and what it liked. He had hosted two CBC television programs, *The Show That Jack Built*, which ran from 1958–59, and *Sitting Back With Jack*, which ran in 1960. Both were variety shows that featured his orchestra. His high public profile helped to resell Manitobans on Rainbow Stage. In his five years on the board before assuming control he had obviously learned how the company worked and how to make it work better.

In his first season, he cut the number of shows from four to two, and extended the run for each. This reduced the overhead of preparing and paying for sets and costumes. Shapira had a knack for knowing what audiences wanted, and delivering it. The deficit, which had ballooned from $42,000 to $95,000, dropped by half in the first season. In the second season, good weather and an extended run wiped out the debt. Shapira also had good people working for him; Gerry Eldred, his first production manager, went on to manage MTC, the National Ballet, and the Stratford Festival. The theatre went on a fifteen-year hot streak, in which, as Wilkins says, "Jack Shapira has been producing audience-proof Broadway and London musicals. Although the Canada Council and hard-line theatre critics take a dim view of Shapira's recycled wonder shows...the theatre's patrons are not so discriminating and turn out by the thousands to applaud whatever's offered." It sounds as if the theatre took the easy way out under Shapira, but MTC did not fare nearly so well with a very similar formula.

In the early days, Rainbow Stage was an open-air theatre. The audience shared the space with the weather, the bugs, and whatever neighbouring sounds drifted into their earshot. Similarly, picnickers who lingered got to hear rehearsals and performances, something that might have encouraged them to pay for the full show a few nights later. A favourite way to entertain visitors during summer was to take them to Rainbow, and if the guests complained about the weather, well, that just proved that Winnipeggers were hardier, that's all. At a 1968 production of *The Music Man*, the weather was so foul that Bill Walker, the star, led the cast in applauding the audience.

Over the years, many Winnipeggers had their first inkling that a theatre career was possible at Rainbow Stage. Before he became Donnelley Rhodes of *Da Vinci's Inquest* and *Soap*, Donnelley Henry acted there. Jennifer Lyons and Jerry Kushnier started their careers there. While some artists used Rainbow as a stepping stone to a career in Toronto or elsewhere, others chose to stay and share their gift with their neighbours. Rainbow Stage helped to make this choice possible for Evelyne Anderson, Doreen Brownstone, Stan Lesk, Cliff Gardner, Paul Fredette, Georges Lafleche, Harry Nelken, Ted Korol and many others.

Of almost equal importance to the local theatre scene is the number of theatre artists who, while they never became professional, learned first-hand what went into a professional-calibre theatre performance. This experience gave Winnipeg an audience with a more sophisticated understanding of theatre than otherwise would have been possible.

But just like summer, all good things must end someday. Jack Shapira's long run ended in a tragic fall from grace. Shapira, who drove around town in a Rolls Royce, faced charges of misuse of funds.

Although Rainbow Stage was in the black, the books did not balance. Further criminal charges led to a brief jail term, and Shapira's days as a force on Manitoba's arts scene were over.

Shapira's replacement, Jack Timlock, ran Rainbow on the up and up, but it lost money. By 1993, the city had a mayor who belonged to the Mulroney school. City hall cut funding to the arts by 28 percent, a move that earned Susan Thompson the nickname Suzie Scissorhands. Rainbow Stage was heavily in debt, and the city announced there would be no more bailouts. Once again, Rainbow Stage announced it would fold.

Still it did not die. A volunteer board took over, and operated for a while without an artistic director. At the insistence of board member and actor Stan Lesk, the company renewed its emphasis on local talent, and gradually earned back its audience. In 2000 the company started a winter season by booking the Pantages Theatre for one show each winter. It also toured to Brandon. Whatever the future holds for Rainbow Stage, it has earned its reputation as a developer and employer of local talent.

The First Theatre Royal

The Second Theatre Royal

Corner of Portage & Main, circa 1870

Winnipeg Opera House, Notre Dame Avenue, circa 1890

C.P Walker, Manager of the Walker Theatre, 1907

Harriet Walker, 1921

Exterior of the Walker Theatre

Interior of the Walker Theatre, 1907

Dominion Theatre,
October 1, 1941

Rainbow Stage, opening of
Bye Bye Birdie, March 7, 1963

Manitoba Theatre Centre Opening,, November 2, 1970

John Hirsch, MTC Artistic Director, August 4, 1964

Cercle Molière rehearsal of *Du Vent,* April 25, 1969

PTAM's Margo Charlton

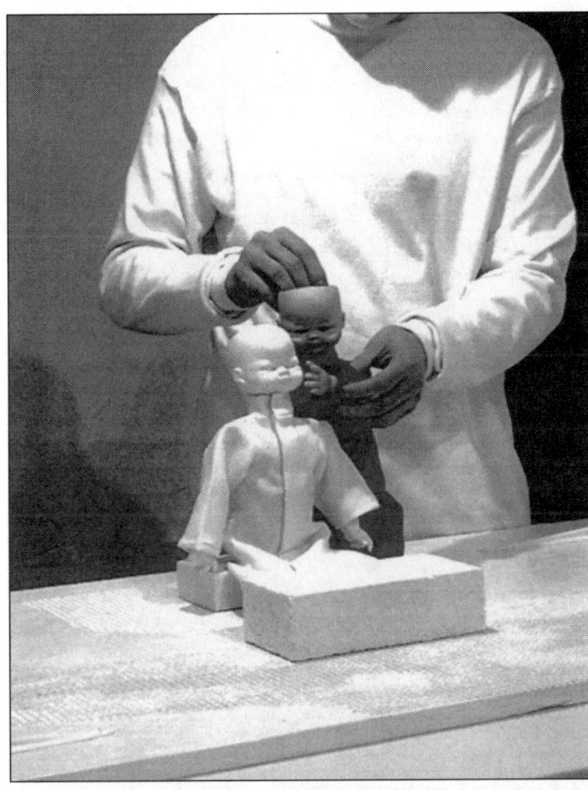

Adhere & Deny production of *Found & Lost,* 2000

Tracey McCorrister and Marsha Knight in Prairie Theatre Exchange's production of *fareWel,* 1996

12

Breaking down the Walls: Alternative Theatre

"By limiting the Factory to only new Canadian plays, we were forced to abandon the security blanket of our colonial upbringing. We found ourselves in a vacuum without roots, and indeed without playwrights. The plays soon surfaced."

—Factory Theatre Lab's founder Ken Gass, about the Toronto theatre's beginnings.

Just as farmers and gardeners have learned that you can't stop thistles from sprouting where they want to sprout, repressive governments everywhere have learned that you cannot stop the flow of the written word. Writers just cannot help themselves, and playwrights, even with the added impediments of needing actors and a space, are no exception. While the situation in Manitoba did not by any stretch qualify as repression, it stopped considerably short of benign neglect. In the late 1960s and early 1970s, playwrights found little outlet for their work.

Other centres shared the same problem, with the alternative theatre movement as the result. Although its intent was nationalist, this movement borrowed a lot from similar movements in the United States and Britain. This was the "flower power" period, when experimentation in new methods and approaches was the thing to do. The establishment houses, run as they were by very establishment boards, could not be expected to buy into this movement. Given the very conservative nature of the Manitoba establishment, the chances here were even slimmer than elsewhere.

And yet, the new play movement had a Manitoba champion. When Tom Hendry left Winnipeg in 1963, he became executive secretary of the Canadian Theatre Centre. He went on to become the first literary manager at Stratford, and to co-found the Playwrights' Co-op, which later became the Playwrights' Union of Canada. In 1974 he also co-founded the Banff Playwrights Colony.

In 1971, Hendry was on the first board of Toronto Free Theatre. Its mandate was free admission and free experimentation. Hendry's play, *How Are Things with the Walking Wounded,* was the first play Toronto Free Theatre produced, in 1972. Toronto Free Theatre, as the on-line *Canadian Theatre Encyclopedia* describes it, was "a house specializing in aggressive and often transgressive theatre like John Palmer's *The End*, Martin Kinch's *April 29, 1975*, Hrant Alianak's *Passion and Sun* and Michael Hollingsworth's *Clear Light.*"

This was a time when governments around the world wondered what to do with their restless youth, who seemed to want to raze the established world and start over. While the other world leaders were grey men in grey suits, Canada had Pierre Trudeau. Even John Lennon approved of him. One program Trudeau instituted was Opportunities for Youth, also known as OFY. A later version, the Local Initiatives Program or LIP, also funded projects. These programs granted money to individuals and groups so they could take on projects of their own choosing. Naturally, the conservative elements in society howled, and highlighted some of what they considered to be the most flagrant abuses of government largesse. Jane Stewart's Human Resources Development Canada (HRDC) scandal of 2000 comes close to the outrage expressed. In Winnipeg, a group of young people got funding so they could hand one-dollar bills to drivers at stop signs and red lights who had their seat belts buckled up.

No doubt some of the criticism was well founded. At the same time, even the seat belt bounty program had good intentions, and it drew attention to an important safety issue.

One positive outcome of these two programs was that independent theatre projects sprang up across the country. Just as Canada Council funding slowed to a trickle, this funding from non-cultural ministries caused a creative flowering in the arts, disproving the old notion that you do not solve a problem by throwing money at it. While the people who set up the OFY and LIP programs did not set them up to revitalize theatre, perhaps that was why they were so successful.

Theatre Winnipeg was one Winnipeg group to spring up out of this program. With a $60,000 grant, Winston MacDonald set up a program of noon-hour and weekend family shows in 1973. Wayne Nicklas and Jim Mezon often acted with the company. Shakespeare in the Ruins board member Richard Howell was the group's stage manager, assuming that position because at 29 he was the oldest person in the group and would therefore be seen by the powers that be as responsible. Grant Guy was involved with the company as well. As was the case across the country, the participants worked very hard to get the program on a good footing, often working though the night to get the production ready. Their audience grew, but not fast enough for them to survive once the federal funds ran out.

A similar group was Winnipeg Community Theatre, founded by Reg Skene and Geoffery Sperl in the 1970s. Its members included Jim Mezon, Albert Patenaude, Chris Lowther and Bernie Boland (an Englishman who spoke good enough French to work at Le Cercle Molière). This group also had a relatively short life.

Agassiz Theatre fared a little better. The company started in 1980 with the goal of producing "a season of alternative theatre." The first chairs were Brian Richardson and Martin Reed. Among the many Agassiz people still active today are Judy Cook, Coral McKendrick, Margo Charlton, Chris Hurley, Paul Walsh, and Nancy Drake, who chaired the company's first artistic committee. Agassiz was the first stage to produce a Maureen Hunter script, *Poor Uncle Ernie in His Covered Cage.* They also produced her *Queen of Queen Street* and the acclaimed *Footprints on the Moon*. *Footprints on the Moon* received a Governor General's Award nomination and has had other productions across Canada.

Agassiz also produced Nick Mitchell's thriller, *House,* and Rosemary De Graff's *Fields of Sorrow.* Nancy Drake was a frequent director, as was Craig Walls. They performed at the Warehouse, the Planetarium, the Gas Station and PTE. The company also ran workshops. The run ended for Agassiz in 1988 when arts council operating funds dried up.

Most groups foundered after the money ran out, but a few survived in various incarnations. Winnipeg's Prairie Theatre Exchange (then called the Manitoba Theatre Workshop) received funding so that students could renovate a city-owned building at 160 Princess Street. This building became the group's first home, and the place where many believe its best years took place.

While some writers lament that the federal "make-work" programs did not produce the playwrights and blossoming of new plays that happened elsewhere in the seventies, the Manitoba OFY/LIP legacy was substantial. As for the new plays, Manitoba found its own way to search for them.

13

Prairie Theatre Exchange's Legacy

"Our intention is to put much energy in the next few years into developing 'alternative' professional theatre in Manitoba, a theatre whose bias would be towards indigenous material and performers."

—Colin Jackson, quoted in Peter J. Spencer's doctoral thesis, The History and Contribution of the Manitoba Theatre Workshop/Prairie Theatre Exchange

"From the first day, they had the sense that this was a space where they could create something."

—Deborah Quinn, ibid.

It must have felt like a dark day when the Manitoba Theatre Centre announced it was closing its school in 1972. The telltale signs were there, but those involved must still have felt shocked and perhaps a little betrayed to learn that the school would close. It had not adjusted well to the move from the Theatre Across the Street to the Warehouse. With a dangerously high deficit to contend with, MTC knew something had to give, and the school was an obvious choice.

Still, enough people felt a strong sense of loss that a group of concerned parents met with Eddie Gilbert, MTC's returning artistic director, and some teachers from the school, including Colin Jackson. Charles Huband, a parent who was also a city councillor and later leader of the Liberal Party in Manitoba, made sure the meeting did not adjourn before some concrete steps to start a new enterprise had taken place. The result was Prairie Theatre Exchange's (PTE's) predecessor, the Manitoba Theatre Workshop (MTW).

As was the case with the first days of MTC, MTW had the good fortune of having the right people come together at the same time. In

Huband they had a passionate civic leader. Eddie Gilbert sat on the first board, ensuring continuity. Another founding board member was Brian Watkins, on sabbatical from his position as the head of drama at the University of Birmingham in England. In Colin Jackson they had a youthful spokesperson with a talent for organizing and marshaling support.

The initial staff included the talented Deborah Quinn, who later replaced Colin Jackson as Executive Director, and Chris Hurley, who would later found the Manitoba Puppet Theatre.

The timing was also right. Besides the funding the federal government offered for projects oriented towards youth, the city was trying to revitalize the inner core (some things never change) and offered the old Grain Exchange Building for a dollar a year.

Although it was a necessity, using OFY funds to pay students to renovate the building was also a master stroke in motivation. The early students formed a solid attachment to the theatre, and some, such as Shawn Kettner, later became teachers there. Like MTC in its early days, the Manitoba Theatre Workshop had a family feel to it, with its young staff willing to work long hours at low wages to make it succeed. At first funding was dangerously low, but eventually the theatre achieved a measure of financial stability.

The new school also differed from MTC in some important ways. A look at its initial objectives reveals a very different philosophy:

1. To provide an access point for individuals to explore their interest in theatre to whatever level they so choose.
2. To provide professional resource people to all those individuals and organizations interested in the theatre arts.
3. To provide a professional theatre which promotes the development of local artists.

These objectives are different from those of MTC both substantively and philosophically. The difference is not just a product of the times each list arose in. While MTC's stated objectives were easily quantifiable (such as an audience of 150,000) and couched in businesslike language, MTW's were more open-ended and at the same time more rooted in the community. While MTC strove to create a theatre *centre* (and succeeded), MTW strove to create a theatre *community*, not just for the larger community, but *by* and *about* the community. Both organizations have stumbled from time to time, and both have had triumphs, but MTW's legacy (and PTE's) is the creation of indigenous Manitoba theatre. Without the chain of events that MTW started (and, to be honest, inherited from MTC), it is difficult to imagine the success that Manitoba playwrights later achieved.

From the beginning, Prairie Theatre Exchange has had a focus on outreach. While in the early days MTC tried to sell the idea of professional theatre to Manitoba, MTW's focus was in the opposite direction. It instead tried to find out what people's specific theatre needs were, and tailored its activities to meet those needs.

Neither approach is good or bad in itself, and without MTC pioneering professional theatre in Manitoba, people might not have realized they had needs when MTW came calling.

Planting the Seeds of Indigenous Theatre

Someone at MTW must really have paid attention in Sunday school to the passage in Matthew about the mustard seed, because its greatest achievement is the many groups that MTW spawned, sponsored, or inspired into existence. It liked to think of itself as a seedbed in the early days, and in a province renowned for its fertile soil, its harvest is unmatched.

Although the Manitoba Theatre School under MTC had become what Peter Spencer called "a recreational drama centre," MTW's goal from the beginning was much more ambitious. Its first stated objective, "To provide an access point for individuals to explore their interest in theatre to whatever level they so choose," was deliberately open-ended. This broad focus caused MTW grief from time to time, but someone had obviously also heard of Wordsworth's advice about reach exceeding grasp.

MTW hosted classes at its Princess Street facility, but it also took its programs to schools, hospitals, and prisons. Its Creative Arts in the Schools Project, in which Kevin Burns and Elisabeth Coffman met with teachers to develop a curriculum-oriented program similar to Dorothy Heathcote's in England, was a major success. The program sought to help teachers develop teaching methods in the arts. Eventually the planning and research branch of the Department of Education took over this program, and it eventually evolved into the Artists in the Schools program the Manitoba Arts Council operates today.

The salary that MTW offered its instructors ($144 per week in 1973), while not princely, was still enough to attract qualified people.[39] (University graduates working at entry-level jobs in the federal public service at the time would have earned perhaps $15 to $20 more per week.)

Perhaps the best example of the can-do thinking MTW employed in the early years is the correspondence between Colin Jackson and John Cleese of Monty Python fame. Jackson learned that Cleese wanted to have a holiday in the wilderness as a spiritual refresher, and started a correspondence aimed at combining a canoe trip with a comedy writing workshop for the school. Between June of 1974 and October of 1975, the two exchanged letters trying to set up a mutually beneficial date.[40]

The event never worked out, but Cleese's letters show he was keenly disappointed that BBC commitments kept preventing the trip. Clearly, no goal was deemed too lofty for MTW to attempt, and if it occasionally missed, as it did with Cleese, more often than not it succeeded. A group that would invite someone who was at the time one of the hottest comedy stars in the world to teach at its school obviously had the courage to make other things happen.

MTW continued the High School Drama Festival as a non-competitive event with professional adjudication, but decided to drop it in 1976 because of budget constraints. In doing so, it hoped education officials would pick up the costs. In 1978, however, Leslee Silverman gave up waiting for outside support and organized the festival. She eventually secured lottery funding and set up Manitoba Drama Festivals, headquartered at MTW. In 1980 Tacey Lawrence, the coordinator, extended the program over the school year and included community amateur theatre groups. (Silverman is not the only future artistic director to have worked at MTW in the early days. In 1975, future Winnipeg Jewish Theatre artistic director Kayla Gordon was house manager for MTW's *Jamboree.)*

The expanded festival participation eventually resulted in the formation of the Association of Community Theatres (ACT), a vibrant theatre group that survives to this day. The annual ACT theatre festival is a descendant of the Manitoba Drama Festival.

Another case of MTW acting as a seedbed was Confidential Exchange. This group of actors, armed with a LIP grant, sought to establish alternative professional theatre, and included many people familiar to Manitoba audiences today: David King, Brian Richardson, David Gillies, Fred Penner, Al Simmons, Harry Nelken, Jim Mezon and David Huband. MTW and Confidential Exchange worked cooperatively for a few years. The first production, in February 1975, was a two-play evening of David King scripts, *New Canadian Drivel* and *Finite Junction*. In 1975–76, MTW registered the Confidential Exchange name and worked with the group to produce a season. David King's *Sandhills* was the first show MTW produced under a full Equity contract. It was famous for using over 8000 kilograms of sand for the set. Stage crew members still complain about the sand, but it was otherwise well received.

Eventually Confidential Exchange and MTW parted ways, and Confidential Exchange folded soon after. When MTW decided to change its name to reduce confusion with MTC, however, it borrowed the Exchange part and incorporated it into its new name.

Professional children's theatre also got its start at MTW. From the beginning it offered children's theatre, often using students presenting material they had written themselves. Deborah Quinn proved that children's theatre could be as challenging and grounded as adult theatre. The company's work drew rave reviews in the media and enthusiastic audiences. Quinn eventually founded TNT, The Neighbourhood Theatre. With the arrival of TNT in 1977, Manitoba was no longer the only province in Canada that did not have a professional children's theatre company. She also produced a television program, *Let's Go,* which ran on CKY television for a couple of seasons.

Chris Hurley's work with puppets eventually developed into the Manitoba Puppet Theatre, a group that enjoyed an international reputation. When Hurley's work with the Puppet Theatre constrained his work teaching, the Puppet Theatre spun off to become an independent organization housed at 160 Princess Street. The Puppet Theatre still survives, in a limited form.

During this time Shawn Kettner launched Puppet Tree. Kettner trained under Hurley and Quinn, and her troupe became a natural replacement for the Manitoba Puppet Theatre. She also developed Patient Puppets, used to demystify the hospital experience for children around the world.

Another group that shared the early MTW experience was the Contemporary Dancers. This partnership did not go as smoothly as some other mutual arrangements. The Contemporary Dancers had trouble paying the rent MTW charged, $6400 annually for about one-third of the space. Even when the MTW reduced the rent to $3000, this proved too much of a burden for the Contemporary Dancers. The dancers left 160 Princess Street in 1978. MTW used some of the liberated space, and rented the rest to the Manitoba Fencing Association.

Calling All Playwrights

As MTW moved towards a season of adult professional theatre, it realized that to fulfill its mandate to develop indigenous theatre it would have to find locally written plays that would tell Manitobans' stories to themselves. In 1979 it launched the Playwright's Search. The success of the Search led then-Executive Director Ernie Stigant of the Manitoba Arts Council to start the Playwrights Development Program, under which four playwrights each received $500 and workshops in 1979 and 1980:

1. Brad Leiman for *Showdown*. Leiman also wrote *Love and Chicken Soup*, which appeared at the Warehouse as part of its showcase program.
2. Bruce McManus for *Fragile Possibilities.* This was McManus' first script. In a letter to Michael Snook, executive producer for radio arts and drama at CBC, Colin Jackson wrote "some of the poetry of language is very strong...radio in particular should assist and encourage him."
3. Martin Reed for *The Reluctant Knight*. Brian Richardson reports that John Hirsch claimed this play was "just right the way it is." Richardson, who helped found Agassiz Theatre, said they certainly would have produced it if children's theatre had been part of the company mandate. Reed would also have a script workshopped in 1982.
4. Alf Silver for *Dud Shuffle.* Under the title *Thimblerig,* this play was the first Manitoba script to appear in a full production at MTC in over a decade.

The initial series of workshops benefited from having three professional directors: John Hirsch, Jace Van Der Veen from Vancouver's New Play Centre, and Colin Jackson. Leslee Silverman was the assistant director. The sponsors were Imperial Oil, the Manitoba Arts Council, the CBC, MTW, and the provincial department or tourism and cultural affairs.

After a one-year gap, five Manitoba playwrights received workshop productions at a MAP-sponsored series of workshops in 1982:

1. *House* by Nick Mitchell (*House,* a suspenseful psychodrama, eventually had an Agassiz production, and has had several

productions since. It is in the anthology *New Works 1*. *Mum* also had an Agassiz production. Mitchell later had a PTE main stage premiere of his historical drama, *Tin Can Cathedral*.

2. *221-B Baker Street* by Martin Reed. Reed, a medical doctor and professor of medicine, also wrote two children's plays, including *The Reluctant Knight*.
3. *Fields of Sorrow*, by Rosemary De Graff. Richard Ouzounian expressed interest in this play, but it never made the MTC stage. Later it had an Agassiz production. De Graff also had several radio plays produced.
4. *Climate of the Times*, by Alf Silver. This play had a Warehouse production in the 1982–83 season. Silver later had several plays appear on the Warehouse stage. He now lives in Nova Scotia and has had several books published.
5. *St. Peter's Asylum*, by William Horrocks. This play premiered at PTE in the 1982–83 season. Horrocks was playwright in residence at PTE for a while, moved to Thunder Bay, and then was associate dramaturg at the Playwrights' Centre in Montreal until the early '90s. His play *Vandal* is in the anthology *Eight Plays for Children* published by NeWest in 1983.

Of these nine scripts, then, at least five later received professional productions, and all playwrights went on to other successes. This proves that Manitoba was seething with playwriting talent at the time of the search. As administrator Michael Utgaard said in a letter to Colin Jackson, "We seem to have tripped over [a] proverbial sleeping giant."

What happened to these playwrights? Two, Silver and Horrocks, left town. Rosemary De Graff has died, but she kept on writing while she was alive, and wrote a very touching short play for MAP's Short Shots festival. Mitchell has gone on to a moderately successful career as a playwright, and Martin Reed's medical activities have kept him from being more prolific. Of course, the writers found in the search were not the only ones writing quality scripts. Brian Richardson, Charles Wilkins, and Dennis Noble, among others, were all creating successful scripts, Wilkins and Richardson locally and Noble across North America. What the search did was give what Shakespeare called the "ocular proof" that quality playwrights existed in Manitoba.

The Playwrights Development program evolved into the Manitoba Association of Playwrights (MAP). After the first search, Brian Richardson, Alf Silver, Charles Wilkins, William Horrocks, and Colin Jackson sent a letter to everyone who participated (there were 76 entries) inviting them to join a scriptwriters' association.

In the early years, MAP worked out of the PTE building on Princess Street. PTE can justifiably claim that Manitoba playwrights got their first real professional start under its wing. This has not been a passing flirtation, either. In PTE's 25th anniversary program, General Manager Cherry Karpyshin claimed that of the 214 plays it had presented, 119 (just over half) had been original works. Only a few of these were not by Manitoba playwrights. Those who wrote the Gaspé Manifesto would have been proud.

PTE Finds Its Stride With a New Name

The names of the two major theatre groups had caused confusion for some time, especially since the Manitoba Theatre Workshop had grown out of an MTC program. Although it was a topic of debate for some years, in 1981 the board finally instructed Colin Jackson and Artistic Director Gordon McCall to come up with a new name. Prairie Theatre Exchange was the result. It also adopted a new logo. The following season was a landmark one.

During a Manitoba Association of Playwrights meeting upstairs at PTE, Colin Jackson burst in carrying a bottle of wine and some glasses. Jackson had left MTW in 1976 to work at the CBC, and had returned as Executive Director in 1981. "I'm 37 years old, I left a secure job at the CBC, and it's just magic down there. They're eating out of her hand!" he announced, referring to Juliana Saxton's performance in *The Women of Margaret Laurence* then happening downstairs. The meeting abruptly adjourned and the aspiring playwrights helped Jackson celebrate his dream coming true.

Over the years a lot of magic has happened at PTE. In the early 1980s, it was the place to go to see exciting theatre. Plays regularly sold out and enjoyed extended runs. *The Fighting Days*, *Section 23* and *The Shunning* reflected the Prairie experience to a hungry audience. Sometimes the plays even travelled outside Manitoba's borders. *The Ecstasy of Rita Joe,* for instance, toured Canada to rave reviews. It may be hard to believe today, but this was the first production of George Ryga's play that used an exclusively First Nations cast.

In the 1982–3 season, PTE took the brave step of hosting a season that comprised entirely premieres, with three scripts by Manitobans. Unfortunately, the season resulted in a $20,000 loss, and PTE did not repeat the experiment.

PTE on the Move: A Misstep Followed by a Stumble

Of course, life at PTE was not all beer and skittles. Money was an almost constant problem, and the desire to be all things to all people caused a lack of focus at times, and sometimes contributed to the stress staff felt. Looking back at the lasting institutions that PTE spawned, contributed to, rescued and inspired, its accomplishments are nothing short of miraculous. One should remember, though, that this legacy resulted from the contributions and sacrifices that staff, board, and volunteers made.

As the professional performances became more successful, the need for a larger performance space became more pressing. For one thing, the demand often outstripped the supply in the 150-seat theatre. For another, the company needed the extra revenue that added seats would provide. PTE found itself caught in the traditional price-revenue squeeze common in the business world. One solution to balance the books is to raise prices. If sales volume remains constant, the books come into balance. That is a big if, however, and if the buying public resists the price increase, volume and revenue can actually drop, aggravating the balance sheet problem.

Another solution to this squeeze is to try to increase volume. At the very least, this involves an increased marketing effort. This did not apply well to PTE's situation, though, because it had a capacity problem. PTE had more than enough customers, but the current facility could not accommodate them. Adding shows to a run is one solution, but the margin on a performance was limited by the small seating capacity. It did not want to increase prices, because that would put the theatre out of reach to many people it had created its theatre for.

Solutions for capacity problems are expensive, though, and PTE did not have bags of money to throw around. The Winnipeg Core Area Initiative, launched in 1981, seemed to offer a solution. PTE's lease at 160 Princess Street was to expire in 1983, and this program seemed to offer the opportunity to move to a larger facility. Colin Jackson and Charles Huband began searching for a building that would house 450–500 patrons. They considered the abandoned Bank of Commerce building on Main Street, and even put an architect on retainer. These plans never came to fruition.

A second initiative, which Jackson started while he was still at the CBC, was to found a cultural centre similar to the Vancouver East Cultural Centre. The result was the Gas Station Theatre on River and

Osborne. The 250-seat theatre was seen as a possible stopgap until PTE found its larger space. PTE used this space only once, however (*Playing the Fool)*, and instead eventually moved to the third floor of the new Portage Place Shopping Mall.

The Portage Place Mall today stands as a monument to poor political and civic planning. Originally conceived as an upscale mall that would attract suburbanites to Winnipeg's fading downtown, it instead became a graveyard for failed commercial enterprises. The mall originally excluded local businesses, focusing instead on major retail chains. Eventually the mall's high-blown concept altered as the recession and the folly of this concept had their dual effect. Today the mall has a dollar store and other discount operations. The most successful store in the mall is McNally-Robinson Booksellers, a local independent bookstore chain that has expanded its space in the mall twice and is today Canada's second-largest bookstore chain.

Unfortunately, someone convinced PTE that it would be a good idea to move there, although civic authorities strongly urged PTE to become the anchor tenant at the renovated Playhouse Theatre. In 1989 PTE began its life at its new facility with a bad stumble. The second production, *Lloyd's Prayer,* by Kevin Kling, was the first non-Canadian play at PTE. It comes up often when people discuss the worst theatre experience of their lives. The Portage Place facility ate up two artistic directors before Allen MacInnis found a way to bring audiences back in 1996.

When PTE moved from its charmingly decayed Princess Street building to the glitzy mall on Portage Avenue, something stayed behind, and it was not just audience members. Some, perhaps most of their audience visited the new facility in the first year, but most complained that the experience was not the same.

For one thing, although the old building was in the rundown Exchange district, people complained that they did not feel safe in the new mall. As reports of swarmings, people being attacked by large groups of rogue youths and roughed up for their running shoes or jackets hit the media, these fears became stronger. A low point for the Portage Place Mall, and a black eye for the whole city, happened when visiting U. S. servicemen were swarmed at the mall. One was seriously injured. The Portage Place Mall took on the unfortunate and largely unfair reputation as being an unsafe place.

Second, the market economy mall did not appeal to the people who loved the old PTE with almost religious fervour. Many people who went to PTE also went to the Folk Festival and other remnants of the counterculture.

The new facility also opened as a recession took hold. People who would once attend theatre and concerts as a matter of course now found themselves wondering where the rent money would come from. Attendance in all areas of the arts dropped.

Finally, the playbill was not as strong as it had been. Besides the regrettable *Lloyd's Prayer,* the season included *Cruel Tears,* a musical remake of *Othello* featuring Humphrey and the Dumptrucks, a jug band. Although the theatre did continue to make strong choices, such as Wendy Lill's *Sisters* and Joan MacLeod's *Amigo's Blue Guitar,* they were just as likely to put on a colossal flop like *A Flush of Tories.* Kim McCaw, who had created magic time and again on Princess Street, left after two years in the mall. When one compares the plays he produced at the Princess Street theatre to the ones that saw the stage at Portage Place, a few differences become apparent.

First, the mall plays were more often experimental in form: *Lloyd's Prayer, Cruel Tears, Sisters* and *Cornflower Blue.* Second, the playbills shift slightly away from local playwrights. Although plays with a prairie focus still predominated, a subtle shift had started. This shift eventually caused a counter-shift to new theatre companies. In the meantime, another problem surfaced: a battle over theatre aesthetics erupted.

14

THIS ISN'T A POPULARITY CONTEST: Audiences vs. Aesthetics

"Benefit to the public is not a consideration with grants to individuals because we are not assessing whether the public will ever see or enjoy (the art)."
—Then-executive director of the Manitoba Arts Council Marlene Neustaedter, as quoted in *The Winnipeg Sun*, September 18, 1992

During this time, PTE (and its big sister, MTC) became caught in another, more precarious squeeze than the price-revenue squeeze.

As Canadian artists sought to assert themselves, they faced an uphill battle against American cultural dominance. For one thing, the American market dwarfed the Canadian one, and gaining notice was a little bit like trying to get someone's attention from the other side of a football stadium. For another, the economies of scale worked against Canadian artists. For instance, a Canadian television station could pick up a hit American show for a fraction of what it would cost to produce an original series.

Serious artists the world over must come to terms with the market forces that reward slick mass-market imitations more handsomely than the genuine article. In large economies, both the popular and the serious artist can earn a living, but in a small economy located so close to the dominant world economy, being an artist is much less than an even-money survival bet. The only way for an artist to survive is through subsidy in the form of grants.

(Do not assume from the foregoing a bias against popular art. For one thing, the terms "popular" and "serious" are far from mutually exclusive, and for another, both have their place.)

The two strikes Canadian artists faced, then, were dominance from a foreign culture and participation in a form that is a minority taste in any culture. The call, therefore, was for funding bodies and others to support serious art, which became codified as works with "artistic merit." An easy distinguishing mark for artistic merit was experiment in form. Popular culture, aimed as it is at the vast majority (or, if you prefer, the lowest common denominator) uses tried-and-true forms. Movies aimed at mass audiences adhere to the beginning-middle-end model, and usually follow linear time. The protagonist and villain are obvious to even to those with the most limited attention spans.

Artists of merit, on the other hand, "move the form forward." They experiment. Their experiments do not typically have audience reaction as part of their evaluation criteria; at least, they do not include the average Joe or Jane. During this time, the term Kitchen Sink Play, meaning a play in which the kitchen sink worked, became a pejorative term.

As Doug Arrell explains in "Paradigm Shifts at the Box Office," alternative theatre, with its emphasis on realism, was seen as "propaganda for the status quo." Critics, academics, and even some artists and theatre managers began to have misgivings about prairie realism just as it was reaching an audience that for decades had hungered for a theatre that reflected their lives.

Post-modernism, the eventual successor to New Criticism, cast a jaundiced eye on realism, because it often tends to perpetuate the idea that the current reality is the best of all possible worlds, and because its supposed objectivity often denies other realities. "Linear" became a pejorative term for people who could not appreciate the new forms post-modernism advocated. The result, however, is often indistinguishable to audiences from the high art, New Criticism aesthetic it replaced; they don't understand what they see. In both aesthetics, the result often does not relate to the person who pays for tickets, much less the person who subsidizes the product through taxes without the benefit of witnessing the result. These people gain their attitude to the art they pay for through the filter of press reports, which often deal only with sensational aspects, such as a virgin's ritualized penetration by a unicorn's horn in MTC's *Not Wanted on the Voyage*. Conservative taxpayers then start to question why they should support artists who seem to be getting their kicks from offending them: the people who pay their freight.

PTE faced an even more difficult dilemma. Its theatre was community-based from the beginning, and when it produced René-Daniel Dubois' *Don't Blame the Bedouins* in 1987, much of its audience expressed outrage. PTE patrons who had abandoned MTC for the humble theatre on Princess Street must have felt a particularly sharp sense of betrayal. Here was a theatre that had lured them by producing theatre that related to their lives and was now abandoning them, going over to the dark side to force-feed them high art.

Loyal audience members suffered the double indignity of critics complaining that they were just not sophisticated or open-minded enough to appreciate what was to them self-indulgent dross. The problem that a lot of the post-modern theatre of the period shared was a lack of internal logic, and often, incomplete execution. One could ask of Mrs. Noah in the 1992 *Not Wanted on the Voyage*, "If life was so great in the old days, why did she spend so much time on the porch drinking straight gin?" Similarly, in PTE's *The End of the World Romance*, the lead character has stolen the wind, but strangely, musical instruments, which depend on wind to transmit their sound, still worked. At its best, this theatre tantalized audiences with unrealized potential. Audiences were expected to accept this often half-baked art at a time of downsizing, when they had to exhibit hyper-competence just to keep their jobs.

The problem is that the Kitchen Sink play, a variant of the well-made play, is the best form for people to explore their mutual experience. Variations of the well-made play formula launched vital theatres in Norway, Ireland, and late 19th-century Paris. Unfortunately for Manitobans, their turn came just when leading thinkers expressed supreme boredom with the concept.

Someone who has studied dozens of classic plays in university and then spent a career either teaching or writing about them can be forgiven for finding the formula tiresome. The same goes for actors and directors in the second or third decade of their career. It is natural, then, to long for something new in terms of form and narrative. It is much less forgivable to expect the average person to share that longing.

Unfortunately, "serious" art became a catchphrase with funding bodies and serious artists, in all fields. Grants to so-called "literary" authors allowed some valuable books to emerge, and kept some writers from abandoning their calling. Over the years, some "literary" writers developed loyal followings, and a few began to earn a livable income. Others secured posts at universities. Unfortunately, popular success became synonymous with selling out. The same politics applied to other art forms.

A bizarre manifestation of this prejudice was the first search for a new Manitoba novelist. Bess Kaplan of the Canadian Authors' Association and others pressed the funding bodies to sponsor an award similar to the Alberta New Novelist award. This award helped launch Janette Turner Hospital's career, and the idea was that it could work in Manitoba as well.

When the event finally happened in 1982, Kaplan and some others felt a sense of dismay bordering on betrayal. When the judges announced the winning entries at the Chamber of the Black Star in the Legislature, they proudly recalled their decision to limit their scope to "literary" novels. The catch was that the contest no longer had a publisher, and without a publisher, the authors had little chance of finding readers. It would be years before book awards made their way back onto the Manitoba scene, although the three prize winners eventually found publishers.

The same bias worked against theatre. If a play that was traditional in form packed audiences in, that was proof that the work lacked merit. A theatre could either please the people who paid for tickets, or please the funding bodies and intelligentsia.

This was a real catastrophe for PTE and its audience, because alternative theatre was what it did best, and what its audiences loved about it. While other cultures might have had centuries of traditional drama that explained their lives to them, Manitoba's tradition had just begun when the people who mattered most in terms of funding—the arts councils, critics, and academics decided the form was obsolete. This shift created a sense of betrayal for audience members who had a fleeting taste of what they had yearned for for years, only to have it snatched away after just a few bites. Since PTE relied on ticket receipts for only about half of their revenue, it faced a difficult dilemma.

Nor was this new aesthetic helpful for emerging theatre artists. Doug Arrell writes about this dilemma in an article in *Aesthetics* titled "Teaching Aesthetics to Artists." He explains that "young artists are afraid that what they may gain from [aesthetics] is an overdeveloped artistic conscience that will make it more difficult for them to make the hardheaded career choices they sense they will soon have to make." For the students at Winnipeg's two universities, this choice might play out in deciding whether to audition as a spear carrier in the latest MTC classic, fearing that the professors they had placed their faith in would see them making a career-based choice instead of following the higher path, even if that path meant unemployment and competing for restaurant jobs instead of acting ones.

At a different level, artistic directors and their staffs faced an equally difficult choice. If they chose plays that audiences would love, more often than not, the critics and academics would scorn the choice as pandering. If they chose "artistically sound" plays, they ran the risk of alienating their audience. What they might gain in prestige and funding, therefore, they were likely to lose in box office revenue and community goodwill.

Artistic directors caught in this squeeze often used the popular but seldom successful strategy of trying to please everyone. This solution was popular with neither the audience nor the intellectual movers and shakers. Kim McCaw left PTE after two years at the mall.

His replacement, Michael Springate, came from Montreal via the Canada Council with a reputation for being a playwright's director. If so, the result often did not look like it on stage. New scripts often appeared to be thrown together on opening night. Often the plays themselves did not seem fully conceived, such as the promising but ultimately disappointing *End of the World Romance.* Whatever his skills as a dramaturg might have been, it was evident that his product fell short somewhere between the read-through and opening night. Springate left after four seasons, with the theatre in deep financial trouble.

There is some evidence that had he stayed, he might have overcome his deficiencies. With season ticket sales at a record low of just over 2000, however, time ran out. Still, the Springate legacy is far from a total failure. He opened a second stage that premiered some important new works and introduced Winnipeg audiences to works they might not have seen otherwise. His forays into international companies, Odessa Ukrainian Music and Drama Theatre's *Marilyn Mudrow* and Traverse Theatre of Edinburgh's *Bondagers,* brought an international flavour to Winnipeg without ignoring the theatre's prairie roots. The Ukrainians and the Scots, after all, sent many of the people who opened up the prairie soil for agriculture.

Springate also kept local playwrights on the main stage. Nick Mitchell, Bruce McManus, William Harrar, Carol Shields (twice), Patrick Friesen, and Margaret Sweatman all had productions. Tannis Kowalchuk, Lora Schroeder, Carol Matas, Per Brask and others saw their work appear in the Young Audiences program. His Theatre with

Bite! series in the Colin Jackson theatre gave more local playwrights exposure, and brought outside groups such as Mump and Smoot in from the Fringe circuit.

15

Dark Days at MTC:
The Popularity–Aesthetics Squeeze

"The Manitoba Theatre Centre is the Fatty Arbuckle of Winnipeg show business. Big ambitions, big sets, big sweats."

—Charles Wilkins, in *The Winnipeg Book*, 1984

From the late 1970s until well into the 1990s, MTC must have felt as if people were firing on it from all sides. It must have seemed almost a comfort that their main stage was in "a big concrete bunker of a building, once described by columnist Shaun Herron as "a Siberian bus station," as Wilkins said in *The Winnipeg Book*.

Local actors did not like MTC because they did not get enough work. Playwrights did not like MTC because they had grown tired of being hired as playwright-in-residence, only to have their scripts gather dust. Intellectuals did not like MTC, accusing it of becoming a "regional roadhouse for whatever plays the rest of the world deems worthy." When MTC did try to be adventurous, its courage often failed, making what was groundbreaking theatre elsewhere seem bland. Even then, its loyal audience blamed it for abandoning them in the name of elitism. Artistic Director at MTC became the toughest gig in town. The job chewed up and spat out a number of artistic directors until Steven Schipper found a precarious path through the minefield during his tenure, which started in 1989.

Until Schipper's regime, and to a lesser extent afterwards, the great grey building became known as the place where grey great plays took place. Perhaps in response, MTC developed a justified reputation for excellence in set design. The building itself is so cold, so lacking in intimacy, that the stage almost begs for ornamentation. Occasionally, though, MTC would overcome its surroundings and produce some magic, usually with Shakespeare.

In the spring 1991 issue of *Canadian Theatre Review,* University of Manitoba Theatre professor Chris Johnson refers to the Gilbert/Hasnian period (1966–69 and 1972–1980) as the "bad old days." (Presumably, Johnson does not include Len Cariou's one-year stint in this condemnation.) Their replacement, Richard Ouzounian, did not always find an artistic high ground, but at least he put theatre on the map in Winnipeg.

Ouzounian cut quite a figure in Manitoba's artistic scene. Not until the Winnipeg Symphony Orchestra's Bramwell Tovey did the province have such a flamboyant figure. Even people who didn't attend theatre knew who Richard Ouzounian was, and people who did not attend theatre started to. His flair for razzle-dazzle sometimes fell flat, as it did with his 1982 *Taming of the Shrew,* in which he put a full-sized swimming pool on stage and set the play in Tuxedo. Most of the time, though, he brought people and excitement to the theatre. Audiences at his *Black Bonspiel of Wullie MacCrimmon* marvelled at the curling match, and the stagecraft that made the rocks go where the script told them to. Canadian content increased. His *Balconville* showed his show business acumen at its best.

David Fennario's *Balconville* is a Marxist look at life in the Montreal slums. Its inhabitants live in an uneasy truce across the language barrier, broken at times when outside events threaten their precarious existence. The gritty reality uses even grittier language; it is a tour de force of swearing and other bad behaviour. Ouzounian soon had the sold-out sign appearing at the box office, only to have some patrons head to the exits as the air went blue in two languages. His solution was to tell people who had arrived too late to get seats to wait, and if they didn't mind missing a few minutes, he would probably be able to squeeze them in.

MTC was the talk of the town, and Ouzounian was a popular after-dinner speaker around town. For all his success, though, Ouzounian had his detractors. Purists said he often went for the sizzle instead of the steak. Chris Johnson says, "He probably cares more about show business than theatre." Some members of the local theatre still look down and spit on the ground each time his name is mentioned. They blame him for importing a resident company they called the "gang of incompetents" instead of using local talent. Opportunities to work became fewer under his reign, they accused. In the almost two decades since he left, however, most would at least grudgingly admit that actors such as Richard Hurst and Robbie Patterson have enhanced the theatre scene.

Ouzounian ended a fifteen-year moratorium on Manitoba playwrights by producing three Alf Silver plays in three years at the Warehouse. *Thimblerig* created positive attention and seemed to mark the beginnings of better times for local playwrights. Unfortunately, the two later plays did not continue the momentum, and Manitoba plays' appearances again became sporadic on MTC stages, although not as rare as before.

When Ouzounian performed the rare MTC artistic feat of leaving by choice, he left a void. Just as when Hirsch left, MTC had problems finding a replacement who would carry them forward. It was not alone. In an essay in *Canadian Theatre History,* Mark Czarnecki points out that only two regional theatres did not change artistic directors between 1983 and 1984. He goes on to express the hope that Ouzounian's replacement, James Roy, would use his experience at the Blythe Festival to launch new Canadian plays at MTC. History does not bear this out.

Roy's tenure at MTC was short and largely unhappy. His major triumph was reportedly Ted Galay's *Tsymbaly,* a play for and about Manitoba's Ukrainian community. The play was a huge popular success, but Roy (and his replacements) did not repeat the experiment. His other mainstage shows often lacked life; he even made *Tartuffe,* the play that caused such a stir that it shut French theatre in Quebec down for more than a century, dull. Added to these woes was Roy's personality: he had none of Ouzounian's Barnum and Bailey appeal. He left under a cloud, with many in the community, if not sorry to see him go, at least outraged about the way it happened. On the plus side, he did produce one Manitoba play, Alan Williams' *The Last Doors' Bootleg* in 1986.

His replacement, Rick McNair, fared little better. Ironically, Czarnecki mentions him in the same *Canadian Theatre History* essay as someone who had proved that Canadian playwrights could write for the regional theatres' large stages. He had produced Sharon Pollock, John Murrell and W.O. Mitchell at Theatre Calgary. Unfortunately, he soon had MTC board members grumbling. Manitoba playwrights complained that they received commissions but not productions, and some questioned the wisdom of spending public money in this way when other theatres did a better job of putting local scripts on stage.

Once again, when the axe fell, MTC suffered a public relations disaster. Perhaps more embarrassing for it in this case, McNair stayed in town and often produced independent theatre.

Despite his lack of popular and artistic success at the theatre, McNair's legacy is much more important than that of any of his predecessors, except for John Hirsch. For one thing, he instituted the practice of using local amateurs in touring productions, giving people outside Winnipeg an inside look at professional theatre, and making a stronger link to local audiences. While he did not win any gold stars for his use of local professional talent, he did them an important favour.

The Winnipeg Fringe Festival started during his tenure, under the skilled guidance of his assistant, Larry Desrochers. It has become the second-largest Fringe in North America, and has helped to launch many careers. Playwrights Dennis Trochim, Ian Ross, Rick Chafe, Yvette Nolan, James Durham, Harry Rintoul, and Bruce McManus either launched or revived careers there. Chris Sigurdson had his first directing success with Rick Chafe's *Zac and Speth*. Many actors have established credentials with solid Fringe performances.

As the 1990s started, MTC found the heat a little less intense. This was in part because its board hired Steven Schipper, an artistic director who knew how to make the theatre viable, and in part because other groups took up the artistic slack.

16

THE FRINGE FESTIVAL

"See you at the Fringe..."
—Fringe devotee's version of "Next year in Jerusalem."

Ironically, the greatest vehicle Winnipeg has had for introducing new ideas and forms is an MTC creation. Manitobans first experienced Ronnie Burkett, Mump and Smoot, and many other innovative groups at the annual July festival.

The only Fringe Festival sponsored by a major theatre started during Rick McNair's tenure, but the seed germinated a little earlier. As McNair tells it, he was walking from interviews at MTC to a party at PTE during a light snowstorm. As he glanced around the Exchange district, he thought, "Hm-m-m. This would be a great place to have a Fringe."

Fast forward a few months, and McNair is artistic director at MTC. Larry Desrochers is a young director looking for work. It so happened that McNair had seen something Desrochers had directed. They discussed it, and what impressed McNair was that Desrochers was willing to discuss it intelligently, not defensively, as many young directors do. McNair sensed that this intelligent and well-organized young man might be just the person to launch a Winnipeg Fringe. He supported a Desrochers project to take a play to the Edmonton Fringe as a way to get an insider's view of what worked and what needed improvement. This proved invaluable: when Desrochers arrived in Edmonton, he learned that the stage dimensions the Fringe sent were wrong, and his set did not fit.

Since its inception, the Fringe has been a model of good organization, a tribute to both Desrochers' organizational ability and McNair's eye for talent. The Winnipeg Fringe is now a major tourist attraction, and a key spot in the community of touring Fringe companies. Fringes start in the east, and move across the country in a roughly western itinerary. The big time for Fringes, however, starts in Winnipeg. Companies hope to have their show in shape, both artistically, and financially, when they arrive in Winnipeg. Toronto, Montreal, and Ottawa are the Fringe equivalent of touring the provinces.

The first Winnipeg Fringe in 1988 created a lot of curiosity. To Winnipeggers it seemed like a curiosity from a previous decade, but the good-time feeling that emanated from the Market Square was unmistakable. The memory most people who attended the first Fringe talk about is The Cauldron. This second-floor venue earned its nickname. Jessica Burleson recalls acting in a play that called for her to be on a swing set with another actor. She temporarily lost consciousness. The other actor reached over to catch her, she shook her head, and continued with the show.

Fringe legends Three Dead Trolls in a Baggie found a creative way to deal with the heat. They hired a Dickie Dee salesman to come in during their intermission. Every night they hauled him up the fire escape. Although the ice cream salesman had apprehensions, he kept coming back, because he sold out every night. The Fringe proved to be a godsend for local playwrights. It was a way to gain exposure and critical attention. Since Winnipeg had no shortage of underemployed actors, a writer with a good script could attract a cast good enough to do it justice. The Fringe was also a way for local directors to show that they had the ability to pull a show together. Chris Sigurdson, Kelly Daniels, Megan McArton, and Arne MacPherson all used the Fringe to establish credentials.

Almost immediately, however, artistic tensions arose. For one thing, Fringe participants have never developed a consensus on what the event's purpose is. For one faction, the key word is Fringe. They see the festival as a way to explore aspects of theatre not available during the regular season. For this group, the Fringe circuit is the true home of experimental theatre. Primus launched itself at the Fringe.

A second group, that at least partly overlaps the first, holds that the Fringe is for new plays. The Fringe is an economical way to audience-test a play, and some playwrights (Lora Schroeder, Tannis Kowalchuk, Dale Lakevold, Ian Ross) have established themselves this way. It's a double-edged sword, however. Fringe plays have acquired a reputation for being "edgy" in a negative way, self-indulgent scripts with community theatre production values. The reason is that for less than $1000, anyone can mount a Fringe production. The Fringe proudly (and quite rightly) claims that there is no quality control. It is both its blessing and its curse. Theatre reaches a public without the filter of current aesthetic fads, board interference, or local arts politics. Artistic directors therefore sometimes shy away from Fringe plays, worried that what gets positive attention at an artistic free-for-all might just look lame in a formal setting.

The third group who stake a claim to the Fringe are ambitious actors at the start of their careers. Sometimes these actors take a chance on a new script, either through friendship or because it represents an opportunity to work. At least as often they decide to put on a classic script by George F. Walker, Sam Shepard, or someone else they studied or otherwise learned about. As might be expected, sometimes, as in the case of *Laundry and Bourbon* at the 1990 Fringe, the results are great. In the worst-case scenario, the company at least has a familiar and loved play to draw a house with.

The fourth group is less ambitious than the previous three. This group comprises community theatre groups and others who do theatre because they enjoy it. Theatre is not a career or even a potential career for these people. It is, however, an important part of their lives, important enough that they willingly sacrifice their spare time and sometimes their dignity to be a part of the festival. Often the product they put on stage is very enjoyable. Some groups, like the Tara Players, put on shows (like *Someone to Watch Over Me* in 1995) that stand up well against the fare in the regular theatre season.

The fifth group, Fantasy Theatre for Children, falls somewhere between this group and the next. Under Tony Frost, it produces traditional children's theatre, using a cast of aspiring younger performers. These shows usually sell out to the daycare audience. While theatre purists might look down on Fantasy Theatre, it satisfies a specific audience. Actors who work in Frost's shows learn the basics of the craft, such as showing up for rehearsals on time, paying attention in rehearsals, and enunciating well.

The sixth and final group is the professional touring companies. Early on, some groups learned that they could make a modest living by touring a show on the Fringe circuit. Some groups, like the English Suitcase Theatre Company or Sensible Footwear, have come from England. Others, like Three Dead Trolls in a Baggie or Real Canadian Mounted Productions, have come from other Canadian centres. Some groups create their own scripts, while others choose existing scripts and put their own stamp on them. Some local groups have gained enough confidence to tour their shows, such as Angus Kohm has done with his parodies of formula films.

Touring is a perilous way to make a living, as any vaudeville act could have told these companies. Sometimes their vehicle (both transportation and dramatic) breaks down, resulting in unplanned, costly repairs. Sometimes the best productions fail to catch on with the public. A prime example of this phenomenon is the ironically named show *Justice is a Red-lipped Whore.* It played in 1993 at Prairie Theatre Exchange, the first year the Fringe used a venue so far away from the Market Square. Noises in the Attic, an Edmonton company, presented a superbly surreal production that played to tiny houses, partly because people were reluctant to make the 20-minute walk, and partly because people were unfamiliar with the show.

In 1994, another touring show died at the box office through no fault of its own. David Stocton Rand of West Lafayette, Indiana brought a 35-minute jewel called *i dreamed i was a baseball card* to Winnipeg. This show also played in a first-time venue. An added handicap was a three-day hiatus in the middle of the run. His best time was on the first day, an 8 p.m. slot. Unfortunately, Rand did not have time to establish a name for himself. The Saturday *Free Press* printed a three-star review that dismissed the play's impact. The noon-hour show on Monday drew only 15 people, who nevertheless gave him a sustained ovation. After he left, the audience took a few minutes to collect themselves before venturing back into the world. The show started to get some 'buzz," including a rapturous review by Robert Enright. Thursday at 1:15 pm, (dead time for Fringe shows), 50 people lined up outside the door to see Rand's performance. It was too late. Rand had run out of money and had to leave for home on Wednesday, without learning that he had finally found his audience.

If the Messenger's Guilty, Why Can't I Shoot Him?

Over the years, the Fringe has had an uneasy relationship with the media. On one hand, people need to know that the event is happening, and they want to know which of the dozens of shows they should choose to see. (Seeing all the shows is a mathematical impossibility.) On the other hand, Fringe purists see the event as largely proletarian. Their ideal situation is one in which productions find their own level with an audience adventurous enough to take a chance on unknown artists.

Both elements—media attention and an artistically brave audience—are necessary for a successful event. As with most things in life, the question is one of balance. Too much media attention, and the event becomes a carnival. Too little attention, and the event becomes irrelevant. At the same time, the purists' wary attitude to the press has some justification. The period leading up to and containing the Fringe is long past Manitoba's golden age of theatre criticism. The *Free Press* theatre coverage, in particular, has mirrored the paper's general decline. At a 1989 Canadian Authors Association conference, the *Edmonton Journal*'s entertainment editor asked a group of Manitoba authors over lunch: "What's wrong with the *Free Press*? It used to be such a good paper."

At first, the *Free Press* coverage was perfunctory: a few feature articles, and one reviewer writing a few reviews a day. The CBC gave the event the coverage it traditionally gives a major arts event, and assigned its key people, Robert Enright and Jacqui Good. The *Winnipeg Sun* gave the event some coverage, but in fairness, its target audience is not an artsy one in general. Still, the informed, balanced reviews that John Baert and Riva Harrison have provided put the more uptown *Free Press* to shame.

This lack of print media attention changed in 1991 with the *Jenny*. Coral McKendrick, a former *Free Press* theatre reviewer and Agassiz board member, launched this unique newsletter to give Fringe fans and performers a way to communicate. Anyone willing to sign their name can pen a review, and companies are free to submit promotional copy. They can also pay for ads. McKendrick's entertaining daily editorials are an added bonus, often explaining and apologizing for a production delay caused by *Jenny*'s meagre human and financial resources. Michele Cook, Rosey Goodman, Dave Pruden and Dave Cramer often work around the clock to make sure the *Jenny* arrives in the kiosks every day.

This shoe-string operation has a large and loyal readership. Often lively debates over the merits (or lack thereof) of a show erupt. (One year, the participants of *The Happy Cunt* roamed the beer tent with fire in their eyes, looking for the author of a scathing review.)

Mainly, however, the *Jenny* is a much-loved institution. Touring companies say the *Jenny* is unique, and they look forward to the feedback the newsletter affords. Often performers comment on each other's shows, offering a rare chance for dialogue (and perhaps some mutual box office boost). Robert Enright thinks enough about the *Jenny* that he often submits reviews for shows he deems worthy of attention.

The admiration society does not apparently include the Fringe administration. The *Jenny* receives no funds or endorsement from them, and often has to tread lightly. Just getting media passes is often a problem. Despite chronic lack of funding and official support, the *Jenny* has been part of every Fringe since 1991 except for the 1999 Fringe, when scheduling conflicts caused by the Pan-Am Games kept most staffers at the Folk Festival instead. That year, a volunteer group put out *ReVIEW from the Edge.*

The *Jenny* also hosts an awards night at the close. These mostly nonsense awards are a good-natured way of recognizing people who have made a mark at the current Fringe.

Perhaps because of the *Jenny,* and perhaps because of numerous letters to the editor complaining about the lack of coverage, the *Free Press* began printing a pull-out Fringe section in 1993. This has proved to be a decidedly mixed blessing for performers and Fringe patrons alike. Those groups favoured with a rave review (deserved or not) can expect to sell out for the rest of their run. Those who run afoul of the reviewer's sensibilities often play for crickets during the rest of the run.

This situation would perhaps be fair if the *Free Press* hired knowledgeable critics for this effort (or perhaps not, given the many historical examples of critics panning future classics). The *Free Press* does not use established critics, however; it sends whomever it can from the news room, often an unwilling accomplice to the event he or she covers. Worse, sometimes these reviewers seem to take evil delight in finally being able to trash someone in print that they do not have to cover on a daily basis.

An example of how badly out of tune a reviewer can be was when the *Free Press* sent the legislative reviewer to cover *Herds,* a performance art piece. Performance art is a minority taste at best, so it is not surprising that the reviewer found himself at sea during the performance. Instead of admitting that, however, he tried to pass himself off as somewhat of an expert, and accused the work of being a Spalding Gray knock-off. In approach and content, the work was diametrically opposite to Gray's, meaning that even the small audience for performance art was misled. In contrast, the other performance artists on the program, a seasoned duo from New York, raved about the show. In their *Jenny* review, they said, "Perhaps the potential is there to be the future Warhol, or Woody Allen—a budding genius in the raw."

The key word there is potential. Often the mainstream media ignore or forget that for local performers, the Fringe is an opportunity to explore their potential. Without an adequate crowd, however, they do not get the primary feedback they need. Plays such as Kirsten Jay Brooks' *Mask* received negative reviews because the reviewer could not see the potential the work displayed.

On other occasions the *Free Press* coverage has brought the paper perilously close to being sued. The first time was in 1994, in a review of Lorraine Bowen's show. Bowen is a British comedian whose show is a rough mixture of Barry Humphries' Dame Edna and Gilda Radner's Anna Rosanna Danna, except she is not in drag and not adenoidal. Bowen also draws from the same spring as the Steve Martin. In one of his skits, Martin plays banjo and puts a fake arrow through his head for comic effect. In an interview, Martin expressed impatience with people who believed that he thought putting a fake arrow through his head was funny, while the gag was one layer deeper: he played a guy who thought it was funny.

Bowen's stage persona was someone who might be anyone's friendly but slightly loopy neighbour. The character sees herself as God's gift to entertainment, despite empirical evidence to the contrary. She smiles and charms her way through the show's many technical and musical flubs. The *Free Press* reviewer did not get it. His review took the show straight, which was bad enough. The reviewer compounded ignorance with foolhardiness when he suggested the venue technician might have been drunk: "Her show….lacks formal discipline. Either that or the sound and light tekkie, who missed half his [sic] cues on opening night, was drunk." Stage technicians with drinking problems have the same career prospects as neurosurgeons with Parkinson's disease. The technician wanted to sue for libel, but cooler heads persuaded her not to, and the affair died down.

In 1999, the same reviewer stumbled into the same problem. This time the victims were Crumbs, a group of three former MTYP Young Company members who had branched out into long-form improv.

This is the most difficult form of improv. It requires both comic invention and performers who know and trust each other well enough to build a performance out of scraps the audience throws them. Crumbs had built a loyal following by this time, despite the flogging the *Free Press* regularly gave them. This time the reviewer grudgingly admitted that the group had talent, but also said, "In a 50-minute skit advertised as improv but actually scripted (with a plot and everything) the Crumbs show signs of imminent wit." Accusing improv artists of scripting material is the comedic equivalent of accusing Celine Dion of lip-synching, or an academic of plagiarism. It's not the sort of accusation a competent journalist makes without corroborating evidence. A quick interview with the venue technician would have provided that evidence, if such evidence existed. The reviewer instead chose to risk his professional reputation on instinct. One Crumbs member wanted to sue, but the others persuaded him that the best course was to turn the accusation to advantage. They began to advertise themselves as "so good the *Free Press* thinks we're scripted."

In the same Fringe, the same reviewer ran a slight risk of a lawsuit by supermodel Kathy Ireland, when he trashed a Theatre Essential production and attributed most of the blame to her. Fortunately for the reviewer, Ireland probably does not read the *Free Press*, and the real playwright, Kimberly Ireton, just laughed it off.

The Machinery behind the Wizard

The Fringe is now a major event that has developed its own legends and legacy. For the almost two weeks the event lasts, Winnipeg is a city for and about theatre. Some careers have started here, and some great plays have seen their first audience. None of this would have been possible, however, without the staff and volunteers that keep the machinery moving.

The Fringe has been very fortunate in its executive directors. Larry Desrochers set a high standard for his successors and fortunately left behind a solid organization to carry on the tradition. His four-year tenure put the Fringe on solid ground. Craig Walls had the misfortune of taking over the job during a recession, but he kept the event afloat and eventually rebuilt the audience base. When he handed the controls over to current executive producer Bertram Schneider in 1996, it was breaking attendance records again.

Schneider brought extensive Fringe experience to the job, as a performer, director and producer. He added some advertising flair, coming up with a new theme each year. These themes, such as 2000's double-0 theme, gave advertisers and the media something to hook into. He also innovated the sign-up procedures, going to a lottery system instead of having people line up outside in February, hoping for a choice spot. A hiccup occurred for the 2001 Fringe when he instituted e-mail registration. Some numbers were left off the draw, and the Fringe had to redraw names. The overseas registrants sometimes could not communicate with the MTC server. During his tenure also, the bring-your-own venue flourished. Under this scheme, a company rents space other than a standard venue, and provides its own technical support. It guarantees good performance times, but it also dilutes the audience during prime time.

Schneider's advertising innovations helped to boost the Fringe attendance to new heights, and it came at a time when local artists began to come into their own.

Some people complain that the "Hollywood" approach to the Fringe detracts from the serious art they try to produce. Others are glad to have the larger audiences. Probably the only instance of serious mismanagement came during the 2001 Fringe. Since the Eaton's building on Portage Avenue was vacant and slated for demolition, the Fringe set up three venues there. Unfortunately, they put two venues side by side on the main floor. Noise bleed between venues was so bad that the English Suitcase production of *Betrayal* moved to a bring-your-own.

As important as the sound management the Fringe enjoys are the thousands of volunteers who keep the event running for over twelve hours a day. These volunteers come from all walks of life: professional artists wanting to give something back to the community, retired people (some in their late 80s), high school students hoping either to flesh out their résumés or meet someone cute, and people who take holidays from work to help make the event a success. Many romances (and at least one marriage) have resulted from the community spirit among Fringe volunteers.

While the artists and audiences benefit from the event, an indirect beneficiary is the city itself, particularly the downtown core. During the Fringe it is a lively, friendly place teeming with people. It shows the city what the downtown could be with some forward thinking.

17

And Now for Something Completely Different:

From Theatre X to Primus

"When I came back from Europe after 12 years, I honestly thought the (theatre) work was just the same as it was in the 1960s and 70s.... A friend of mine said that with most things you see, by the time you've got your car keys in your hand, you've forgotten what they were about. Entertainment is only part of the show. The rest is what's going to resonate afterwards, how the audience is going to talk about it, think about it, dream about it."

—Richard Fowler,as quoted by Garth Buchholz
in *Theatrum*, Summer 1994

As the twentieth century drew to a close, a few groups staked out territory that MTC and, to a lesser extent, PTE either avoided or stumbled on when they visited. The universities and other training programs had been graduating theatre students impatient to explore the more adventurous theatre styles that the main stages avoided. By the late 1980s, a critical mass accumulated. Before long Winnipeg had a variety of theatre groups scrabbling in the fringes for their place on the theatre scene.

The first of these was Theatre X. Its alumni stand up well against the province's establishment theatre companies: Rob Slade, Steve McIntyre, Kyle McCulloch, Ellen Peterson, Ron Jenkins, Brian Drader, Leith Clarke and Wayne Buss! (The exclamation point is part of his name, and he did it before the artist formerly known as Prince got the idea.) The group also played a part in developing younger artists, such as the three men who formed Crumbs: Steve Sym, Lee White, and Devin McCracken.

In any list of classic Fringe shows, the Theatre X crowd would have many plays. Fringe veterans still cite its *Mind of the Iguana,* which played at the first Fringe in 1988, as the quintessential Fringe play. Drader and McIntyre wrote this surreal script about a woman's obsession with her pet and her boyfriend's attempts to cope with that obsession. In one of the most physically demanding performances ever seen at the Fringe, McIntyre played the lizard to perfection, using his arms to drag his body all over the set in a silent but mesmerizing performance.

Trial By Bus, by Kyle McCulloch, took audiences on a city bus ride as the action unfolded. This environmental theatre production unfolded unpredictably as each audience influenced the action. Steve McIntyre's *TREEhouses* was a lesser success, but it still created enough attention that Liam Lacey of the *Globe and Mail* chose it as one of the four plays he would write about in his 1990 Winnipeg Fringe article.

Theatre X also presented scripted evenings throughout the year, but its major claim to fame was improv. It was one of the very few companies of the time that performed true improv, with the audience calling out sketch elements as the action proceeded. Slade and McIntyre, with help from McCulloch, became legendary for their amazing ability to make cutting-edge comedy on the run. McCulloch starred in several Guy Maddin films before leaving for Los Angeles and becoming a scriptwriter on *South Park.* McIntyre also left Winnipeg, for Calgary, but he still returns frequently, either to team up with his former partner Rob Slade, or to work as an actor in other projects. Slade has established himself as one of the finest actors the province has ever seen. He is equally at home doing Shakespeare (with Shakespeare in the Ruins) theatre for young audiences (for MTYP) or experimental works (with Adhere and Deny). Movie lovers might remember his poignant performance as Scotty, the doomed pilot in *For the Moment,* an early Russel Crowe film produced by Aaron Kim Johnson.

Primus: A New Vision Means Changing the Focus

Coming from a completely different but equally adventurous perspective was Primus. This theatre collective grew out of a class that founder Richard Fowler taught at the National Theatre School in the 1980s. Fowler left Canada early in his theatre career to become part of Denmark's Odin Theatret, where he stayed for 11 years in the 1970s and early 80s. Italian-born Eugenio Barba created this theatre group in Oslo, Norway, using the innovative Polish director Jerzy Grotowski's ideas. Later the Odin Theatret moved to Denmark.

Some students at the National Theatre School felt so drawn to Fowler's methods that they asked for further instruction. When Fowler moved to Winnipeg, they followed him. The result was Primus.

Primus followed many practices Fowler learned in Denmark, including a communal company structure, an emphasis on physical training, and organic performance development. Joining this company was not too different from joining a monastery whose god was theatre. Not surprisingly, Actors' Equity did not know how to deal with this company, so Primus operated outside the Equity agreement throughout its life.

Describing what Primus did is not an easy task. Its works provided stunning visual and aural experiences unlike anything experienced in Winnipeg before. Perhaps the best gateway to explaining the theatrical experience Primus created is to look at the six aspects of drama that Aristotle described:

1. Plot
2. Character
3. Thought
4. Diction
5. Music
6. Spectacle

The traditional, MTC-style theatre has focused on plot, character, thought, and for MTC especially, spectacle in the form of sets and costumes. Prairie realism often emphasized character and thought to the detriment of plot, and used spectacle as a kind of statement against the elaborate sets and costumes the country's main stages used. For Primus, the emphasis was on diction, music and spectacle, but spectacle for Primus was the performance itself, built through rigorous physical and vocal training. Whereas in other theatres thought would find its expression in the unfolding of plot and the characters' reactions to it, in Primus the thought emerged organically from the theatrical experience. For Primus, the line between process and performance did not exist.

Part of the reason its work differed so greatly from that of other groups is the way it developed a performance. Instead of working from a script and using the text as a foundation for the performance, Primus members used their training and rehearsal process to develop the finished work. The text emerged from this process more or less concurrently. As Stephen Lawson said in an interview with Rick Skene, "I felt really strange at the Playwrights Union of Canada conference when the MC came out and put this script down and said, 'Well, we all know it starts with this.' Well, in our case, it doesn't start with a script."[41]

This process might have produced chaotic results if Richard Fowler had not been part of the process. As the director, he sifted and shaped the elements until they coalesced into a unified artistic expression. In 1998 he received the Chalmers Award for artistic direction.

It is also important to note that the Primus did not consider itself part of the experimental theatre movement. As Fowler explained in a 1994 *Theatrum* article, Primus did not experiment. It followed "a well-delineated, comparative performance technique."[42] It belonged to the so-called Third Theatre Movement.

He did not, however, impose his artistic vision on the company, as many traditional directors do. At the end of each rehearsal, the performers and Fowler debriefed. Also, unlike many so-called avant-garde companies, Primus always considered audience reaction in its performance development. It did not belong to the self-expression into self-indulgence school. Primus offered an open invitation to the theatre community to attend rehearsals. Afterwards Fowler would hold a debriefing session, to test his goals for the performance elements with how outsiders perceived them. Their productions evolved during rehearsals, with all the input affecting the performance.

Primus from the first developed a special connection with its audience. Before the performance started, the company members would usher the audience into the performance space. Often the company would have constructed this space especially for the performance: in an abandoned bank, the Winnipeg Art Gallery, or a park. The company also took on community projects, such as the ill-fated First Night Celebrations.

First Night was a combined indoor and outdoor New Year's Eve celebration that took place in downtown Winnipeg. This alcohol-free celebration copied similar events in other cities. The idea was to provide a way a family could celebrate New Year's together. For two years the company worked with community volunteers to develop *Caravan of the Midnight Sun*. It involved stilt walkers, a choir, a Chinese dragon dance, and many other multicultural elements in a procession to the legislative building, where the countdown and fireworks took place.

While the event was an artistic success and helped forge permanent bonds between the company and the larger community, poor festival management and brutally cold weather ended the festival in the second year (1992–3). The funding bodies refused to cover losses, so Primus and many other participants found themselves facing bankruptcy. Primus survived this disaster, at least partly because the artists had become used to a Spartan existence, but also because the community responded to its fundraising appeal.

The company maintained its community connection by offering workshops to interested people and performing at events such as the Blizzards, Manitoba's film awards. The group's work also appeared on CBC radio.

Besides Fowler, the company comprised Tannis Kowalchuk, Steve Lawson, Donald Kitt, Karen Randoja, and Ker Wells. Sean Dixon, Jane Wells and Richard Clarkin also belonged to the company for a while. Dixon contributed textual elements to the process.

Primus' first work was *Dog Day/Jour de Canicule* in 1988. After that came *Alkoremmi* (1991), *The Night Room* (1994), *Wait for the Dawn, Far Away Home* (1997), a children's theatre piece, and *Madrugadi,* a collaboration with Groundswell using text by Patrick Friesen. The group also took part in the New Music Festival, setting Patrick Friesen's poetry to music. Unlike other companies that develop a performance and then move on to the next project, Primus kept its works in repertoire, continually shaping them as new ideas developed.

Primus also organized Survival in the Ice Age, an international theatre conference held at the St. Boniface College in 1997. The conference combined performance and workshop discussions, with a cabaret night each evening. The magazine *Canadian Theatre Review* devoted an entire issue to the conference. In 1997 the group presented Show Girls, A Festival of Women's Performance.

Its work received international acclaim and toured widely in North America and Europe. Of a 1996 performance of *The Night Room* in Cleveland, reviewer Linda Eisenstein said, "As an experimental ensemble, Primus' strength is in its ability to manipulate a beautifully designed environment, creating a series of dream insights out of what are essentially variations of flashlights, gauze, and actor's bodies. The piece also boasts two highly skilled performers, who are able to command an audience's attention regardless of the material they're given: Ker Wells and Stephen Lawson."

Unfortunately, nothing lasts forever. Primus folded in 1998. Some members stayed in Winnipeg or return on occasion, but most have permanently located elsewhere. Prince Edward Island-born Ker Wells returned east to set up Theatre 11, based out of Halifax. This company continues the tradition Fowler and his company started. Fowler set up permanent residence in Italy, Tannis Kowalchuk married and relocated to the United States, and Karen Randoja moved to Toronto. The first time Manitoba audiences saw a Primus alumnus on stage after the breakup was in 2001, when Stephen Lawson performed in Spatial Relations' contribution to Beckettfest, *Act Without Words*. The ideas the company presented to Manitoba audiences live on, however.

Adhere and Deny: Great Does Not Necessarily Always Mean Big

Grant Guy's Adhere and Deny theatre gives little theatre a whole new meaning. Intellectual without being pretentious, his small-scale productions live with the audience long after, as Richard Fowler once said in an interview, you start reaching for your car keys.

Adhere and Deny grew out of a company called Shared Stage, a cooperative effort including Agassiz Theatre, the Manitoba Association of Playwrights, and the Winnipeg Film Group. The company, founded in 1981, offered a mixed program of theatre, performance, music, poetry and prose readings, and film and video screenings. In 1987 the company became Adhere and Deny, gradually narrowing its focus to object and puppet-based theatre in 1998. The key player and continuing influence has been Grant Guy.

Guy has directed and designed for a number of local companies; most notably he has been the designer for a number of Shakespeare in the Ruins productions. He has also had a close collaboration with Ace Art gallery. He has had his best success as a dramatic artist, however, with his company, which develops unique presentations of slightly obscure (by Winnipeg standards) artists. Among his creations are productions of *Ubu Roi, Bell* (1996), *John the Baptist, Woyzeck*(1998), *Kleist: fragments* (2000), *Salome* (2000) and *Found and Lost* (as part of Beckettfest). In 1998 he curated Ace Art's Ground Zero productions. Adhere and Deny co-produced *The Harrowing,* by Scott Douglas, with Theatre Projects. Guy directed this 1996 production.

His works often include puppets of one form or another, and always explore new ways of expressing the text. He uses Rob Slade frequently and other noted Winnipeg actors such as Graham Ashmore and Carolyn Gray and Sharon Bajer. Another common feature is the small performance space Adhere and Deny uses. Often the house capacity is no more than a few dozen. The small performance scale forces audiences to concentrate on the performance to a greater degree than normal, but Guy's creations reward that experience. His audience is a rather small and cohesive one, primarily (but not completely) made up of fellow theatre artists. These people understand the theatre's conventions. These small events have an enormous impact on audiences and an influence out of proportion with the theatre's size.

Adhere and Deny's scale is not always small, however. In 1994 it collaborated on the Light/Light series. One event was *While Angels Sleep,* Sharon Alward's performance art piece. As she describes it, "I rode a motorcycle…while wearing purple neon wings and dragging 12 crucifixes. Five video monitors, interspersed between burning barrels, played a continuous tape loop of my hand lighting a match and shaking out the flame during the performance." This took place outdoors, on the banks of Omand's Creek.

Over the years, Adhere and Deny has held an important place in Manitoba's theatre landscape. The Manitoba Arts Council recently recognized this by awarding the company operating funds (as opposed to project grants). Operating funds go only to groups that have established a record of good productions and sound management.

Shakespeare in the Ruins: Pioneer Quest

Part of the pioneer spirit that historians romanticize is self-sufficiency. For years, the Manitoba acting community faced a number of unpleasant choices:

1. Leave town to pursue opportunities. If fortune smiled and talent provided the engine, an actor could establish a career and expect to return to Winnipeg occasionally to act in an MTC production as a local who had made good.
2. Stay in town and land the odd minor role at MTC, plus the odd starring part at PTE, MTYP, the Winnipeg Jewish Theatre, or a personal Fringe project. The occasional film and teaching gig might add up to a below-average but livable income.
3. Start a company, and take on long hours of preparing grants, arranging for rehearsal and performance space, schmoozing the media for coverage, and managing an unruly bunch of

very articulate and creative fellow artists. The result would be the same level of income as option 2 (or worse, if you consider the hours involved).

We have already described a number of artists who chose option 1: Judith Evelyn, Tom Hendry, Len Cariou, Jim Mezon, Bill Walker, and Heath Lamberts. Maggie Nagle also eventually took this route. To Manitoba's great benefit, a number of talented people have exchanged almost certain fame and fortune to stay in the province and share their gift with the community that nurtured them: Evelyne Anderson, Doreen Brownstone, Nancy Drake, Ted Korol, Cliff Gardner, Vic Cowie, Paul Fredette, and so on.

In 1993, a group of Manitoba theatre artists chose option 3. Tired of subordinating their artistic drive to the traditional top-down method of putting a theatre performance together, they decided to form a cooperative that would stage Shakespeare outdoors, in the ruins of a Trappist monastery just outside town. (Prophetically, in *Curtain Time*, Ruth Harvey describes this monastery in a wistful description of life in Winnipeg at the turn of the 20th century.)

The three founders were Lora Schroeder, Ann Hodges, and B. Pat Burns. They all brought impressive credentials to the project. Lora Schroeder was the gold medallist in her 1993 graduating Honours Drama class at the University of Winnipeg. She had acted in a number of professional companies, including a stunning performance in Theatre Projects' *See Bob Run*.

B. Pat Burns directed the MTYP Young Company for a number of years. This company produced a Shakespeare play each year. Some productions approached professional quality, especially *The Tempest*. He had been Schroeder's director for *See Bob Run*. Burns had also taken over as interim Artistic Director when Theatre Projects founder Harry Rintoul quit. Ann Hodges graduated from the National Theatre School's directing program. She had acted and directed professionally, including some experimental works.

Schroeder had been involved in restoring the ruined Trappist monastery just south of Winnipeg in St. Norbert. The site offered rare potential for staging Shakespeare in settings close to those that existed in Elizabethan times. Besides the walls of the ruined church, the site had an abandoned orchard, surrounding forest, and the LaSalle River running along the border. A group of determined artists had successfully fought government plans to level the site, and had established a fledgling artists' colony on the site.

The founding trio gathered some of Manitoba's most talented artists to work on their first production at the ruins. Their first grant application failed, but on the second try the project went forward. Although it had only a limited run, 1994's *Romeo and Juliet* was a critical and popular triumph. The company list reads as almost a who's who of Manitoba's ambitious and growing theatre community: actors Derek Aasland, an MTYP Young Company graduate, Michelle Boulet, B. Pat Burns, Lee J. Campbell, Maggie Nagle, Debbie Patterson, Gene Pyrz, Lora Schroeder, and production staff Marc Beaudry, Katie R. East, Ann Hodges, Grant Guy, Rick McPherson, and Rick Skene. The only person imported for the show was Matthew Moreau, a Bishop's University graduate who had worked with Ann Hodges at that university. He took part in the first five productions and also did some MTC work.

A unique aspect of Shakespeare in the Ruins, besides the promenade style of theatre it uses, is that it is, like Primus, an artist-run company. Unlike Primus, though, it does not have a senior guiding artist. It uses a cooperative management style, which is both its blessing and its curse. The group decision-making process has helped give the artists the creative input they craved, but it has also led to friction. The company has never seemed to suffer artistically, but members often complain about collective meetings being an emotional and physical strain.

From the start, this group, like Primus, has had trouble fitting into the existing organizational patterns. It obtained permission to operate as an Equity co-op for the first few years, on the grounds that no one else locally was doing what it was doing. As the popularity of Shakespeare grew, this position became untenable, and it had to change its Equity status to the Independent Artists' Agreement. This meant appointing a board with both community and artistic members.

Official control of the company therefore had to pass from the co-op to the board. For most other theatre groups in the province, this arrangement meant that the company became more a board entity than an artist-driven one. Shakespeare in the Ruins did not want to surrender the artistic autonomy it had worked so hard to establish. The solution was to have a board with both company (artist) and community members. So far the company has succeeded in finding community members who admire the artists' artistic achievement enough to leave that aspect to them, while providing the administrative and management support the company needs to succeed. Gradually the two groups have developed a level of mutual trust that allows them to function effectively.

A key prerogative for the company was avoiding the single point of artistic control that marked almost all other companies in the province's theatre history. It therefore made a conscious decision not to hire an artistic director. It has instead a paid chair for the artistic committee, appointed to a two-year term. The first person to hold this position is Arne MacPherson.

While the company's management structure was evolving, the artistic component also underwent change. Although the original plan was to have Burns and Hodges share directing duties, for a variety of reasons Hodges directed the first four productions. This established her as the de facto resident director, so when Arne MacPherson got the nod to direct *Much Ado About Nothing*, the company faced its first artistic challenge. Could it succeed under another director? Since then, the company has rotated the directing task, with Chris Sigurdson directing *Richard III,* Dawn Mari McCaugherty directing *Love's Labour's Lost,* and MacPherson doing *The Tempest.* McCaugherty was the first non-company member to direct, although the company had in the past hired her as a vocal and text coach.

Throughout all the directorial changes the company's artistic reputation has grown, to the point where in 2000 it began to attract national media attention. Sponsors began to seek out the company, a rare event in the tight market for corporate donations.

The year 2000 marked what was perhaps the company's most significant artistic achievement. In that year it presented an original script for the first time. It had earlier commissioned Winnipeg playwright Rick Chafe to do an adaptation of *The Odyssey,* and presented a workshop production in the fall of 1999 to a select audience. In September of 2000 it presented the finished script for a two-week run. No one knew if its audience would come out to support a new script at a non-traditional time. Thanks to the quality of the script, and the company's ensemble work under director Chris Girard-Pinker, the production was an artistic and popular success. It could not have come at a better time, because the company faced a deficit due to poor houses for *Love's Labour's Lost.* The rains that had caused a record number of cancellations for Shakespeare in the spring largely stayed away in September.

Odyssey: the Islands was visually stunning and featured some of the best work the company had done so far. Megan McArton was particularly effective as Penelope. With this production the company proved a number of things: first, its audience was as loyal to the company as it was to Shakespeare. Second, Shakespeare in the Ruins proved that it could be an effective vehicle for developing a script. Third, the company proved that the fall could be as effective a time as the spring and summer for a production, although limited daylight hours imposed extra technical demands. Last, and most important for the community at large, Shakespeare in the Ruins proved that Manitoba playwrights could work effectively on a large canvas if given the opportunity.

For decades, Manitoba playwrights have been told that they did not write plays that were "big enough" for MTC's main stage. If one looked at their output to date, that might have been a reasonable deduction. Manitoba playwrights seldom got the chance to work with large stages, and when they did, as Maureen Hunter did on MTC's main stage, the cast size was small. Until *Odyssey: the Islands,* the ocular proof was missing. It is not missing any more. Although he had written "small" scripts before, Chafe proved that given the scope he, and by extension his colleagues, could rise to the occasion. On the strength of that success, Shakespeare in the Ruins has embarked on a plan to expand its season to two plays a year, one from Shakespeare's canon, and one contemporary work. The 2001 production was an *Odyssey* remount, and in 2002 Shakespeare in the Ruins will headline MTC's Brechtfest with a production of *Threepenny Opera* at the Warehouse. In 2003 the company hopes to premiere another original work.

The company's biggest challenge, however, will be one that has daunted many other Manitoba companies: change of venue.

Its original site at the ruins has given Manitoba audiences some of the most memorable moments in their theatre history: Puck dropping out of a tree, torches illuminating Romeo and Juliet's crypt, Titania arriving on a barge, Lady Macbeth washing that damned spot out in the river, a lone piper playing a pibroch while lightning flashed in the distance, Canada geese accompanying the lovelorn Don Adriano in *Love's Labour's Lost,* and the climactic battle scene in *Richard III.* In many ways, the ruins are the perfect site to do Shakespeare.

Unfortunately, Shakespeare in the Ruins is not the only group with a claim to the site. Its landlord, the St. Norbert Arts Centre (SNAC), also uses the site and has a prior claim. As Shakespeare in the Ruins has grown in reputation and popularity, natural tensions have surfaced between the two groups. SNAC wants to expand its outdoor activities, and its desire to use the space runs into direct conflict with Shakespeare in the Ruins' desire to expand its season. There is also a conflict in mandates. SNAC is a residency-based company dedicated to contemporary works. While Shakespeare in the Ruins considers itself to be contemporary artists, to SNAC it is a group which performs traditional scripts.

In 1999 SNAC announced that they could no longer accept Shakespeare at the site. Their solution was for SIR to become part of SNAC and develop predominantly contemporary works. SIR negotiated a three-year transition period, and through a mediation process agreed to a two-year moratorium on Shakespeare at the site, starting with the 2003 season. The 2002 *Hamlet* will therefore be the last Shakespeare script at the site until 2005, although the company may decide to do a contemporary script there if SNAC also agrees to it.

At this point, it seems unlikely that audiences will see Shakespeare at the original ruins site again. A search committee hopes to find an equally magical site for future productions. This committee, in keeping with the new structure, has both company and community members. The company is fortunate in the people who agreed to serve on this committee. The chair, Richard Howell, an architect who was stage manager for Theatre Winnipeg, understands both sides of the theatre business.

Regardless of what the future holds for Shakespeare in the Ruins, in its eight years of existence, it has proved that Winnipeg can be a world-class venue for theatre.

Heritage Theatre: Manitoba's Most-Produced Playwright

Brian Richardson formed Heritage Theatre in 1989 to bring local history alive for visitors to the Forks National Historic Site, a park at the confluence of the Red and Assiniboine Rivers. His bilingual plays take place outdoors with actors playing many roles. They make rapid costume changes to create this illusion.

The plays have a strong family orientation and move at a quick pace, with enough broad humour to keep antsy children interested. In 1995 he did *Sketchy History* at the Fringe. Because of his work at the

Forks, Richardson is the only Manitoba playwright to have had a script in professional production every year for the past 10 years. And because his shows take place at a popular tourist site, he probably has had the largest audience of any Manitoba playwright.

Heritage Theatre uses local actors from both the French- and English-speaking communities. Perhaps the best known of these is Wayne Nicklas.

18

THE MANITOBA THEATRE FOR YOUNG PEOPLE

"You people are saving lives".
—Tom Jackson speaking about MTYP, at the launch of the fundraising drive for the new building

---

Professional children's theatre was slower in coming to Manitoba than any other province. Manitoba has since made up for lost time, with the Manitoba Theatre for Young People being the flagship.

The Manitoba Theatre for Young people grew out of Actors' Showcase, a group dedicated to showcasing local talent. Daphne Korol formed the company in 1965. Later Tony Pydee ran it. It produced plays by Rosemary De Graff and offered a chance to see new material on its Studio nights. It later became a semi-professional company performing children's theatre in the traditional vein. A desire for higher standards and change in direction led to a bitter fight for control of the company. In 1982 this conflict was resolved and Leslee Silverman emerged as artistic director. (Pydee changed his name to Tony Frost and formed Fantasy Theatre for Children, a semi-professional company that survives to this day.)

Under Silverman's guidance the company blossomed into an internationally acclaimed theatre company. Besides its children's program, MTYP offers a teen drama series and classes for all ages in various aspects of theatre arts. For some working professionals in Winnipeg, MTYP classes have been all the training they have received.

The school has been an underrated asset in Manitoba's artistic community. Besides providing a second source of income for many local theatre professionals, it has an enviable record of training people who later became professionals. Among these are Devin McCracken, Steve Sym and Lee White from the improv comedy troupe Crumbs.

Paul Anthony made a name for himself as the obnoxious car thief in Manitoba Public Insurance Company ads. Anthony also starred in a seminal series of anti-drinking and driving ads, Nobody Walks Away, which became a teen fad. With each new ad, high school students struggled to be the first to memorize the lines. The Manitoba Public Insurance Company reported that arrests and deaths due to drunken driving dropped significantly during those ads.

Derek Aasland also had a successful career acting in Winnipeg before he left for Toronto to pursue composing and film acting opportunities. Meredith McKeechie also went to Toronto, where she worked at Stratford and later starred in the McCain frozen pizza TV ads. Angela Chalmers, Stanis Anthony, Mike McFadden (Toner) and Jennifer Villaverde also took courses at MTYP.

In a community where professional companies have had their artistic ups and downs, MTYP has been a paragon of stability. For years the company worked out of cramped rented quarters on Princess Street and presented its works at the Gas Station Theatre and other venues. MTYP plays offer children an intelligent look at the issues they face, performed to the highest professional standards. In 1990, the *Canadian Theatre Review* said, "If an award was given for the highest achievement in Winnipeg theatre, Manitoba Theatre for Young People would have won it hands down."

MTYP has a long string of honours, among them two nominations for Chalmers awards (for the best play of the year). It won in 1998 for *Old Friends,* developed with Ronnie Burkett. Leslee Silverman received a 125th commemorative medal from the Governor General in 1992, in recognition of her contribution to Canadian life.

Unlike other professional theatre companies in Manitoba, MTYP has maintained an unbroken record of artistic and popular success. Also unlike the others, MTYP's audiences grew when it changed locations. Its 1999 move to a new facility at The Forks resulted in record crowds and allowed it to become a landlord instead of a tenant. Audiences noticed no drop in quality, or loss in direction, as happened with other companies. How has MTYP escaped the turmoil that has plagued others?

One answer is stability at the top. Leslee Silverman has been the artistic director for the company's entire history as a professional company. Another answer, closely related to the first, is sound, yet courageous artistic decisions. MTYP has always been a company that respected its audience and considered its needs and wants. At the same time, it has never been afraid to challenge its viewers. MTYP has produced theatre in a variety of styles: realism, puppets, *commedia dell'arte*, dramatized fairy tales, and post-modernism. The common denominator has always been the desire to produce works that related to young people at a personal level.

Another answer is that MTYP learned from PTE's early days and went into the community to discover its needs. MTYP's theatre is not art imposed from above. Often a play will emerge from a recognized community need, but the development does not stop there. MTYP has worked with the Canadian Mental Health Association, Winnipeg Child and Family Services, the Addictions Foundation of Manitoba and other groups in developing drama of relevance to young people. In developing *See Saw,* a play about bullying, Director Silverman and playwright Dennis Foon went to 35 schools in Winnipeg, interviewing children from grades two to seven. The result is that MTYP plays have an authenticity often missing from other productions.

A third factor is that MTYP has largely stood apart from the debate over audiences versus aesthetics. By choosing an aesthetic that respects young people as people, MTYP avoided the audience-aesthetic squeeze.

The key to its success, however, is probably that MTYP has always presented works that matter to its audiences. MTYP has tackled divorce, poverty, mental illness, bullying, learning disabilities, and substance abuse, without being preachy or too morbid. The scripts have been intelligent, dramatically sound vehicles for their subject matter, whether it is mental illness (David Gillies' *There Is no Shame*) or poverty (Ian Ross' *Baloney*).

Although MTYP has always maintained a high standard of presentation, this has not been at the cost of opportunities for local artists.

Over the years, MTYP has regularly commissioned local playwrights, including Ian Ross, Rick Skene, and David Gillies. Young Manitoba audiences have also had the opportunity to see the best local actors, an experience their adult counterparts do not always enjoy. David Warburton, Rob Slade, Jan Skene, Chris Sigurdson, Martine Friesen, Maggie Nagle, Steve McIntyre, and MTYP Young Company alumnus Derek Aasland all have regularly graced MTYP's stage.

Its first touring show, *Feeling Yes, Feeling No*, developed by Dennis Foon of Green Thumb Theatre in Vancouver, is a good example of how and why MTYP works. The play explores the dangers of sexual abuse from a child's perspective. It is a series of vignettes illustrating the various risks a child might encounter, and how to avoid them. Interspersed with the vignettes are narrations that explain what has happened and introduce the next segment. Before the company would perform for students, however, the director and actors would conduct an in-service with staff and an orientation with parents to prepare them for what would happen. In one school division, fewer than 10 of the 3600 students opted out. The outstanding aspect of this show is that it differentiates between positive physical contact with adults (yes feelings) and negative ones (no feelings). It respects the children enough to trust them to make the proper judgments, and gives them strategies for avoiding bad choices.

This program toured schools from 1983 until 1991, a good indication of its quality. In all, it reached over 80,000 children in 241 elementary schools. It also provided steady employment to theatre professionals, another area in which MTYP excels. Most important, though, is that the program produced results. In a September 22, 1988, *Winnipeg Sun* article, a Winnipeg police spokesperson said that referrals to child and family services went "way up" when the program started each fall. "One program can go to one school for the afternoon...they get from seven to eight phone calls right away." There is no way of knowing how many young people were spared or freed from abusive situations.

Today, MTYP tours perform over 100 shows per year to tens of thousands of young people: in Manitoba, across Canada, and occasionally abroad. These shows always have a purpose beyond pure entertainment, but MTYP has always been wise enough to entertain first, a maxim Schiller put forward more than 100 years ago.

Its strong touring program also acts as a missionary agent for the art of theatre. When an MTYP show goes to a school, it entertains dozens of students who would otherwise never see live theatre. This is where all the wise artistic, aesthetic, and management decisions pay off, for if the theatre did not present very high quality theatre art, it would not have developed the audiences who later visit MTYP and other theatres.

The MTYP success story also shows just how good theatre has to be in Winnipeg before it gets its due. The campaign to secure the funds needed to build the new theatre went on for fourteen years. The final product is a multi-purpose building that boasts a 325-seat flexible theatre.

19

POPULAR THEATRE ALLIANCE:
Descendant of Workers' Theatre

"When you believe in things, it costs."
—Harold, from Bruce McManus' *Selkirk Avenue*

From 1984 to 1998, the Popular Theatre Alliance of Manitoba (PTAM) enjoyed a fifteen-year run, producing socially relevant theatre that often set the standard for excellence on the local theatre scene. It also helped to redefine the theatre aesthetic in Manitoba.

The company was a direct descendant of the political theatre movement of the early part of the 20th century. Like the suffragette theatre and the worker's theatre, PTAM saw its art as a means rather than an end. And like MTYP and PTE, PTAM was a theatre founded on a desire to serve and be a part of a community.

PTAM was part of the Canadian Popular Theatre Alliance (CPTA), a group formed to use theatre for social advancement. This theatre grew out of the alternative theatre movement of the 1970s, but based its movement on Ross Kidd's pioneering use of theatre for popular education in Zambia and Botswana. Kidd in turn based his work on Newfoundland's Mummers Troupe. The popular theatre movement in Canada therefore had its roots in Africa and the Third World, which in turn drew its inspiration from Newfoundland.

In 1981 Kam Theatre of Thunder Bay organized Bread and Circuses, a festival of small, non-Equity theatre groups which included 12 Canadian and seven African and Caribbean companies. The festival generated enough enthusiasm for the Canadian companies to organize the CPTA. Catalyst Theatre of Edmonton hosted the second festival, Bread and Roses, in 1983. PTAM came about in 1984 to organize the third CPTA festival, Bread and Dreams, held in Winnipeg in 1985.

In a fall, 1989 article in *Theatre History in Canada,* Alan Filewod describes the growing pains the popular theatre movement faced. These community-based groups often used the collective process to develop their theatre and manage their affairs. Thus they often fell somewhere between professional and amateur theatre as the arts councils and PACT (the body governing professional theatre in Canada) defined them. Their predominantly left-wing stance also caused some alienation from the larger community.

In its founding statement of principles, CPTA said: "We believe that theatre is a means and not an end. We are theatres which work to effect social change." Popular theatre, therefore, is diametrically opposed to the idea of New Criticism of art that it is "an autonomous social activity subject to its own laws of function and beauty." Filewod goes on to say, "Popular theatre by principle is designed to embody the consciousness and express the experience of the audience to which it is targeted, and thus its aesthetic principles are those of that particular audience community." This aesthetic placed the popular theatre movement outside both the traditional and the post-modern models. Popular theatre found itself in the same bind that workers' theatre found itself in the 1930s, and, like that movement, it had trouble gaining establishment acceptance.

From the beginning, PTAM used a combination of "professional" and "community-based" theatre. Everything it did, however, had a community focus that both looked within the community and took perspectives from outside that had relevance. In its inaugural professional production in 1986, PTAM produced renowned anti-apartheid South African playwright Athol Fugard's *Blood Knot* at Prairie Theatre Exchange's Princess Street theatre. (Fugard's *Road to Mecca* was a hit at the MTC mainstage in the 1987–88 season.) In the very next production PTAM used a Manitoba playwright, Harry Rintoul. The play, *Forget Me Not,* was the first of many that Margo Charlton, the founding artistic director, would direct.

In the years that followed, PTAM just managed to keep afloat financially, using rented facilities on Selkirk Avenue for offices and classes. Most performances were at the Gas Station Theatre, but it also toured and used other facilities when appropriate or necessary. Besides Rintoul, the company produced and co-produced many local playwrights: Allana Lindgren (*Side Show),* Bruce McManus (*Selkirk Avenue, Calenture),* Valorie Bunce (*Birth of a Dancing Star),* Deborah

O'Neil (*No. 1 Gem*), Yvette Nolan (*Everybody's Business, A Marginal Man*), and Margaret Sweatman (*Hectic*).

The company also helped establish careers for actors and directors. Megan McArton, who directed *Side Show* in 1989, later had a great success with *The Darling Family* at the 2000 Fringe. Her performance in 1992's *If Betty Should Rise* established her as a top-rank actor. Nancy Drake directed *No. 1 Gem* in 1989. (She had earlier directed Agassiz productions.) Monique Marcker had an early success with *Scientific Americans,* and Ken Brand had an early writing and performance success as part of *Testing Ground*. Jan Anderes wrote in *Theatrum* that, "PTAM, under Charlton's lead, has become a source of energy and hope to performers, writers, and audiences."

Equally important was PTAM's community work. Its location in the heart of Winnipeg's North End put it in daily contact with the city's struggling poor. Many plays grew directly from this experience. PTAM also offered training programs geared to its neighbours.

One group to come out of community outreach programming was The Goldenrods, a seniors' acting company. Rosemary De Graff turned the seniors' contributions into a play, *On the Wings of Change,* which toured in 1994 under the direction of Kathy France. Another group France facilitated was the Dream Sharers, a multicultural collective. France was especially suited to this role, since she was both a director and taught English as a second language. The Dream Sharers worked with playwright Donna Lewis to develop *How Do You Do.*

The Krayolas, a group of minority actors, worked with Yvette Nolan to develop a play about racism. Other collective creations explored family violence, unemployment, housing and aging. Lee Anne Block developed Women on the Edge, a dramatic and at times humorous examination of the difficulties women with mental health problems face. PTAM did not limit its activities to Winnipeg. For three years, Margo Charlton and script writer Ellen Peterson travelled to Melita to assist a youth theatre group called The Almost Broadway Players.

Charlton explains that in the beginning, Manitoba did not have a strong aboriginal theatre group, so they "brought in shows like *All My Relations* by Floyd Favel or *Moonlodge* by Margo Kane—they were a great success—showing there was need for plays that reflected the aboriginal experience." They encouraged the development of Red Roots Theatre. Monica Marx received training at PTAM.

Selkirk Avenue, produced in 1990, is perhaps the best example of PTAM's style. Sponsored by the Selkirk Avenue Business Association, it tells the street's story over several generations through the eyes of Harold, the street's photographer. Although the play has elements of prairie realism structure, it does not follow linear time and paints a much broader canvas than most plays of this genre usually attempt. It is Bruce McManus' finest work, and stands up as one of the best Canadian plays of all time. The play received a belated Governor General's Literary Award nomination upon publication in 1998. Part of the production was an historical display in the lobby, showing Selkirk Avenue over the years. It is also unique in that it was the first Manitoba play to receive two productions by two different professional theatres. PTE produced it in their 1991–92 season.

Just as it was for their neighbours, survival was always in doubt for PTAM. Its newsletters reveal an optimistic attitude playing against what must have seemed almost continual catastrophes. A fire destroyed its offices in 1989; PTAM rebuilt with community support. Later rain destroyed the roof and flooded the office, forcing a move to PTE's complex at Portage Place. Funding did not always arrive when expected or needed, but somehow the company continued for fifteen years, supported by and supporting the community around it.

From the beginning, PTAM took the "Popular" part of its name seriously. Besides sponsoring numerous community projects, it offered "pay what you can" performances on Sundays as a way to ensure no one would miss a production because they could not afford it. As Margo Charlton says, "I also think we pioneered the idea of target marketing particular community groups, offering group rates and doing the kind of outreach which is taken for granted now." While MTC and PTE both went out into the larger community to garner an audience, PTAM took it to a new level.

Unfortunately, the word "popular" did not extend to the province's political or cultural elite. While MTC had the establishment solidly behind it, and PTE had Charles Huband in its corner from the beginning, PTAM's lists of boards of directors and major contributors seldom contained blue-ribbon names. Similarly, the reviewers in the major dailies often seemed at a loss when reacting to its work, and much of its community work went unreported.

While PTAM often produced avant-garde, post-modernist theatre such as *Lion in the Streets* and *Calenture,* its main prerogative was social relevance. Margo Charlton signed her messages to audiences with "acting together for change." PTAM shared the same activist roots as the Political Equality League and Theatre of Action. Perhaps that is why its aesthetic succeeded when the same aesthetic often failed at PTE or MTC: the audience related to the subject matter and was therefore willing to filter it though a foreign presentation style.

At the same time, PTAM often found itself on the outs with the establishment. The funding bodies were slow to provide stable funding, insisting instead on project-by-project grants. It therefore had to find unconventional sources of funding, something at which it proved to be very innovative. Still, PTAM often found itself laying off staff or making other economies just to stay in operation.

This problem came to a head in the 1991–1992 season, when the company had to postpone *Calenture* because the Manitoba Arts Council turned down PTAM's project grant application. This decision outraged the local theatre community and played a part in a major upheaval at the Manitoba Arts Council.

To put the event in its proper perspective, however, one has to look at the broader political picture of the time.

Arts Funding in Hard Times

The Opportunities for Youth and Local Initiatives Program funds mentioned earlier did not last forever. Neither did Trudeaumania. As Trudeau's third term as Prime Minister wound down in 1979, patience had worn thin in many areas across the country. The Liberals did not win a single seat in Alberta or Saskatchewan in 1974 (something to keep in mind when people speak of parliaments split along regional lines today) and their grip across the rest of the country began to slip.

The Conservatives were the government-in-waiting, and their key message was that it was time to bring the deficit under control. They formed a minority government under Joe Clark, and a top minister, Sinclair Stevens, began implementing his plan to slash 50,000 public service jobs. Clark's government fell almost as soon as it faced the House, but it marked a change in attitude. Managing the growing deficit became a national priority. Depending on one's political perspective, the Trudeau governments either spent too much or did not collect enough taxes. Either way, journalists began to cover stories about debt reduction, with many examples to put the debt into perspective, and dire warnings about the consequences if we did not give this problem our attention.

Pierre Trudeau won the next election, after returning from a brief retirement. He triumphantly announced to the nation, "Welcome to the eighties!" For the arts community, the eighties meant making do with less. When reporters quizzed Trudeau or his lieutenant, Marc Lalonde, about curbing spending, they had an infuriating response. With cold logic, they would ask what they should cut: Health care? Old age pensions?" Canadians did not want to pay more taxes, so other areas of spending came under scrutiny, and the arts were an easy target, as was the military and some other less-popular programs. The CBC was an easy target, and in the time-honoured tradition of bureaucracies, the regions felt the cuts most. In the early 1980s, CBC Winnipeg producer Dan Wood had his budget for radio drama cut in half. Radio drama had been a way many Manitoba playwrights had cut their teeth, and the royalties paid well enough to make writing in the form attractive. As local drama production diminished, playwriting itself became more precarious.

Trudeau stepped down for good in 1984. The Liberals' choice of a replacement was as unfortunate as the Conservatives' choice of Joe Clark in 1976. John Turner had long appeared as the Liberal heir apparent, but by the time he took over the leadership his time had passed. His personal and campaigning style belonged to a different era. The combination of fatigue with the Liberals, Brian Mulroney's slick campaign for the Conservatives, and Turner's gaffes gave the Conservatives their first majority government since 1958 and one of the largest majorities ever. (Ironically, Turner's leadership campaign dismissed Jean Chrétien as a serious candidate because he was "yesterday's man.")

Brian Mulroney campaigned with the promise to increase trade with the United States, which he said would result in "jobs, jobs, jobs." He also promised to reduce the deficit. During his time in office, the deficit and unemployment both soared. It was not a good time to be an artist in Canada, because people who do not have jobs do not buy paintings, attend the symphony, or go to the theatre. Companies struggling to meet a payroll do not expand their donation lists, and governments find the arts an easy target for reduced funding. People who rise to prominence in the arts rarely do so because they are skilled financial managers. Finding instances of poor financial management is therefore relatively easy. Governments can then sell the public on cuts to arts groups "until they put their financial house in order."

Cuts to the arts caused a nation-wide wave of protest, called the "Masse Appeal," after Marcel Masse, Mulroney's Minster of Culture. Times did not get any better for artists. For one thing, the artistic community was fractured.

One fissure ran along federal-provincial lines. Provincial arts councils provided valuable assistance to artists, but at the same time they caused a focus shift from national to provincial among those seeking a career in the arts. A group usually has to secure regional financing before it can hope for recognition at the national level. This can take many years, during which time the artist or arts group becomes more dependent (and therefore familiar with and emotionally attached to) the provincial funding body. With the Canada Council scaling back during this period, the national option became more and more of a long shot.

Another fissure was caused by tensions between the older, established (and more conservative) arts bodies, and the up-and-coming, experimental ones. The older groups felt that they deserved continued funding because of their status as founders. The newer groups struggled to survive, and thought that the older groups were fossils that deserved to lose funds anyway. (An example of this tension is a series of letters to the Manitoba ACTRA branch newsletter published in 1991. An editorial defending the Arts Council for freezing MTC's funding drew a response defending MTC. The debate went on for several issues.)

Still another source of disunity arose from the debate over strategy. Some artists thought the best response to funding cuts was to defend the arts in terms that budget formulators understood, and advance arguments that demonstrated the arts' value in economic terms. Another camp said that the arts were not about money, and it was specious to use the money argument to defend them. This argument continues today. The ongoing aesthetic debate further weakened the arts and the ability of its champions to defend it against cuts.

The regional focus had numerous effects. Some were relatively benign. While regional arts councils played and continue to play a vital role in our artistic lives, they also diffuse support when the arts in general face a threat. Artists naturally tend to defend funding bodies, but the funding body they feel most loyal to is likely to be the one closest to them geographically. Regional arts councils were therefore more likely to enjoy a vigorous defense, and therefore to suffer less, relatively speaking, than the Canada Council. Unfortunately for both the Canada Council and the artists, this division of loyalties also serves to weaken the ties that local artists feel to their counterparts in other areas of the country. Organizations like the Playwrights' Union of Canada are a vital counterbalance to this trend.

Regionalism can also blind artists to the national issues that affect them. When the Manitoba literary community formed an ad hoc committee to find ways to fight the planned goods and service tax on books, the Manitoba Writers' Guild representative wondered aloud why the committee was spending so much time discussing the federal government, since taxing books was not a federal responsibility. When the bill to introduce a revision to the copyright law stalled in the senate, the Manitoba Branch of the Canadian Authors' Association called the Guild to muster support for a collective protest. To its dismay, the CAA learned that nobody in the Guild office even knew that a bill was before the House. National arts groups therefore found it difficult to mount joint efforts.

Gradually the funding squeeze started to make itself felt provincially. As part of its debt-cutting strategy, the Mulroney government began cutting transfer payments to provinces. As budgets shrank, funding agencies had to make hard decisions. Should they fund a new, experimental group with an uncertain future at the cost of a cultural institution like the Royal Winnipeg Ballet or the Manitoba Theatre Centre? Should they fund professional groups or "community" groups?

The jury process answered that question. The Councils did not award grants on their own. Instead, they appointed peer juries to do this task. Ideally a jury would act as an expert, objective decision-making body. The problem lay in finding people who fit both descriptions in a small pool of potential jurors.

Often this meant choosing jurors from either academic or arts journalism circles, but even this option had limited usefulness. For one thing, these people are often active in the arts themselves, and if they aren't, their former students are. For another, the pool of arts journalists in Manitoba is very small. Finally, members of this co-called arts establishment bring a definite aesthetic to the job, and during this time that aesthetic cared little for, and often disparaged, public tastes.

At the same time, talented people who care enough about the arts and artists to write about them are unlikely to be objective. The solution was to appoint jurors from outside the province, a strategy that would help ensure objectivity, but at the cost of a potentially limited knowledge of the local scene. Peer juries were therefore at least one step removed from the potential audience, and often two steps. This built-in alienation came at a time when the arts community desperately needed support from the larger community if it were to escape drastic funding cuts.

The various strategies used to find knowledgeable, objective jurors almost guaranteed that these people would hold leading-edge views. Their aesthetics probably caused the major theatres some discomfort, and may have prodded them to some of their more regrettable choices. In a July 3, 1993 interview in the *Winnipeg Free Press*, MTC's Artistic Director Steven Schipper blamed the company's deficit on producing "one too many artistically significant plays that we knew in advance would not sell tickets, but we felt would invigorate and consolidate our artistic integrity."

The short-term result for vanguard artists was also questionable. While Sharon Alward, Diana Thornycroft and others gained notoriety and some measure of critical respect, their art came forward in a time ill-suited to receive it. To someone who had suffered downsizing, it must have seemed insane to give someone thousands of dollars to indulge their artistic fantasies. The aesthetics some of these artists subscribed to merely added fuel to the fire. Many people in the art establishment at the time simply did not believe the public could appreciate art. They often expressed this opinion publicly, not a strategy suited to rallying wide-spread support.

Added to this explosive mixture were the inevitable hard feelings among some of the unsuccessful applicants. People were in a cranky mood in the Mulroney years, a decade that historian Will Ferguson calls "ten lost years."[43] To be fair to the Conservative administration, however, this period also saw two pieces of legislation that creators had sought for generations. One was the enactment of Public Lending Right, annual payments to authors whose books were in libraries. The other was the revision of the 65-year-old Copyright Act. The modernization of this act meant that authors could receive payment for photocopying of their works, and it also meant that directors and choreographers owned the copyright to their work. The act also provided for meaningful penalties for violators.

As the funding bodies found their budgets shrinking, they made some difficult choices. In the early 1990s, the Manitoba Arts Council decided that its literary support belonged primarily to the Manitoba Writers' Guild, the province's largest writer's group. The Manitoba Branch of the Canadian Authors' Association lost its funding, and the Manitoba Association of Playwrights had its funding cut severely. Neither of the latter two groups liked the choice.

In the middle of this troubled period PTAM submitted a project grant application for the play *Calenture*. It could be forgiven for expecting to receive the grant. After all, the playwright, Bruce McManus, had received a grant to write the script, as had the composer to write the music. PTAM also received funds for the workshop. The company felt confident enough to announce the play as part of the season before learning if it had the grant. Unfortunately, the jury, comprising three out-of-town members and one local, turned the project down. The theatre community responded with outrage. Criticism of the Manitoba Arts Council had been muted before, but now people called publicly for changes.

The Winnipeg Sun ran a series of articles in September 1992. The articles portrayed Winnipeg's arts community as an incestuous little group that used public money for its private pleasure, with little or no thought to the public that supported it. The *Sun* reporter, Greg Pindera, caught MAC's executive director, Marlene Neustaedter, with some unfortunate quotes that seemed to back up that position. The Council dismissed Neustaedter shortly afterwards. While the reasons for her firing remain unclear, the *Sun* fallout almost certainly played a role.

The *Sun*'s circulation soared for a while: the publisher said he had never seen such a strong response to a series of articles before. The arts community rallied around the Council, some with more enthusiasm than others. The Council could have used this attention to explain itself. It could have tried to initiate a dialogue to find ways to fulfill its mandate without abandoning its principles. Instead the Council and its most ardent supporters adopted a siege mentality.

In October 1992, Bonnie Mitchelson, the Minister of Culture, asked the Arts Council to respond to the five major themes the *Sun* series raised:

1. The wisdom of funding those bodies perceived not to have public appeal;
2. Perceived conflicts of interest in the peer assessment or jury system;

3. The perception that the Council was awarding grants to those who did not need the money;
4. The perception that a small group of people exerted undue influence on the granting process;
5. The apparent lack of accountability for public funds.

The Arts Council announced a review of peer assessment on October 15, 1992. The Council further promised to hold public consultations in January 1993, after releasing a report on this review. The Council never released a report, but on February 5 it did announce a public forum, to be held on February 28. It did not announce this forum to the general public, an omission the *Sun* seized on. The Council invited written submissions, with a deadline of March 1, the day after the public forum. Although Chris Hurley, one of the people the Council invited to organize the event, recommended that the forum's panel comprise people with differing views, all panelists spoke in favour of the status quo. People who expressed dissenting voices from the floor did not receive a warm reception.

A small group of artists wishing to improve on the status quo met after the public forum to develop alternatives and seek a meeting with the Council to discuss their ideas. When the Council finally agreed to meet this group, then-chair Roberta Christiansen refused to allow anyone to take notes. The Council eventually released an updated peer assessment document in which it said, "Council's review committee found Council's peer adjudication process generally effective, efficient in its administration, fair in its determination of grants..."

Of course, the problem was not the Council's opinion, or that of its committee, but the public's perception. One outcome of the apparent lack of self-examination was that a small group of artists formed to pressure the Council into consulting more widely. Some members of this group met at the public forum. They formed the Independent Canadian Artists. Besides sending a series of open letters to the Council, they started activities geared to forging a stronger communications link between artists and audiences. Their leader, artist Robert Mears, lent his studio to the group for meetings and public readings. (The studio soon proved too small, and these events moved to the St. Luke's parish hall.)

The ICA coffee houses featured a multi-disciplinary evening, with a visual artist and musicians sharing the stage. As an encouragement for the artists to create their own audience, the ICA split the gate receipts with the artists. Attendance was typically small, but a number of people, such as Glen Sures, Ian Ross and Bill Fugler found an early audience.

Another activity was *Street,* a magazine that examined issues in the arts and politics. The magazine's staff was never large, and the publication's initial effect on the arts community was at first probably one of annoyance. Over the years, however, some of the magazine's rhetoric has crept into discussion of the arts. A key recommendation, that the downtown become a place where artists can live, work, and attract traffic, has become a popular issue at City Hall. Its attempts to publicize the old Ashdown building on Main Street eventually attracted investors to the idea.

Towards Recovery

The economy gradually recovered in the early 1990s, either in spite of or because of the change in government at the federal level. "Yesterday's man," Jean Chrétien, won his first of three consecutive majority governments in 1993. Regardless of one's politics, the fact remains that the recession diminished during this period.

At the provincial level, official attitudes to the arts changed little. Despite Premier Gary Filmon's appearance at arts events, he frequently appointed weak ministers to the culture portfolio. One minister, Bonnie Mitchelson, could not name a single Manitoba writer during a *Winnipeg Sun* interview, although eventually she recalled meeting a "Sandy somebody."

Despite the improved economic climate, the arts community still faced internal problems. In November 1993 the CBC Radio program *Ideas* broadcast a ten-part series called *Culture in the Marketplace.* In one segment, Andrew Coyne, a right-wing columnist, debated Robert Enright to a sputtering standstill on the subject, "The Future of Public Subsidies."

In another segment, "What Do Audiences Want?" the respected theatre director and critic Urjo Kareda described what he called a splintering of the traditional theatre audience. One, the older, more traditional audience, went to the theatre for an emotional connection with the performance. The other, newer one, deliberately shied away from this connection in favour of maintaining an emotional distance. He said these audiences connected at an ironic level. Naturally, satisfying both audiences was a difficult proposition, especially since the first audience held the money and the second held the future.

This series showed that artists and audiences had reached a point of disconnection. The public attitudes to the arts had changed, and artists had not kept abreast of this change. Some artists seemed willing to pretend that the gap was unimportant, others struggled to understand it and adapt, while still others seemed at a loss.

PTAM Emerges from the Dark and Fades to Black

PTAM's second application to the Arts Council for *Calenture* succeeded, and in 1993 the public finally got to see what the fuss was all about. While it was not a triumph on the scale of *Selkirk Avenue,* it still contained many McManus hallmarks, including poetic language, passionate characters, and an emotional bond to the audience. The play had the most experimental structure McManus had yet tried, and at times it seemed that the cast had not fully bought in to the concept. And yet, it still delivered moments of pure magic.

In 1993 also, PTAM launched the first of three Testing Ground programs, a series dedicated to experimentation. Artists proposed short subjects to a panel which would select the most promising proposals. The goal was for artists to experiment in new genres or disciplines. These highly popular events gave emerging and seasoned artists much-needed opportunities to experiment and gain experience.

Expanding on its tradition of showcasing artists like Megan McArton and Nancy Drake, PTAM's Testing Ground gave Ryan Black, Chorine Scott, Michelle Boulet, Julia Arkos and Ardith Boxall early acting experience, and Arne MacPherson gained some early experience as a director.

In 1994, PTAM went through another period of change. Margo Charlton stepped down from her position as the company's first artistic director. The company had experienced a somewhat rocky year artistically. Yvette Nolan's *A Marginal Man* received a lot of advance publicity but did not live up to Nolan's previous standard of work. She had directed previous scripts (*Blade, Job's Wife)* to good effect, but this production suffered from uncertain pacing, plot and character implausibilities, and didacticism.

Debbie Patterson stepped in and guided PTAM for the rest of its life. Unfortunately PTAM did not long survive Charlton's departure despite some truly fine work after she left. Its final performance was Margaret Sweatman's *Hectic,* as ambitious an undertaking as ever took place on Manitoba's stages.

In keeping with its tradition of community involvement, PTAM and Sweatman worked with prostitutes to develop a script that would tell their story. Some prostitutes became cast members in *Hectic* and earned Equity wages during rehearsals. The rest of the cast were Equity members. PTAM had been experimenting with alternative venues (a 1997 production, *Pissy's Wife,* took place at the Blue Note Café), so this play used the abandoned Big 4 Sales (Ashdown) building as its venue.

While the performances and the script were decidedly uneven, the production was a valuable experience for all involved. The audience saw a side of life they might otherwise never have seen. For most, it was probably the first time they had ever looked at a prostitute as anything but a worker in the sex trade. For some prostitutes, it was the first time they had ever received a regular salary.

The professionals in the cast also found their experiences broadened in unusual ways. The assistant stage manager had a difficult time keeping track of shoes used in costumes, because one of the prostitutes had a fondness for shoes that rivalled Mila Mulroney's. When the assistant stage manager found the culprit and tried to explain the gravity of the situation, she discovered that in the first-time actor's world, confrontations were met with death threats.

In a way, *Hectic* was a fitting way for PTAM to end. The local press had a hard time relating to the play, since it was outside the normal critical aesthetics they employed. The work, although important and valuable to the community as a whole, did not gain enough support to make it succeed in the long term.

20

THEATRE PROJECTS MANITOBA: Homemade Does Not Mean Second Best

"Besides offering a consistently high level of artistic achievement to his audiences, Rintoul gave literally dozens of Manitoba theatre artists their professional debut."

—Article about Harry Rintoul's departure in *Theatrum*[44]

There is never any shortage of people willing to diagnose a problem and suggest solutions, as long as the forum is a coffee shop or someone's kitchen. People who have the courage and energy to start the wheels of change in motion are much more uncommon. Harry Rintoul fits the second mould.

He and Rick Skene founded Theatre Projects Manitoba in 1990 in an effort solve the problem of limited opportunities for professional artists to work in Manitoba. In its first season, Theatre Projects presented two shows: Michel Tremblay's *Albertine in Five Times*, and two short plays by Manitoba playwrights (David Demchuk's *Why the Dishes Can't Wait Until Tomorrow* and Ellen Peterson's *Tickle Trunk*).

Both productions drew a favourable response, and the company was on its way. A measure of just how badly the theatre community needed the company came in its second year. The company stumbled badly in its choice for the season opener, Michael Nathanson's *To Kill the Weatherman,* a poorly developed script that suffered from uncertain direction. The second production, Vern Thiessen's *The Resurrection of John Frum* fared somewhat better, but still fell far short of the quality of the first year's productions. If the company had not satisfied an urgent need, it would probably have died then.

Instead, it went ahead with a third season, and found its stride. Martine Friesen's performance of Joan MacLeod's classic *Jewel* and Yvette Nolan's *Job's Wife* met the best standards of professional theatre and established Theatre Projects as a positive force. As I noted in my *Theatrum* review of *Job's Wife*, "It accomplished what the hundreds of thousands of dollars invested in Kugler and Rose's *Not Wanted on the Voyage* could not; it presented an intelligent alternative to traditional ideas about modern religion in effective dramatic terms."[45]

During PTE's Springate years, Theatre Projects, operating out of PTE's Colin Jackson studio theatre on the same night as PTE's main stage production, often outdrew PTE in the much smaller venue. The company presented a mixture of Manitoba scripts and plays from other playwrights unlikely to see the stage of other theatres. To date it is the only Manitoba professional company to present a Daniel MacIvor script, a stunning version of *See Bob Run* starring Lora Schroeder. One audience member reported having to fight the urge to go on stage, take the actor in her arms, and tell her everything would be all right.

Rick Skene's 1993 *Ce Weekend Là* was a stunning success. Launched as a vehicle to prove that small theatres could present large-cast productions, the play about small-town family conflicts sold out for most of its run. It turned traditional prairie metaphors inside out in a funny, politically incorrect farce about a young man who must decide what to do with his life while the tensions of a family wedding swirl around him. The seething passions on the surface fail to hide the love that binds the family. Another daring move was premiering Elise Moore's *Live With It,* a play she wrote while still in high school. This 1994 production proved that song-and-dance man Richard Hurst also had depth as a serious actor. A year later he starred in William Harrar's superb *InQuest.*

Rintoul's tenure at Theatre Projects did not end happily. Despite the company's outstanding artistic record and established popular support, it suffered from funding cuts that shortened the season by one play in 1995. Rintoul had asked for a raise to better compensate him for the enormous time he devoted to the company. With one less production to worry about, the board instead decided to spend a surplus on a part-time business manager. This caused Rintoul to resign in protest.

Perhaps this was inevitable. In many ways he resembles John Hirsch, MTC's mercurial guiding light. Sooner or later, the struggle to maintain his artistic vision and work with a volunteer board might have caused him to leave. B. Pat Burns took over as interim artistic director, and Bruce McManus soon replaced Burns.

Rintoul's legacy during his five years is enormous. For one thing, the company survives to this day. It did not merely survive, however; it kept its original vision intact. During Rintoul's tenure, Manitoba playwrights wrote 12 of the 17 scripts produced. He used 11 different directors.

In 2000, Margo Charlton replaced Bruce McManus. The company still produces cutting-edge theatre, almost always using locally written scripts, and always using Manitoba artists. Theatre Projects Manitoba is a vital part of Manitoba's artistic scene, a rare opportunity for Manitoba playwrights to receive a full professional production.

21

Don't Kill the Messenger: History of Criticism

"Real criticism, founded on interest, is the lifeblood of the theatre. And it can be adverse without being a timid following of convention or an expression of the universal love of malice."

—Ruth Harvey, in *Curtain Time*

How do you know if the water you drink is safe? How do you know if a company's financial statements are in order? In both cases, you get an outsider's opinion. You want someone impartial, objective, and knowledgeable to confirm quality.

That's the way most of us look at outside quality assessments: as consumers. They have another important function, however; they help healthy organizations improve their quality. An insecure water works department, or a coal mine that is knowingly flouting safety regulations, will treat an inspection as a threat, and will go to enormous lengths to deny and minimize any faults found. They will attack the assessor's credibility, seek changes to legislation, and attempt to suppress the results.

A healthy organization treats the same assessment as an opportunity to improve performance based on the feedback it receives. Even a passing grade often includes suggestions for improvement.

What if the outside assessment is incompetent? Everybody suffers. The same is true for theatre. Just as in a research facility, where one researcher's output benefits from constructive colleague criticism, theatre and other arts forms thrive when the community has perceptive critics who can give artists the feedback and prodding they need to reach their full potential.

In 18th century London, David Garrick gained from the advice of his former schoolmaster, Dr. Johnson. French playwrights had the mixed blessing of the Academy, and other great playwrights have had similar mentors. As Oscar Wilde said, "An age that has no criticism is either an age in which art is immobile, hieratic and confined to the reproduction of formal types, or an age that possesses no art at all."

Winnipeg has also had its era of great critics. Unfortunately, their period passed before Manitoba playwrights started finding their way onto professional stages.

Theatre Criticism: The Early Days to the Golden Age

Theatre reviews appeared in Winnipeg newspapers soon after theatre started. The earliest extant review dates from 1873, when a critic chided the Garrison Theatre's production of *Poor Pilicody* because the actors did not know their lines and improvised entrances and exits. Reviews in 1874 made Mrs. Collins and her husband the first legitimate stars of Winnipeg stages.

During its golden age, Winnipeg had three daily papers with talented critics: Charles Handscomb (1867–1906) wrote for *The Free Press*, Charles Wheeler (1838–1917) for *The Tribune*, and Ernest Beaufort for *The Telegram*. Wheeler and Handscomb waged a bitter literary feud, which, whatever its merits, added spice to the theatre scene. This feud gave rise to *Town Topics,* an entertainment weekly that Handscomb published. Harriet Walker, who occasionally contributed reviews to *The Free Press* under the pseudonym Rosa Sub, used the pseudonym Matinee Girl in *Town Topics.* In the 1920s, her daughter Ruth wrote reviews under the pseudonym Matinee Girl.

These people were not merely journalists assigned to theatre because somebody had to do it and they had drawn the short straw. Charles Handscomb was a celebrated tenor who had toured with Haverly's minstrels for two years and who at age 19 had written a popular comic melodrama, *The Big Boom,* about the Winnipeg land boom. The star was the American actor, E.A. McDowall. *The Big Boom* toured with the Winnipeg Operatic Society to Emerson, where it had a holdover performance the same night. Charles Wheeler was a bass soloist for Holy Trinity Anglican Church and an architect. His firm designed many buildings in Winnipeg. Despite the demands this business must have placed on his energies, he started writing a column for *The Sun* in 1887, switching to *The Tribune* in 1890. Ernest Beaufort had co-authored a prize-winning play for the Drama Festival and won praise for his acting at the same event. Harriet Walker was of course the most experienced and accomplished theatre artist of the group.

During the early days of the 20th century, therefore, Winnipeg had four critics with an inside knowledge of professional theatre. This is a luxury few cities today can boast, and Winnipeg's current coterie of theatre journalists certainly falls far short of this mark.

Viewed with today's perspective, these critics have their limitations. While he praised *Ghosts* for its dramatic structure, Handscomb denounced its moral "depravity." As Doug Whiteway says in his essay in *Torch on the Prairies,* "they were rarely in conflict with the values of their audience," and that audience was "the plutocrats and their wives who dominated Winnipeg's cultural scene."

This view is only partly true. A Walker Theatre production of Shaw's *Mrs. Warren's Profession* in 1907 closed after one performance and a scathing *Manitoba Free Press* review. ("No more unwholesome nor repulsive play has ever been seen in Winnipeg.") The whole story is not as simple as that, however, because Harriet Walker was a member in good standing of not only the critics' circle, but also the Political Equality League. And as owner of the major theatre house in western Canada, she had standing in a third party: the business side of theatre. Charles Handscomb was also part of the progressive element in Manitoba society.

The Walkers and Handscomb were certainly trying to nudge the world a little bit, although their critical perspective was still pretty conservative. Nonetheless, if a brilliant playwright had emerged and had found a company with a similar vision to produce his or her plays, there is no doubt that at least one of these critics would have recognized the event.

Reviewing in the Daily Papers

Later years produced other notable theatre journalists, such as Frank Morriss. Doug Whiteway's essay "And the Band Played On" in *Torch on the Prairies* gives a brief history of these journalists. Often, though, theatre and the other arts found themselves relegated to the women's pages, while the latest Hollywood epic caught all the popular attention.

Starting in 1928, Frank Morriss contributed a weekly theatre column to *The Free Press*. Charles Laughton said of him, "He is a man of great taste and knowledge of the theatre. I would say he is one of the most listened-to critics on the continent." He wrote for *The Free Press* until 1959, when he left to write for the Toronto *Globe and Mail,* and then was the *Winnipeg Tribune* entertainment editor from 1966 to 1971. The Manitoba Theatre Centre has a bust of him in its lobby.

After Morriss, the Winnipeg dailies still used people who knew theatre from the inside to write about it. Ken Winters and Christopher Dafoe covered the *Free Press* theatre beat in the 1960s and earned respect for their work. Brian Richardson, a playwright, actor and organizer, wrote for *The Tribune*. Coral McKendrick, who was part of the first Agassiz production, also reviewed theatre for the *Free Press.* Later, University of Winnipeg Drama department head Reg Skene reviewed for the *Free Press*. Winnipeg therefore had knowledgeable writers covering the scene.

In the late 1980s, that began to change. For one thing, *The Tribune* folded. The *Winnipeg Sun* then became the *Free Press'* main competition, but the *Sun* did not place much importance on covering the arts, although Riva Harrison outshone the *Free Press* writers in both her command of the form and writing style. *Uptown,* a weekly entertainment paper, uses Janice Sawka, a theatre graduate, to review theatre.

Meanwhile, theatre writing has become a bit of a backwater in the *Free Press*. While it dutifully sends reporters to the main professional productions, the results, from both a critical and stylistic viewpoint, have been disappointing. One rarely sees insightful comments and almost never any attempt to probe the edges of the theatre scene to discover unheralded talent.

Unfortunately the daily newspapers are still where many people gain their impressions. They are also the place of first resort for people choosing a night's entertainment. The *Sun's* readership by and large does not fit the theatre demographic, although its writers do provide knowledgeable (if thin) coverage. The *Free Press*, meanwhile, does have the theatre demographic in its readership, but has not recruited or developed anyone who can write well about theatre. Frequently the reviews are a summary of the plot with a few evaluative comments, the type of review that would earn a "C" or less in a high school writing assignment. Other reviews skirt the bounds of journalistic ethics. Even at its best, the *Free Press* coverage never provides what the theatre community needs most: insightful, constructive criticism worth reading on its own merits. This is the only type of writing that will help Manitoba theatre travel outside its boundaries to make its mark in the world.

The national dailies occasionally cover significant theatre events. Even *The Calgary Herald* sent a reviewer to Keanu Reaves' *Hamlet*. *The Globe and Mail,* in particular, has sent reviewers to Winnipeg. Liam Lacey has written about the Fringe Festival. At least once, however, playwright Maureen Hunter wished *The Globe* had not bothered. A late plane connection and illness had rendered Lacey unconscious before the end of *Beautiful Lake Winnipeg's* first act. Unfortunately, he snored.

Theatre Criticism in Magazines

For a while, Canada had two national magazines dedicated to theatre: *The Canadian Theatre Review* (*CTR*), and *Theatrum*, which ceased publication in 1995. *CTR* covers theatre from an academic point of view, while *Theatrum* was more of a news magazine.

CTR's format is theme-based, covering such topics as Native theatre and Western Canadian theatre. Although it has a scholarly approach, the articles are usually written in an accessible style and often are entertaining in themselves.

Theatrum's value was that it gave theatre artists across the country a way to keep in touch with events. The contributors were almost all working theatre professionals. I was a *Theatrum* correspondent myself from 1990 to 1995.

Besides the regular feature articles and editorials, the magazine offered a current events section that listed short news items, coverage of local festivals, and reviews of performances from across the country. This section helped create a historical record, and it also helped give local artists a national profile. The book review section discussed plays as dramatic literature. Another important feature was the centre section, printed in a heavier stock. This section contained a play's text, often the first time a text would appear in print.

The magazine was a labour of love for all involved. The founders, Sarah Hood and Nigel Hunt, took alternating voluntary periods of unemployment so that one of them would have time to keep the magazine running. The correspondents occasionally received honoraria, but these were so infrequent and small that the major benefit of writing for the magazine were the media comps that came with the job.

Over the years, coverage in *Theatrum* helped a number of Manitoba theatre artists further their careers. Reviews helped Theatre Projects establish credibility with funding bodies early in its life. Yvette

Nolan's plays *Blade* and *Job's Wife* appeared first in the magazine. Coverage helped Primus secure touring dates in Ontario. A positive review of David Gillies' *There is No Shame* resulted in queries about the script from across the country.

The stakes for someone being written about or writing for *Theatrum* were therefore high. There was a continuous tension between writing honestly and avoiding career damage. While some artistic directors and theatre artists have the courage and self-esteem to accept negative press, others do not.

Besides being a national forum for theatre artists, *Theatrum* had been a window to the rest of the world. For instance, the *Winnipeg Free Press* relied on Maureen Hunter's perspective when reporting on the Royal Shakespeare Company's production of *Transit of Venus:*

> I feel it was a very strong production, but I don't feel we have anything to apologize for about any aspect of the MTC production. All the reaction I heard was positive.[46]

Theatrum gave a different report:

> That the Royal Shakespeare Company took up a Canadian piece for the first time sounded promising. In fact, strangely, Maureen Hunter's *Transit of Venus* was mounted for just three performances in the 150-seat Pit in London. [*The Independent*'s Robert] Hanks was cool: "There's something suspiciously contrived," [he said] and "it rather precludes emotional engagement.[47]

Both perspectives are of course valuable and valid, but neither is complete without the other.

When lack of federal funding finally caused *Theatrum* to close in 1995, a valued national voice died.

Of course, *Maclean's* and other national newsmagazines occasionally cover significant events in Manitoba, such as when Keanu Reaves played *Hamlet*. Mainly, however, they focus on the Toronto scene.

Electronic Journalism

Manitoba's theatre scene has fared better in the electronic media. The CBC has, perhaps predictably, taken care to cover the local scene. Robert Enright has tirelessly covered the local arts scene for over 20 years. He is one person in the local arts journalism scene who will take the trouble to promote artists he believes are worthy of greater notice. Besides Enright, the CBC has provided such skilled arts reporters as Jacqui Good, Claudia Garcia de la Huerta, and Janet Ringer. Reg Skene occasionally contributes to CBC radio. CBC Manitoba's coverage of the Fringe Festival outstrips even that of CBC Edmonton, and the Edmonton Fringe is the largest festival on the continent.

The local commercial stations also give theatre wide coverage. Perhaps the best example is the smallest television outlet, the A Channel. This shoestring operation more than makes up in enthusiasm what it lacks in budget and experience. Its focus on emerging artists helps give them a much-needed profile. This channel also hosts *The Big Breakfast*, a current affairs show. CKY and CKND, a Global affiliate, also cover theatre, and often sponsor events.

The university radio stations, although small, give ample wide coverage to the arts. Justin Olynick of UMFM has a weekly program that covers theatre.

The French-language radio and television stations, although they serve a small audience, do a thorough job of covering the arts, regardless of which official language the artists speak on stage.

Theatre criticism in Manitoba today is therefore in approximately the same place as theatre itself was in the late 1950s: it does not exist at a full professional level, but an urgent need exists. If a daily newspaper were to make theatre a priority, or if a general-interest magazine were to emerge with a significant interest in theatre, there is no doubt that talented local writers could fill the posts. It would be the final piece in the jigsaw puzzle of an important indigenous theatre scene.

22

Playwrights:

Manitoba's Theatre Outcasts Unite

"For it is a fact that a theatre without playwrights, living, breathing, surly, cantankerous, loving dedicated playwrights is a dead theatre."

—Michael Cook, from an essay titled "Ignored Again" in the *Canadian Theatre Review*, Spring 1976

Faced with the difficulty of finding a place on the city's main stage, Manitoba's playwrights used the frontier cliché of making do for themselves. The Manitoba Association of Playwrights (MAP), an outgrowth of the Playwrights Search, has over the years fostered the existence of a healthy playwriting community. This community has often succeeded in spite of the indifference shown it by the city's major stages.

A guiding force at the beginning was William Horrocks, a Tec Voc High School graduate who eventually became playwright-in-residence at PTE, a position which involved a lot more work than most residencies. The theatre did not have money in the budget to pay a playwright-in-residence, but it did have a vacancy for a janitor. Horrocks thus became what is probably the only instance of a playwright-janitor in modern history.

Besides Horrocks, MAP had a nucleus of energetic writers who wanted to make their mark: Nick Mitchell, Bruce Hunter, Bruce McManus, Rosemary de Graff, Alf Silver, Vera Redstone, Martin Reed, Charles Wilkins and Brian Richardson. From the beginning they made ambitious plans and worked to create their own opportunities. They helped organize workshops and arranged for professional feedback on members' scripts. A frequent analyst was the future administrator Rory Runnells. He amazed the group with the speed with which he returned his analyses, and often annoyed them in equal measure with the acerbic nature of his comments. Other times MAP would bring in a dramaturg from outside Manitoba to comment on its members' plays. At one early meeting Horrocks hauled then-artistic director Gordon McCall into a meeting to explain what PTE looked for in scripts and playwrights.

A handicap MAP had early on in its attempts to stage workshop productions was a shortage of local directors. MAP felt it essential that emerging playwrights have the benefit of an experienced director if the event were to contribute in a meaningful way to their development. It used Dan Wood, a talented CBC radio producer, Gordon McCall, Richard Ouzounian and Bob White, to name a few. McCall and Ouzounian obviously had their hands full in their regular jobs, so the opportunity to use their talents was rare. Still, McCall staged the William Horrocks script (*St. Peter's Asylum)* he workshopped, and Ouzounian publicly expressed the desire to stage De Graff's *Fields of Sorrow*, although an MTC production never happened.

Another difficulty playwrights faced was that the Manitoba Arts Council was slow to understand their needs. At one meeting in January 1984 Sevelia Sytnick, who was then the Council officer responsible for playwrights, proudly explained changes that the Council deemed necessary to fund playwrights properly. Among the changes was a requirement that playwrights be at arm's length from the theatres that would fund them, to avoid potential conflicts of interest. She then stood stunned at the front of the meeting for almost an hour while Bruce McManus and others explained angrily that the changes ignored the climate under which plays develop, and that the Council plans would actually make it harder for playwrights to succeed. In the early 1980s, companies such as Theatre X included actor-playwrights who developed their works collaboratively within a company structure.

When the Manitoba Arts Council appointed first Linda Huffman and later Margo Charlton as Theatre Arts Officer, it marked an improvement in the quality of support the Council offered and a recognition of the importance of Manitoba plays.

MAP did not always get the funding priority that the playwrights thought was fair. It felt the sting of funding cuts during the years of restraint, while the Manitoba Writers' Guild survived almost untouched. MAP answered that challenge by becoming as well-connected and vocal as the Guild, and by establishing a reputation for excellence. After the first round of cuts in 1991, Rory Runnells and board members

Per Brask and Larry Desrochers went over the head of then-theatre officer Pat Carrabré and met directly with then-chair Marlene Neustaedter to press their case. This was not a group that passively awaited its fate. In comparison, the Manitoba Association of Composers took a more diplomatic tone, and it disappeared.

An early example of MAP's excellence was the Playwrights Development Program. This program, started in 1982, matched playwrights with professional actors and directors. Everyone was paid for a one-week development workshop, in which the actors rehearsed, the playwright rewrote, and everyone explored.

In the MAP publication *On the MAP,* a collection of scenes workshopped in the program's first five years, Doug Arrell describes the program's strengths and pitfalls. The obvious benefit is that playwrights get to see their words on stage. This simple experience gives a playwright more information on how to revise the script than any other exercise. The quality of this feedback, however, depends heavily on the quality of the people doing the workshop. A professional director and cast are the best guide to learning what works and what does not. Even in the worst situations, where the director and playwright either do not mesh or the director cannot control the process properly, the playwright learns important lessons about the rehearsal process. Playwrights also learn what might happen to their scripts when they go out into the wide world alone. A second major benefit for the playwright is the script-in-hand staged reading. At these events the public attends a presentation of the script as a work-in-progress. The public seldom expands beyond the theatre community and the playwright's friends and family, but the experience still gives the playwright an inkling of how a "real" audience might react to the play.

Of the 19 scripts in *On the MAP,* at least 12 later had professional productions. Rick Chafe's *Player Pool* later had a Fringe Festival production. Four of these (*House, Why the Dishes Can't Wait Until Tomorrow, Departures and Arrivals,* and *refugees*) have received multiple productions and taken a place among Canada's celebrated plays. William Harrar's *Bolshie Bash* had an Agassiz production and an independent Fringe production in 1999. (Harrar performed it himself at the 1990 Fringe.) Since these workshops were not attached to any theatre and did not have an opening night commitment, their track record is remarkable.

Another of MAP's programs that helps playwrights earlier in the development process is the Open Door. University of Winnipeg professor Alan Williams was the first dramaturg during his stay in Winnipeg. The open door is literally that: a playwright can bring a script to the MAP office on a Sunday afternoon. If the coordinator and actors are not already busy with someone else's work, the playwright can listen to people sitting around a table read the script. Afterwards the coordinator and readers (and anyone else present) comments on the script. The free-for-all can be confusing and contradictory, but it beats writing in a garret. Fortunately, MAP has chosen wisely in the coordinators it has hired, thereby reducing the potential for chaotic feedback.

MAP also coordinates the playwrights' colony. Once every two years a playwright works with a director, dramaturg and cast for a two-week intensive workshop. Although there is no public performance as such, directors often use the colonies to work on plays they already know they will be producing in the fall.

MAP has hosted readings by playwrights, often teaming a visiting playwright up with at least one local writer. These events have helped to establish contacts with the theatre world outside Manitoba. Besides readings, MAP sponsors workshops when visiting theatre artists are available and willing. Although these workshops sometimes have embarrassingly poor attendance, those who do attend receive development and contacts they would not have received otherwise.

In a unique project in 1995, MAP sponsored a dramaturgy program, led by Per Brask. MAP chose six playwrights to spend two years studying scripts and dramaturgy, moving from the classics to Canadian plays, and finally to works in progress. The group studied and contributed to the development of Dale Lakevold's *Never, Never Mind, Kurt Kurt Cobain*. The play had a Theatre Projects premiere in 1998. Brask brought in other academics, prominent Canadian playwrights, and local theatre artists to share their perceptions with the group.

An underrated benefit MAP bestows on its membership is *ellipsis…*, its newsletter. Over the years, a number of talented and generous playwrights have devoted their energies to communication with the membership. Harry Rintoul, Michael Nathanson, Ross McMillan and Angus Kohm have served as editors. This newsletter goes beyond the parochial cheerleading that professional organizations often publish. While births and marriages occasionally find their way into the newsletter, the bulk of the content is craft talk, market information, and lively discussion. In the December 1991 issue, editor Ross McMillan took on Robert Enright for accusing people who did not like *Not Wanted on the Voyage* of "reacting either to its 'blasphemy' or its heavily narrative undramatic form." McMillan went on to say, "I, for one, objected to its intellectual emptiness." A few paragraphs later he defended Sean Dixon's *End of the World Romance* against criticism that it lacked a strong sense of story. McMillan concluded his editorial with "The difference is that Dixon's problems are of the type that can be fixed. In his play, Findley had nothing to say, and that's not something you can fix." It takes a brave man to attack Manitoba's premier arts critic and one of Canada's most beloved authors in one brief essay, but then MAP has always had the courage of its convictions.

A tangible proof of that conviction is MAP's second publishing venture (other than its two fundraising cookbooks). *A MAP of the Senses,* which Runnells edited and Scirocco published in 2000, contains 12 plays by Manitoba playwrights. To use the obvious pun, it puts Manitoba playwrights on the map. The book resulted directly in Theatre Anywhere's decision to mount Rick Chafe's *Zac & Speth* in 2001.

Although MAP has had good luck in the many talented and active people who have served as chair, executive members and newsletter editors, much of the credit for its success in promoting Manitoba playwrights must go the person who has had the longest direct association with the office, Rory Runnells. Besides serving capably as administrator, he has kept his finger on the pulse of drama in Manitoba, showing up at most premieres (although seldom staying for small talk afterwards) and adding his often acerbic, but always considered, opinion to the discourse on drama in the province.

In the past few years, Manitoba playwrights have begun to cross international borders. Bruce McManus has had a Minnesota production of *Selkirk Avenue.* Harry Rintoul has also had several productions of his plays in the United States. Maureen Hunter's work has travelled even further, to the Royal Shakespeare Company in England (and a BBC broadcast). In July 2001, Ian Ross' *fareWel* travelled to the Edinburgh Fringe.

Another positive aspect to local playwriting to arise recently is the arrival of playwrights from ethnic groups outside the mainstream. Ugandan George Seremba, although he now lives in Toronto, spent his first years in Canada teaching and acting in Manitoba. He wrote a stunningly evocative play called *Come Good Rain.* (Strangely, although

Manitoba has a growing African population, no Manitoba theatre has seen fit to produce this play.)

Yvette Nolan, Ian Ross, and Doug Nepinak have all written good plays that reflect the aboriginal experience (although Nolan's plays have a broader outlook). Two young playwrights with Filipino roots, Mike Realba and Primrose Madayag, show promise. The Mennonite Theatre company sponsored a Millennium playwriting competition. As a result of this competition they produced Benjamin Wiebe's *The Right Reason* in 2001. They will produce Veralyn Warkentin's *Mary and Marthe* in 2002. (The Mennonite Theatre company has contributed more than playwrights to Manitoba, of course. The current head of the Winnipeg Fringe Festival, Bertram Schneider, got his start there.)

And while they do not represent an ethnic group per se, gay playwrights David Demchuk, Brian Drader and Dennis Trochim (and some Rintoul plays) have added some valuable work to Manitoba's dramatic literature. Unfortunately for Manitoba, Demchuk, like Seremba, has left Manitoba.

Will one (or more) of these playwrights break through to become an international figure in dramatic literature? From the viewpoint of pure volume, one would have to vote yes. On the basis of quality, especially when you look at Ian Ross, Bruce McManus and Harry Rintoul, it also seems inevitable.

A truism in marketing says that to succeed, a new product must stand out from the crowd. It cannot just be good; it must fulfill an unmet need. Art does not succeed with an audience purely on mass appeal, though; it must communicate on a different level. Great dramatic art both forces us and helps us face our demons and make sense out of the chaos that daily living entails. A demon that Manitobans, Canadians, and other people around the world must face is coping with the damage civilization has done to indigenous peoples. For that reason, the witty and wise works Ian Ross has developed seem to point him out as the most likely candidate to be Manitoba's first great crossover artist. His success at the 2001 Edinburgh Fringe supports this possibility.

23

Now What?

"Predictions are for gypsies."
—Legendary Montreal Canadiens' coach Toe Blake

We have seen that over the 150 years of documented Manitoba theatre, a great indigenous theatre has not arrived...yet. We have had some great writers, some great artists, some great administrators and even some great critics. The pieces have not come together yet at the same time and place.

If one looks at world models of small populations that have produced great drama, the best bets seem to be Ireland and Norway. In both countries the emergence of a transcendent indigenous theatre coincided with a period of growing national pride and confidence. Manitoba seems to be entering just such a period. Long-stagnant real estate values have started to climb. Two polls published in July of 2001 cite buoyant confidence in the province's economy and future. Manitoba has developed a crop of playwrights, directors, and other theatre artists who would not look out of place on any world stage. The one shortfall seems to be in print media, but perhaps if an exciting theatre emerged, a talented critic might come forth to write about it.

What theatre would this critic cover? On first glance, MTC is the logical place to look. It is the biggest house, it has the biggest budget and, during Steven Schipper's tenure, it has entered a period of stability. Schipper has held this post longer than any of his predecessors, and many key people have stayed part of his team. The 2001–2002 season will see two Manitoba playwrights on its main stage, for the first time in the theatre's history (Maureen Hunter's *Vinci* and Olaf Pyttlik's *The Wave,* which appeared at the 2000 Fringe in a test run).

The downside is that neither play could be said to emerge from Manitoba's daily life and trials. The theatre of Ireland and Norway confronted the audience's demons. The great plays did not always open to warm response: brawls broke out during O'Casey's plays at the Abbey. More troubling for Manitoba playwrights is that the Warehouse has not produced a play by a Manitoba playwright since 1990. MTC has, regardless of its merits, become the home of comfortable theatre: polished, professional, occasionally daring, but rarely challenging.

MTC's boldest move over the past ten years has been the introduction of a February festival celebrating a great world playwright. In 2001, the inaugural festival, the Irish playwright Samuel Beckett was honoured. In 2002 it will be the German Bertolt Brecht. The next playwright to be honoured is anyone's guess, but it will not likely be a Manitoba playwright, or even a Canadian.

If a great Manitoba drama does emerge, however, MTC will have played at least an indirect part. It plays to the largest number of people each year. That audience helps to keep theatre alive. More importantly, MTC gave us the Fringe Festival and continues to support it. In interviews conducted for this book, the most commonly mentioned seminal event was the Fringe.

PTE staked a claim to native theatre early in its life, but lost that fire sometime during the Springate years. Allen MacInnis has proved to be the theatre's financial and popular saviour, and a real asset to Manitoba's theatre life. He knows how to get a play to life on opening night, and he has shown the ability to work with premiere plays. The downside to his stewardship is that often the Prairie part of Prairie Theatre Exchange does not exist. If one looks at his playbills, Prairie writing does not seem to hold much importance. Indeed, the strongest trend one can discern in surveying his play selection is a correlation with past MTC Warehouse and main stage plays. PTE will most likely continue to produce good theatre worthy of audience attention but, at least under MacInnis' stewardship, it does not hold out much hope for spawning a great local theatre.

The remaining theatres are constrained by either their size or mandate. The Winnipeg Jewish Theatre has been presenting professional theatre for years, and its work compares favourably with theatre on other professional stages in Manitoba. The downside is that its concentration on Jewish themes, while in keeping with its mandate and certainly within its prerogative, means that it often uses plays from outside sources.

Similarly, MTYP's youth mandate often precludes Manitoba playwrights. It is not shy about using local talent, and does well by it when it does, but its focus to serve youth means that it must take a broader stance artistically.

Some small companies, like Ross McMillan's Persona, Grant Guy's Adhere and Deny, and Ann Hodges' Spatial Relations produce cutting-edge theatre that excites audiences. They use almost exclusively local talent. Each company, however, is more about form than it is about geography. They all do great work, but they choose primarily outside texts, such as ones by Wallace Shawn, Samuel Beckett and Oscar Wilde.

A promising development has been Shakespeare in the Ruins' choice of Rick Chafe to become its first playwright other than Shakespeare. Logically, its first non-Shakespearean playwright might have been Marlowe, Jonson, or perhaps Molière. Choosing a local playwright shows an ability to think outside the box, and thankfully, Chafe proved to be more than up to the task. The company deserves credit for proving conclusively that no stage is too large for a Manitoba playwright. The company has also expressed willingness to work with other local playwrights.

For this company, too, though, mandate gets in the way of its becoming a home for new scripts. Shakespeare in the Ruins could have stayed at the St. Norbert site if it had been willing to embrace contemporary work and abandon Shakespeare. The St. Norbert Arts Centre asked it to do this as a condition for staying at the site, but Shakespeare in the Ruins decided to move instead.

To its credit, it refused to compromise its artistic integrity. Nonetheless, its next non-traditional choice was Bertolt Brecht. While this company is a vital part of Manitoba theatre life, therefore, it is unlikely to be the cradle of a Manitoba drama. Its most likely role will be maintaining a company of vital theatre artists who are available for other projects.

Theatre Projects seems the best bet to take up the mantle. It has a long and honoured history. In Margo Charlton it has an artistic director who knows how to get things done. The workshop production of Margaret Sweatman and Glenn Buhr's *Flux* shows that it can mount works that break the mould. Charlton also has strong links to the gay and lesbian community, a community that has produced some of Manitoba's most interesting and intelligent works to date. Its playbills show a wealth of work that expresses the Manitoba experience dramatically. Theatre Projects' handicap has been a lack of funds and media attention. Charlton's experience as a Manitoba Arts Council Theatre Officer should help alleviate this problem.

Le Cercle Molière has a long history, and a record for producing Manitoba scripts that shames most other professional companies in Manitoba. Playwrights Claude Dorge and Roger Auger have developed a reputation beyond Manitoba's borders, and English-speaking audiences often have the pleasure of seeing Dorge on stage with English-speaking companies. Unfortunately, because the French-speaking population in Manitoba is small, it does not reach the audience it deserves.

While it may not seem likely on the surface, Red Roots Theatre is also a strong candidate. If confronting a society's demons is a mark of great theatre, this company has the mandate and ability to confront what is perhaps Manitoba's greatest demon, its handling of First Nations people. In Ian Ross, Manitoba's First Nations have a great playwright who writes with humour and a clear eye about the aboriginal experience in Manitoba. His writing also has poetic depth. Yvette Nolan and Doug Nepinak have also written great scripts. Besides writers, Red Roots has some talented theatre artists to draw from: actor and director Tracey McCorrister, actor and artistic director Mike Lawrenchuk, actors Ryan Black, Bernelda Wheeler, Monica Marx, Tom Jackson, Adam Beach and Tina Keeper.

Red Roots' recent collaboration with the University of Winnipeg, with which it shares space and other resources, gives the group stability. Its challenge will be to draw the benefit of academic expertise from the university without falling into the academic trap of worship of form at the expense of audience pleasure.

Another challenge for Red Roots, and one that the Abbey also faced, will be having the courage to confront society's demons squarely. *Winnipeg Free Press* columnist Jordan Wheeler mentions this problem in his July 13, 2001 column about child prostitution when he says, "The irony that strikes me now is that you will never read about that kind of story in a native newspaper. Our leaders, be they political, entrepreneurial, or otherwise, don't want negativity in native journalism or the small native newspapers are held ransom because they depend on the leaders and the organizations they belong to for advertising dollars."

While the column addressed native issues, the same problem holds true for our theatres: they will have to find the courage to tell their stories the best way they can, and let the chips fall where they may. History proves that once the right group makes this leap of courage, a world audience follows.

Predicting the future is a dodgy game at best, as anyone who has read predictions about the future after the fact knows. Manitoba may never produce a great theatre, and if it does, it might not come from any of the sources mentioned above (or it may come from those dismissed, such as MTC). It might come from Nancy Drake's New West Theatre in Brandon, the first professional theatre company to emerge outside Winnipeg. Drake is a highly skilled director who knows how to get the best out of a playwright and actors.

Regardless of the future, the past and present is known. Theatre in Manitoba has produced, and continues to produce, a great legacy for all Manitobans.

Production Appendix

List of Productions for Manitoba theatre companies

The following is a partial list of professional theatre productions in Manitoba, listed in alphabetical order by company name. Plays by Canadian playwrights are noted with • before the playwright's name; plays by Manitoba playwrights are noted with •• before the playwright's name.

Productions listed for the 2001-2001 season were the upcoming productions announced at the time this book went to press.

.

Note*:* defining a Manitoba playwright is a difficult process. Here it refers to a play someone wrote while living in Manitoba, regardless of the playwright's place of birth. This sometimes involves splitting hairs. For the purposes of this list, Wendy Lill's *Fighting Days* qualifies as a Manitoba play, but her 1995 *All Fall Down* does not, because she wrote it after she moved to Nova Scotia, and also because she set the play there.

Date	Play Title	• Cdn / ••MB / Playwright

ADHERE AND DENY

1993	Nightclub	•• Grant Guy
	Bear With Me	•• William Harrar
	Photogenic	•• Grant Guy
	Lost	•• Grant Guy
1994	Light/light series (with Ace Art)	
1995	Washing Spider Out	•• Ross McMillan
1996	Ubu Roi	Alfred Jarry, ad. Grant Guy
	Bell	
1996	The Harrowing (with Theatre Projects)	• Scott Douglas
	Parables and Paradoxes: The Kafka Project	•• Chafe, Boxall, Friesen, Guy, Sigurdson
1998	John The Baptist	•• Grant Guy
	Woyzeck	Greog Büchner
	Ground Zero (with Ace Art)	•• Grant Guy (curator)
1999-2000	Blood Wedding	Fredrico Garcia Lorca, ad. Grant Guy
	Kleist: Fragments	Heinrich von Kleist, ad. Grant Guy
2000-2001	Salome	Oscar Wilde
	Found and Lost (part of Beckettfest)	Samuel Beckett, ad. Grant Guy
	Katarsis	Stanislaw Witkeiewicz, ad. Grant Guy
2001-2002	Prometheus Bound	Aeschylus, ad. Grant Guy

CERCLE MOLIÈRE

1968-1969	Jacques ou la soumission et Délire à deux	Eugene Ionesco
	Du vent dans les branches de sassafrass	René de Obaldia
	Les Rosenberg ne doivent pas mourir	Alain Decaux
	La Princesse Turandot	Claude Satès & Ahouva Lion
1969-1970	Plouft le petit fantôme	Maria Clara Machado
	Du vent dans les branches de sassafrass	René de Obaldia
1970-1971	Les Belles Soeurs	•Michel Tremblay
	Les Jouets du père Noël	Charles Vildrac
	Plouft le petit fantôme	Maria Clara Machado
	Monserrat	Emmanuel Roblès
	Soirée de poésie (poetry evening)	
	Fantômes, clowns et citrouilles	Marcel Sabourin
1971-1972	On demande un ménage	Jean Letray
	Le Violon du temps qui passe	A.C. Charpentier & M. Mayan
	A toi, pour toujours, ta Marie-Lou	• Michel Tremblay
	Monserrat	Emmanuel Roblès
1972-1973	Double jeu	Robert Thomas
	Les Éléphants de tante Louise	•• Roger Auger
	A toi, pour toujours, ta Marie-Lou	• Michel Tremblay
	Tailleur pour dames	Georges Feydeau
	Mistère de Noël	
1973-1974	Molière 300	Molière
	La Princesse et le perroquet	
	Soirée de poésie	
	Mistère de Noël	
	Les Vilains	André Gille
1974-1975	Le Petit coq désobéissant	Ion Lucian, trans. Laura Riga
	Tit-Jean Margoton	
	Tit-Coq	• Gratien Gélinas
	L'Auberge des morts subites	Félix Leclerc
	Je m'en vais à Régina	•• Roger Auger
	Plouft le petit fantôme	Maria Clara Machado
1975-1976	Le Roi qui aimait trop les fleurs	
	Fanfan le finfin	•• Louise Rochon
	Il était une fois dans une grande plaine platte	Jean-Louis Hébert
	L'Avare	Molière
	Piège pour un homme seul	Robert Thomas
	Le Roitelet	•• Claude Dorge
1976-1977	Bousille et les justes (tour prod.)	• Gratien Gélinas

	John's Lunch	•• Roger Auger
	L'Extase de Rita Joe	• George Ryga, trans. •• Roger Auger
	Double jeu	Jean Thomas
1977-1978	Molière-Gascon	Molière
	Les Manigances d'une bru	•• Paul Ruest et Roger LeGal
	V'là Vermette	•• Roger Auger
	Marlot dans les merveilles	Pierre Morency
	Quatre pour vous	
	Gulliver (tour prod.)	
1978-1979	Sonnez les matines	• Félix Leclerc
	Amorphe d'Ottenburg	Jean-Claude Grumberg
	OK d'abord	•• Jean-Guy Roy & Claude Dorge
	CM2	
1979-1980	Le Journal de Anne Frank	
	Maria Chapdelaine	Louis Hémon
	Nico et Niski et la Raquette volante	•• Claude Dorge
	Célimare le bien-aimé	Eugène Labiche
	CM2	
1980-1981	Oscar	Claude Magnier, ad. Jean-Guy Roy
	Florence	Marcel Dubé
	Séraphin Poudrier	•• Roger Auger
	Icare (tour prod.)	
	CM2	
1981-1982	Bonne fête, maman	Élizabeth Bourget
	Le Noël de Frisson, Flocon et Fricon	•• Claude Dorge et Janine Tougas
	Une drôle de vie	Brian Clark, trans. Éric Kahane
	Piège à rebours de Ira Levin	trans. Michel Beaulieu
	CM2	
1982-1983	Nico et Niski et l'Étoile de Noël	•• Claude Dorge
	'Cré Sganarelle	Molière, ad. Claude Dorge
	L'Avocat du diable	Thierry Maunier & Pierre Sabatier
	Moman (tour prod.)	Louisette Dussault
	Et ta sœur?	Bricaire & Lasseygues, ad. J-G. Roy
1983-1984	Katchauchen	Jean-Guy Roy
	Coup de sang	Jean Daigle
	Ah, les hommes !	F. Dorin, ad. I. Mahé & C. Dorge
	C'était avant la guerre à L'Anse-à-Gilles	Marie Laberge
1984-1985	Le Temps de lilas	Marcel Dubé
	La Chaire	Bill Davis
	Emmanuel à Joseph à Davit (tour prod.)	Antonine Maillet
	L'Article 23 (co-prod with PTE)	•• Claude Dorge & David Arnason
1985-1986	Georges Dandin	Molière
	K2	Patrick Meyers
	Les Tremblay	•• Claude Dorge & Irène Mahé
	Avant la nuit, Offenbach (tour prod.)	• Michel Garneau
	Voisin, voisine/Of Mimes and Clowns	•• David Gillies, trans.Irène Mahé
1986-1987	Frenchie	Jean-Guy Roy et Irène Mahé
	Je m'en vais à Régina	•• Roger Auger
	Letinsky Café	•• Louise Fiset
	Tremblay 2	•• Claude Dorge & Irène Mahé
1987-1988	Avant qu'les autres le fassent	•• Claude Dorge & Vincent Dureault
	Les trois coups de Minuit	André Obey
	Agnès de l'Enfant-Dieu	John Pielmeier
	La Passion de Narcisse Mondoux (tour prod.)	• Gratien Gélinas
	Le Noël de Frisson, Flocon et Fricon	•• Janine Tougas & Claude Dorge
1988-1989	Monsieur Fugue	Liliane Atlan
	Paris-Berlin (tour prod.)	Monique Leyrac
	Guili-guili	ad. J-G. Roy, from Babour, F. Marceau
	Victor	•• Gilles Cop
	Le Voyage du train	Claudine Dailly
	Rock en ruine	•• Jean-Louis Hébert
	Magicien au secours	•• Claude Dorge & Janine Tougas
1989-1990	Au Lac-des-bois	Ernest Thompson
	Les Tremblay—Noël en famille	•• Claude Dorge & Irène Mahé
	La Menteuse	Bricaire & Lesaygues, ad. J-G Roy

	Vol 217, Calgary	•• Robert Thomas
	Rock en ruine	•• Jean-Louis Hébert
	Passe-muraille	David Holman, ad. Anne Nenarokoff
1990-1991	Miracle en Alabama	William Gibson
	Les Dernières Fougères (co-prod.)	Michel D'Astous
	L'éducation de Rita (tour prod.)	Willie Russell
	Soirée Félix Leclerc	• ad. Irène Mahé & Jean-Guy Roy
	Les frères Mainville	•Norm Foster
	Passe-muraille (co-prod.)	David Holman, ad. Anne Nenarokoff
1991-1992	Le Tartuffe	Molière
	Piaf	•• Jean-Pierre Dubé
	La Petite-Poule-d'Eau	•• G. Roy , ad. C. Dorge & I. Mahé
	Noël, Noël	•• ad. Jean-Guy Roy & Irène Mahé
	Les Rogers	Robert Bellefeuille
	Le Voyage du train	Claudine Dailly
1992-1993	J'vais revenir avant minuit	• Peter Colley
	Les Belles-Sœurs	• Michel Tremblay
	Quand on n'a que l'amour	•• Jean-Pierre Dubé
	Il était une fois Delmas, Sask (touring prod.)	André Roy
	Jeunesse à la une, deux créations collectives	••
	Le Voyage du train	Claudine Dailly
1993-1994	Zone	Marcel Dubé
	Toasté des 2 bords	•• Janine Tougas
	Haute Fidélité	Ray Cooney
	Le Chien	Jean-Marc Dalpé
	La Vie après le hockey (tour prod.)	Kenneth Brown, ad. André Roy
	De bouche à oreille—Jean-Paul…	•• Élaine Tougas
1994-1995	Huit femmes	Robert Thomas
	L'Ampoule magique	Woody Allen
	Des Minous et des hommes (tour prod.)	D. Chartrand & L. Theriault
	Traces d'étoiles	Cindy-Lou Johnson
	Moinopoli	•• René Ammann
	Toasté encore	•• Janine Tougas
	Gabrielle Roy (co-prod.)	•• Lise Gaboury-Diallo
	De Bouche à oreille	•• Élaine Tougas
1995-1996	Translations	Brian Friel, ad. Charles Leblanc
	Cendres de cailloux (tour prod.)	• Daniel Danis
	Les Aiguilleurs	Brian Phelan
	Les Grandes Chaleurs	• Michel-Marc Bouchard
	Le Faucon	• Marie Laberge
	De Bouche à oreille	•• Élaine Tougas
1996-1997	La Femme D'Urie	Rhéal Cenerini
	Québec/Canada 2000	Richard Neilsen, trans. Nicole Coziol
	Lonely Planet	Stephen Dietz, •• trans. Claude Dorge
	Les Tremblay	•• Claude Dorge & Irène Mahé
	L'Examen de passage (tour prod.)	Israël Horovitz, ad. Benoit Girard
1997-1998	Fugues pour un cheval et un piano	Hervé Dupuis
	L'homme aux trésors (tour prod.)	Marie-Louise Nadeau
	La Trahison (tour prod.)	Laurier Gareau
	Salvation	•• Robin Wilcock, trans. M. Prescott
	U.F.O.R.E.X	•• Edward Roy, trans. Marc Prescott
	De Bouche à oreille	•• Élaine Tougas
1998-1999	7 étages, 7 histoires	• Morris Panych, trans. J. van Burek
	Les Guerriers (touring prod.)	Philippe Minyana
	Laurie ou la vie de galérie (tour prod.)	Herménégilde Chiasson
	Chat en poche	Georges Feydeau
	Les Molière	Molière, add. text by •• M. Prescott
	De Bouche à oreille	•• Élaine Tougas
1999-2000	Une Lune d'eau salée (tour prod.)	• David French, trans. Antonine Maillet
	La Visite de la vieille dame	Friedrich Dürrenmatt, trans. J-P. Porret
	À toi pour toujours, ta Marie-Lou	• Michel Tremblay
	Cap-Enragé (tour prod.)	Herménégilde Chiasson
	De Bouche à oreille	•• Élaine Tougas
	La Quête	•• Suzanne Kennelly
2000-2001	Le Happening 2000	Dubé, Gaboury-Diallo, Nayet, Saint-Pierre, Tougas, Véron

	La Tentation d' Henri Ouimet	Rhéal Cenerini
	Poissons	Marc Prescott
	Récits et Chansons du Manitoba	
	Frenchie	•• Jean-Guy Roy et Irène Mahé

MANITOBA THEATRE CENTRE (MAIN STAGE)

1958-1959	A Hatful of Rain	Michael V. Gazzo
	Blithe Spirit	Noel Coward
	Teach Me How to Cry	• Patricia Joudry
	The Glass Menagerie	Tennessee Williams
	Born Yesterday	Garson Kanin
	Ring Round the Moon	Jean Anouilh
	The Diary of Anne Frank	Frances Goodrich & Albert Hackett
	Of Mice and Men	John Steinbeck
1959-1960	Solid Gold Cadillac	G. F. Kaufmann & H. Teichman
	Tea and Sympathy	Robert Anderson
	On Borrowed Time	Lawrence Watkin
	The Reclining Figure	Harry Kurnitz
	Look Back in Anger	John Osborne
	Volpone	Ben Jonson
	Teahouse of the August Moon	John Patrick
	Anastasia	Marcelle Maurette
1960-1961	Mr. Roberts	Thomas Heggen & Joshua Logan
	Gaslight	Patrick Hamilton
	A Streetcar Named Desire	Tennessee Williams
	Biggest Thief in Town	Dalton Trumbo
	Dark of the Moon	H. Richardson & W. Bernay
	Juno and the Paycock	Sean O'Casey
	Visit to a Small Planet	Gore Vidal
	Four Poster	Jan de Hertog
1961-1962	The Lady's Not for Burning	Christopher Fry
	Speaking of Murder	Audrey & William Ross
	Playboy of the Western World	J. M. Synge
	Arms and the Man	George Bernard Shaw
	The Boyfriend	Sandy Wilson
	Separate Tables	Noel Coward
	Thieves' Carnival	Jean Alouith
	Look Ahead!	• Len Peterson
1962-1963	Bonfires of '62	•• Tom Hendry, music by N. Harris
	Once More With Feeling	Harry Kurnitz
	An Enemy of the People	Henrik Ibsen
	Mrs. Warren's Profession	George Bernard Shaw
	Pal Joey	Rogers & Hart; book by J. O'Hara
	Summer of the 17th Doll	Ray Lawler
	The Caretaker	Harold Pinter
	A Very Close Family	• Bernard Slade
1963-1964	Private Lives	Noël Coward
	Pygmalion	George Bernard Shaw
	The Hostage	Brendan Behan
	A Midsummer Night's Dream	William Shakespeare
	Little Mary Sunshine	Rick Besoyan
	Five Finger Exercise	Peter Schaffer
	The Gazebo	Alec Coppel
	Cat on a Hot Tin Roof	Tennessee Williams
1964-1965	Hay Fever	Noel Coward
	All About Us	Revue, compiled by Tom Hendry
	Mother Courage	Bertolt Brecht
	The Taming of the Shrew	William Shakespeare
	Irma La Douce	More, Heneker, and Norman
	Heartbreak House	George Bernard Shaw
	Who's Afraid of Virginia Woolf?	Edward Albee
	The Tiger and the Typist	Murray Schisgal
1965-1966	The Private Ear and the Public Eye	Peter Schaffer
	The Importance of Being Earnest	Oscar Wilde
	Andorra	Max Frisch
	The Tempest	William Shakespeare

	The Threepenny Opera	Bertolt Brecht
	Nicholas Romanov	William Kinsolving
	The Fantasticks	Harvey Schmidt & Tom Jones
	The Dance of Death	August Strindberg
1966-1967	Charley's Aunt	Brandon Thomas
	The Rainmaker	N. Richard Nash
	Galileo	Bertolt Brecht
	A Funny Thing Happened on the Way...	Shevelove, Gelbart, Sondheim
	Romeo and Juliet	William Shakespeare
	Lulu Street	•• Ann Henry
	Luv	Murray Schisgal
1967-1968	Major Barbara	George Bernard Shaw
	Oh, What a Lovely War	Joan Littlewood & Theatre Workshop
	Antigone/Sganarelle	Euripides/Molière
	The Three Sisters	Anton Chekhov
	The Fantasticks	Harvey Schmidt & Tom Jones
	A Thousand Clowns	Herb Gardiner
	A Delicate Balance	Edward Albee
1968-1969	Fiddler on the Roof	Bock, Harnick & Stein
	A Man for All Seasons	Robert Bolt
	Hotel Paradiso	Feydeau, adapted by Peter Glenville
	Cactus Flower	Abe Burrows
1969-1970	Man of La Mancha	Leigh, Darion, Wasserman
	Cabaret	Kander, Ebb, Masteroff
	Marat/Sade	Peter Weiss
	You Can't Take it With You	Kaufmann & Hart
	After the Fall	Arthur Miller
1970-1971	A Man's A Man	Bertolt Brecht
	Long Day's Journey Into Night	Eugene O'Neill
	Salvation	Peter Link & C.C. Courtney
	Hobson's Choice	Harold Brighouse
	War and Peace	Piscator & Neumann
	Little Murders	Jules Fieffer
1971-1972	What the Butler Saw	Joe Orton
	Alice Through the Looking Glass	Lewis Carroll, ad. Keith Turnbull
	The Homecoming	Harold Pinter
	The Sun and the Moon	• James Reaney
	Lady Frederick	W. Somerset Maugham
	A Comedy of Errors	William Shakespeare
1972-1973	A Streetcar Named Desire	Tennessee Williams
	Sleuth	Peter Schaffer
	A Thurber Carnival	James Thurber
	Hedda Gabler	Henrik Ibsen
	Guys and Dolls	F. Loesser, A. Burrows, J. Swerling
	Hamlet	William Shakespeare
	Rosencrantz and Guildenstern are Dead	Tom Stoppard
1973-1974	You Never Can Tell	George Bernard Shaw
	A Day in the Death of Joe Egg	Peter Nichols
	The Dybbuk	S. Ansky
	Godspell	S. Schwartz & J-M. Tebelak
	The Plough and the Stars	Sean O'Casey
	Indian and Black Comedy	Peter Shaffer
1974-1975	The Sunshine Boys	Neil Simon
	The Cherry Orchard	Anton Chekhov
	The Boyfriend	Sandy Wilson
	Forget-Me-Not-Lane	Peter Nichols
	Red Emma, Queen of the Anarchists	• Carol Bolt
	Trelawny of the "Wells"	Arthur Wing Pinero
1975-1976	Cyrano de Bergerac	
	The Price	Arthur Miller
	Equus	Peter Schaffer
	Company	Steven Sondheim
	Of Mice and Men	John Steinbeck
	Private Lives	Noel Coward
1976-1977	Twelfth Night	William Shakespeare
	All Over	Edward Albee

	Relatively Speaking	Allen Aykbourn
	Dames at Sea	Maimsohn, Miller & Wise
	The Crucible	Arthur Miller
	She Stoops to Conquer	Oliver Goldsmith
1977-1978	The Last Chalice	• Joanna Glass
	Knock Knock	Jules Fieffer
	The Contractor	David Storey
	The Night of the Iguana	Tennessee Williams
	Measure for Measure	William Shakespeare
	The Royal Hunt of the Sun	Peter Schaffer
1978-1979	A Midsummer Night's Dream	William Shakespeare
	A Doll's House	Henrik Ibsen
	How the Other Half Loves	Alan Ayckbourn
	Death of a Salesman	Arthur Miller
	Veronica's Room	Ira Levin
	A Bee in her Bonnet	G. Feydeau
1979-1980	Travesties	Tom Stoppard
	Artichoke	• Joanna McClelland Glass
	Absurd Person Singular	Alan Ayckbourn
	The Sea Gull	Anton Chekhov, ad. Arif Hasnain
	The Diary of Anne Frank	Frances Goodrich & Albert Hackett
	Dracula	Bram Stoker, ad. Deane & Balderson
1980-1981	Billy Bishop Goes to War	• John Gray & Eric Peterson
	Jitters	• David French
	Balconville	• David Fennario
	Grease	Jim Jacobs & Warren Casey
	The Elephant Man	Bernard Pomerance
	As You Like It	William Shakespeare
1981-1982	Encore Brel!	• ad. Richard Ouzounian
	Candida	George Bernard Shaw
	The Black Bonspiel of Willie MacCrimmon	• W.O. Mitchell
	The Taming of the Shrew	William Shakespeare
	The Little Foxes	Lillian Hellman
	The Importance of Being Earnest	Oscar Wilde
1982-1983	Nicholas Nickleby	Charles Dickens, • ad. R. Ouzounian
	Blood Relations	• Sharon Pollock
	The Man Who Came to Dinner	Moss Hart & George S. Kaufman
	Richard III	William Shakespeare
	The Three Musketeers	Alexandre Dumas, ad. Eberle Thomas
	Mass Appeal	Bill C. Davis
1983-1984	The Mikado	W.S. Gilbert & Arthur Sullivan
	A Tale of Two Cities	Charles Dickens
	Much Ado About Nothing	William Shakespeare
	The Duchess of Malfi	John Webster
	Bedroom Farce	Alan Ayckbourn
	The Dining Room	A. R. Gurney, Jr.
1984-1985	Amadeus	Peter Shaffer
	Old World	Aleksei Arbuzov
	Quiet in the Land	• Anne Chislett
	Born Yesterday	Garson Kanin
	Quartermaine's Terms	Simon Gray
	Tartuffe	Moliere
1985-1986	Barnum	Bramble, Stewart & Coleman
	The Real Thing	Tom Stoppard
	Tsymbaly	• Ted Galay
	Talking Dirty	• Sherman Snukal
	Hamlet	William Shakespeare
	Filthy Rich	• George F. Walker
1986-1987	Brighton Beach Memoirs	Neil Simon
	A Christmas Carol	Charles Dickens, ad. Barbara Field
	Mirandolina	Carlo Goldoni, ad. Olwen Wymark
	Doc	• Sharon Pollok
	I'm Not Rappaport	Herb Gardner
	The Foreigner	Larry Shue
1987-1988	Royalty is Royalty	• W.O. Mitchell
	The 101 Miracles of Hope Chance	• Allan Stratton

Season	Play	Playwright
	Ten Little Indians	Agatha Christie
	You Never Can Tell	George Bernard Shaw
	The Road to Mecca	Athol Fugard
	Morning's at Seven	Paul Osborn
1988-1989	"B Movie," The Play	• Tom Wood
	1949	• David French
	Falstaff	William Shakespeare
	Woman in Mind	Alan Ayckbourn
	A View From the Bridge	Arthur Miller
	Brass Rubbings	• Gordon Pinsent
1989-1990	Broadway Bound	Neil Simon
	You Can't Take It With You	Kaufmann & Hart
	Emerald City	•• David Williamson
	Cat on a Hot Tin Roof	Tennessee Williams
	The Mousetrap	Agatha Christie
	Master Class	David Pownall
1990-1991	The Heidi Chronicles	Wendy Wasserstein
	Macbeth	William Shakespeare
	Noises Off	Michael Frayn
	Sherlock Holmes and the Speckled Band	Arthur Conan Doyle
	Of the Fields, Lately	• David French
	Les Misérables	A. Boubil & C-M. Schönberg
1991-1992	M. Butterfly	David Henry Hwang
	Hedda Gabler	Henrik Ibsen, •• trans. Per Brask
	Not Wanted on the Voyage	• Findley, adapted by Kugler & Rose
	Lend Me A Tenor	Ken Ludwig
	Shirley Valentine	Willy Russell
	The Miracle Worker	William Gibson
1992-1993	Another Time	Ronald Harwood
	A Midsummer Night's Dream	William Shakespeare
	Transit of Venus	•• Maureen Hunter
	Arsenic & Old Lace	Joseph Kesselring
	Democracy	• John Murrell
	Lost in Yonkers	Neil Simon
1993-1994	Dancing at Lughnasa	Brian Friel
	A Christmas Carol–The Musical	Charles Dickens, ad. • Mavor Moore
	Wait Until Dark	Frederick Knotts
	Henceforward	Alan Ayckbourn
	Hay Fever	Noel Coward
	Wingfield's Folly	• Dan Needles
1994-1995	Oleanna	David Mamet
	The Sisters Rosensweig	Wendy Wasserstein
	The Tragedy of Hamlet, Prince of Denmark	William Shakespeare
	Six Degrees of Separation	John Guare
	If We Are Women	• Joanna McClelland Glass
	Homeward Bound	• Elliott Hayes
1995-1996	Keely & Du	Jane Martin
	Season's Greetings	Alan Ayckbourn
	Dr. Jekyll & Mr. Hyde–A Love Story	R.L. Stevenson, ad. James W. Nichol
	Atlantis	•• Maureen Hunter
	Cyrano de Bergerac	Edmund Rostand, trans. A. Burgess
	Little Shop of Horrors–The Musical	Alan Menken & Howard Ashman
1996-1997	Picasso at the Lapin Agile	Steve Martin
	Arcadia	Tom Stoppard
	Death of a Salesman	Arthur Miller
	There Goes the Bride	Ray Cooney & John Chapman
	The Glace Bay Miners' Museum	• Wendy Lill
	Travels with My Aunt	Graham Greene, ad. Giles Havergal
1997-1998	A Perfect Ganesh	Terrence McNally
	Master Class	Terrence McNally
	Office Hours	• Norm Foster
	The Crucible	Arthur Miller
	Three Tall Women	Edward Albee
	Sylvia	A. R. Gurney
1998-1999	Cabaret	Kander, Ebb, & Masteroff
	Of Mice and Men	John Steinbeck

	Proposals	Neil Simon
	Blessings in Disguise	• Douglas Beattie
	Billy Bishop Goes to War	• John Gray
	Lady, Be Good!	Gershwin, Gershwin, Bolton, Thompson
1999-2000	Art	Yasmina Reza
	King Lear	William Shakespeare
	2 Pianos 4 Hands	• Ted Dykstra & Richard Greenblatt
	A Streetcar Named Desire	Tennessee Williams
	Wingfield Unbound	• Dan Needles
	The Overcoat	N. Gogol, • ad. Panych & Gorling
2000-2001	To Kill A Mockingbird	Harper Lee, ad. Christopher Sergel
	Complete Works of Shakespeare (abridged)	A. Long, D. Singer, & J. Winfield
	Camelot	Lerner & Lowe
	The Weir	Conor MacPherson
	The Drawer Boy	• Michael Healey
	Larry's Party	• Carol Shields ad. Ouzounian, Norman
2001-2002	The Wave	•• Olaf Pyttlik
	The School for Wives	Molière
	Syncopation	Allan Knee
	Vinci	•• Maureen Hunter
	Stones in His Pockets	Marie Jones
	The Rainmaker	N. Richard Nash

MTC SECOND STAGE AND WAREHOUSE

1960-1961	Oh Dad, Poor Dad, Mamma's Hung You in the Closet and I'm Feeling so Bad	Arthur L. Kopit
	The Lesson/The Marriage Proposal	Eugene Ionesco
	Under Milkwood	Dylan Thomas
1961-1962	Waiting for Godot	Samuel Beckett
	Who is on my Side? Who?	
1962-1963	The Spirit of the People is a Sometime Thing	
	The Love Merchants	
1963-1964	Endgame	Samuel Beckett

THEATRE-ACROSS-THE-STREET

1967-1968	Happy Days/Exit the King	Eugene Ionesco
	School for Wives	Molière
	Red Magic	
1968-1969	Fortune and Men's Eyes	• John Herbert
	Home Free/The Zoo Story	Alan Ayckbourn/Edward Albee
	How the Puppets Formed a Government	

MTC WAREHOUSE THEATRE

1969-1970	Hail Scrawdyke!	David Halliwell
	Harry, Noon and Night	Richard Ribman
	Mandragola	Machiavelli, ad. • John Murrell
	Indian Wants The Bronx/Escurial	Israel Horowitz
	La Turista	Sam Shepard
1970-1971	The Sun Never Sets	Constantine J. Skourac
	Tomorrow is St. Valentine's Day	
1971-1972	Head 'Em Off At The Pas	
	The Jealous Husband/The Flying Doctor and The Blind Man	Molière
1972-1973	The Promise	A. Abuzov
	En Pieces Detachées	• Michel Tremblay
	On the Air	Tom Shales
	Jacques Brel is Alive & Well & Living in Paris	Eric Blau & Mort Shuman
	Wedding in White	• William Fruet
1973-1974	Mime Over Five	• Theatre Without Words
	Esker Mike and His Wife, Agiuluk	• Herschel Hardin
	You're Gonna Be Alright, Jamie-Boy	• David Freeman
	Jubalay	• Patrick Rose & Merv Capone

1974-1975	Old Times/Hosanna	Harold Pinter/• Michel Tremblay
	Androcles and the Lion	George Bernard Shaw
	The Knack	Ann Jellicoe
	Crabdance	• Beverly Simons
1975-1976	The Collected Works of Billy the Kid	• Michael Ondaatje
	Canadian Mime Theatre	• Canadian Mime Theatre
	Endgame	Samuel Beckett
	Creeps	• David Freeman
1976-1977	Berlin to Broadway With Kurt Weill	Gene Lerner & Kurt Weill
	Fables Here and Then	
	Waiting for Godot	Samuel Beckett
	Alpha Beta	E. A. Whitehead
	Canadian Gothic & American Modern	• Joanna Glass
1977-1978	Hello and Goodbye	Athol Fugard
	Oh Coward!	Noel Coward, ad. Roderick Cook
	Love is Meant to Make us Glad	•
	The Potato People	• Theatre Beyond Words
	Ashes	David Rudkin
	For Love and Chicken Soup	• Brad Leiman
	The Sea Horse	Edward Moore
1978-1979	Forever Yours, Marie Lou	• Michel Tremblay
	Theatre Beyond Words	• Theatre Beyond Words
	The Zoo Story/Sexual Perversity in Chicago	Edward Albee/ David Mamet
	Sizwe Bansi is Dead	Athol Fugard
1979-1980	American Buffalo	David Mamet
	Circus Gothic	• Jan Kudelka
	Waiting for the Parade	• John Murrell
	The Day Jake Made It Rain	• W.O. Mitchell
	Talley's Folly	Lanford Wilson
	Spokesong	Stewart Parker
1980-1981	Betrayal	Harold Pinter
	Macbeth	William Shakespeare
	Bent	Martin Sherman
	1837: The Farmers' Revolt	• Rick Salutin
1981-1982	The Gin Game	D. L. Coburn
	The Tempest	William Shakespeare
	Thimblerig	•• Alf Silver
	A Moon for the Misbegotten	Eugene O'Neill
	Side by Side by Sondheim	Sondheim
1982-1983	Fifth of July	Lanford Wilson
	How I Got That Story	Amlin Gray
	Paper Wheat	• 25th Street Theatre Collective
	Cloud 9	Caryl Churchill
	Climate of the Times	•• Alf Silver
1983-1984	La Sagouine	• Antonine Maillet
	The Actor's Nightmare/Sister Mary Ignatious Explains it All For You	Christopher Durang
	Remember Me	• Michel Tremblay
	Clearances	•• Alf Silver, based on scenario by •• I. Ross
1984-1985	Sea Marks	Gardner McKay
	'Night Mother	Marsha Norman
	Beautiful Deeds/De beaux gestes	• Marie-Lynn Hammond
	Automatic Pilot	• Erika Ritter
1985-1986	Einstein	• Gabriel Emmanuel
	Fool For Love	Sam Shepard
	One in a Million	T. H. Hatte
	Garrison's Garage	• Ted Johns
	The Last Doors' Bootleg	• Alan Williams
1986-1987	The Double Bass	Patrick Süskind
	We Can't Pay? We Won't Pay!	Dario Fo
	Salt Water Moon	• David French
	Henry V	William Shakespeare
	Life After Hockey	• Kenneth Brown
1987-1988	The Rez Sisters	•• Tomson Highway
	Letter From Wingfield Farm	• Dan Needles

	Loot	Joe Orton
	The Unseen Hand/Killer's Head	Sam Shepard
	The Club	Eve Merriam
1988-1989	Frankie & Johnny in the Clair De Lune	Terrence McNally
	When That I Was	John Mortimer & Edward Atienza
	Life Skills	• David King
	A Walk In The Woods	Lee Blessing
	Frankenstein: Playing With Fire	Barbara Fields
1989-1990	Kiss of the Spiderwoman	Manuel Puig
	The Glass Menagerie	Tennessee Williams
	Beautiful Lake Winnipeg	•• Maureen Hunter
	Driving Miss Daisy	Alfred Uhry
	The Dragons' Trilogy	• Théâtre Repère
1990-1991	Dry Lips Oughta Move To Kapuskasing	•• Tomson Highway
	Toronto, Mississippi	• Joan MacLeod
	Burn This	Lanford Wilson
	My Children! My Africa!	Athol Fugard
1991-1992	Wingfield Trilogy	• Dan Needles
	Goodnight Desdemona...	• Ann-Marie MacDonald
	The Affections of May	• Norm Foster
	Medea	Euripides
1992-1993	Unidentified Human Remains...	• Brad Fraser
	Death and the Maiden	Ariel Dorfman
	Gunmetal Blues	• Bohmler, Wentworth & Adler
	Steel Magnolias	Robert Harling
1993-1994	Lips Together, Teeth Apart	Terrence McNally
	Awful Manors	• Ronnie Burkett
	Mrs. Klein	Nickolas Wright
	The Search for Signs of Intelligent Life...	Jane Wagner
1994-1995	Fronteras Americanas (American Borders)	• Guillermo Verdecchia
	Tinka's New Dress	• Ronnie Burkett
	Poor Super Man	• Brad Fraser
	The Monument	• Colleen Wagner
1995-1996	Our Country's Good	Timberlake Wertenbaker
	Angels In America, A Gay Fantasia	Tony Kushner
	The Good Sisters (Les Belles Soeurs)	• Michel Tremblay
	Romeo and Juliet	William Shakespeare
	Lady Day at Emerson's Bar & Grill	Lanie Robertson
	Transit of Venus (Touring prod.)	•• Maureen Hunter
	Mr. A's Amazing Maze Plays	Alan Auckbourn
1996-1997	An Inspector Calls	J. B. Priestley
	True West	Sam Shepard
	Misery	Steven King, ad. Simon Moore
	None Is Too Many	• Jason Sherman
1997-1998	Quills	Doug Wright
	High Life	• Lee MacDougall
	Skylight	David Hare
	Streets of Blood	• Ronnie Burkett
1998-1999	Wit	Margaret Edson
	Cherry Docs	• David Gow
	How I Learned to Drive	Paula Vogel
	The Attic, The Pearls & Three Fine Girls	• Brewin, Cherniak, MacDonald, Palmer & Ross
1999-2000	Patience	• Jason Sherman
	Closer	Patrick Marber
	The Beauty Queen of Leenane	Martin McDonagh
	The Last Night of Ballyhoo (With WJT)	Alfred Uhry
2000-2001	The Gist	• John Krizanc
	Waiting for Godot	Samuel Beckett
	A Penny for the Guy	• Lanie Robertson
	Happy	
2001-2002	The Lost Boys	• R.H. Thomson
	The Three-Penny Opera	Kurt Weill & Bertolt Brecht
	The Blue Room	David Hare
	The Lonesome West	Martin McDonagh

MANITOBA THEATRE FOR YOUNG PEOPLE

1982-1983	The Little Beast	
	Plum Pudding	
	You're a Good Man, Charlie Brown	Charles M. Shultz, ad. Clark Gesner
	School Yard Games	• John Lazarus
	Laughing to Cry	
	Magic & the Supernatural in Shakespeare	
	Provincial Tour: Feeling Yes, Feeling No	• Dennis Foon
1983-1984	The Dream Eater	Christian Garrison
	Trummi Kaput	• Dennis Foon
	New Canadian Kid	• Dennis Foon
	Je Suis Un Ours!	• Gilles Gauthier
	How I wonder What you Are	• Robert Morgan
	Provincial Tour: Feeling Yes, Feeling No	• Dennis Foon
1984-1985	Separate Doors	
	The Little Prince	Antoine de St. Exupéry
	Alligator Pie	• Dennis Lee
	The Bittersweet Kid	• Peggy Thompson
	L'Uniak	
	Everyday Heroes	
	Provincial Tour: Feeling Yes, Feeling No	• Dennis Foon
1985-1986	Not So Dumb	• John Lazarus
	Of Mimes and Clowns	
	Alligator Pie	• Dennis Lee
	Little Victories	• Suzanne Lebeau
	Peter and The Wolf	Prokofieff, ad. • G. Whitehead
	Getting Wrecked	• Tom Walmsley
	Provincial Tour: Feeling Yes, Feeling No	• Dennis Foon
	National Tour: Of Mimes and Clowns	
1986-1987	Peacemaker	David Holeman
	The Mystery of the Oak Island Treasure	• Jim Betts
	Just So Stories	Rudyard Kipling
	Invisible Kids	• Dennis Foon
	Pigiami	
	Skin	• Dennis Foon
	Peace Project	
	Provincial Tour: Feeling Yes, Feeling No	• Dennis Foon
1987-1988	I am a Bear!	• Gilles Gauthier, trans. L. Gaboriau
	Jacob Two-Two Meets the Hooded Fang	• Mordecai Richler
	The Potato People	• Theatre Beyond Words
	Night Light	• John Lazarus
	Robinson and Crusoe	D'introna, Raviccio & Valentino
	The Oath	
	Liars	• Dennis Foon
	Provincial Tour: Feeling Yes, Feeling No	• Dennis Foon
1988-1989	Coconut Clackers	
	Clairiere	
	The Last Voyage of the Devil's Wheel	• Jim Betts
	New Canadian Kid	• Dennis Foon
	The Red Ball	
	Thin Ice	• Jim Betts & Doug Ellis
	Liars	• Dennis Foon
	Identical Islands	
	Provincial Tour: Feeling Yes, Feeling No	• Dennis Foon
1989-1990	Crying to Laugh	• John Van Burek
	Once upon a Story	
	Bedtime & Bullies	• Dennis Foon
	Square Eyes	• JoAnne James
	Comet in Moominland	Tove Jansson, ad. Whitehead, Chesney & Silverman
	Separate Development	• Sean Corbett
	Work it out	
	Mirror Game	• Dennis Foon
	Provincial Tour: Feeling Yes, Feeling No	• Dennis Foon
	Provincial tour: There is No Shame	•• David Gillies
	National Tour: Robinson & Crusoe	D'introna, Raviccio & Valentino

1990-1991	Two Weeks, Twice a Year	• Colin Thomas
	Under One Roof	• Mermaid Theatre
	No Worries	David Holman
	Moving Day	• JoAnne James
	Terre Promise	
	Mask Messengers	Faustwork Mask Theatre
	There is No Shame	•• David Gillies
	Mirror Game	• Dennis Foon
	Burt/Gil	• Suzanne Lebeau
	Provincial Tour: There is No Shame	•• David Gillies
	National tour: Robinson & Crusoe	D'introna, Raviccio & Valentino
	National Tour: Comet in Moominland	Tove Jansson
1991-1992	Serafina & the Big Cat	• David Holman
	Mur-Mur	Dynamo Circus Troupe
	The Red River Valley	•• Alf Silver
	Not So Dumb	• John Lazarus
	Singing in the Rain Forest	
	Wheelie	• Lyle Victor Albert
	Cost of Living	• Morris Panych
	National Tour: Comet in Moominland	Tove Jansson
1992-1993	Whispers in the Dark	Noël Greig
	Jest in Time	• Jest in Time Theatre
	The Secret Garden	F.H. Burnet, • ad. Paul Ledoux
	SeeSaw	• Dennis Foon
	The Power of Harriet T!	• Michael Miller
	The Servant of Two Masters	Carlo Goldoni, •• ad. Rick Skene
	National Tour: Comet in Moominland	Tove Jansson
1993-1994	Land of Trash	• Ian Tamblyn
	The Impossible Balance	• Jim Jackson
	Pinoccio	Carlo Goldoni, •• ad. David Gillies
	Suddenly Shakespeare!	Wm Shakespeare & • K. Selody
	Bill's New Frock	
	Skin	• Dennis Foon
	Desequilibre/The Challenge	• Gilbert Dupuis
	Ntl tour: SeeSaw	• Dennis Foon
1994-1995	Peter and The Wolf	Prokofieff, ad. • Graham Whitehead
	A Tale of Day and Night	• Suzanne Lebeau
	Snowflake	• Gale LaJoye
	Naomi's Road	• Joy Kogawa, • ad. Paula Wing
	Showdown	• Jamie Norris
	Comet in Moominland	Tove Jansson
	A Day at the Improv (teen series)	•• Slade & McIntyre
	Little Sister	• Joan McLeod
	Provincial Tour: Showdown	• Jamie Norris
	Ntl Tour: Comet in Moominland	Tove Jansson
1995-1996	Stuart Little	E. B. White
	Dolphin Talk	
	The Number 14	• Axis Theatre Company
	The Nightingale	• John Lazarus & John Roby
	Night Light	• John Lazarus
	Making Friends, Influencing People	
	The Book of Miracles	
	Crusoe and Friday	
1996-1997	Ice Cream Store and More	• Dennis Lee
	The Mask Messengers	Faustwork Mask Theatre
	Old Friends	• Ronnie Burkett
	I Am a Bear!	• Gilles Gauthier, trans. L. Gaboriau
	The Stupendous Adventures of Don Quixote	• André Lachance
	Toronto At Dreamer's Rock	• Drew Hayden Taylor
	Flippin' In	• Anne Chislett
	Ntl Tour: Old Friends	• Ronnie Burkett
	Acting Sun Smart	
1997-1998	The Lion, The Witch and the Wardrobe	C. S. Lewis
	Health Class (teen)	• David S. Craig & Robert Morgan
	The Potato People Double Play	• Theatre Beyond Words
	Jacob Two-Two meets the Hooded Fang	• Mordecai Richler
	Baloney!	•• Ian Ross

	Liars	• Dennis Foon
	Twelfth Night	William Shakespeare
	Saigon Water Puppet Theatre	
	Intl Tour: Old Friends	• Ronnie Burkett
1998-1999	Peacemaker	David Holeman
	Beauty Machine	• R. Bellefeuille, • trans. L. Gaboriau
	The Rememberer	Steven Dietz
	Square Eyes	• JoAnne James
	Chasing the Money	• Dennis Foon
	The Other Side of the Closet	• Edward Roy
	Borrowed Black	Ellen B. Obed, ad. Mermaid Theatre
	Ntl Tour: Old Friends	• Ronnie Burkett
1999-2000	The Story of the Little Gentleman	
	Snowflake	Gale LaJoye
	MacHomer—The Simpsons Do Macbeth	Wm Shakespeare, ad. • R. Miller
	The Hobbit	J. J. R. Tolkien, • ad. Kim Selody
	SeeSaw	• Dennis Foon
	The Servant of Two Masters	Carlo Goldoni, •• ad. Rick Skene
	Rocks	S. Nantsou & T. Lycos, • ad. K. Selody
	The Star Keeper	Theatre de l'oiel
	The Boy in the Treehouse	• Drew Hayden Taylor
	Prov Tour: SeeSaw	• Dennis Foon
	Milk Int'l festival: The Boy in the Treehouse	• Drew Hayden Taylor
	SeeSaw & The Servant of Two Masters	• Dennis Foon
2000-2001	Comet in Moominland	Tove Jansson
	New Canadian Kid	• Dennis Foon
	Dying to be Thin	• Linda Carson
	Peter Pan	J. M. Barrie, • ad. Gail Bowen
	The Number 14	• Axis Theatre Company
	Illustrated History of the Anishinabe	•• Ian Ross
	Romeo and Juliet	William Shakespeare
	Jake and Pete	Gillian Rubenstein, ad. Kim Carpenter
	Robinson & Crusoe	D'introna, Raviccio & Valentino
	MB tours: New Canadian Kid, Robinson & Crusoe, Rocks	• Foon; D'introna, Raviccio & Valentino; Nantsou & Lycos
	Showcase 2001: Comet in Moominland	Tove Jansson
	Ntl Tour: The Story of the Little Gentleman	

POPULAR THEATRE ALLIANCE

1986	Bloodknot	Athol Fugard
1987	Forget Me Not	•• Harry Rintoul
1988	This Is For You, Anna	Anna Collective
	You Strike The Woman You Strike The Rock	CCFM (South Africa)
1989	Beautiful City	• George Walker
	Women Director and Playwright Project	Co-produced with MAP
	Side Show	• Allan Lindgren
	Birth of a Dancing Star	•• Valorie Bunce
	No 1 Gem	•• Deborah O'Neil
1990	Selkirk Avenue	•• Bruce McManus
	All My Relations	• Floyd Favel
	No Place Like Home	• Shane McCabe/CCFM
1991	Life on the Line	• Steven Bush
	Everybody's Business	•• Yvette Nolan
	Scientific Americans	• John Mighton
	Fringe festival: Common Ground	Collective creation
	Ixok	Teatro Vivo of Guatemala
1992	If Betty Should Rise	•• David Demchuk
	Moonlodge	• Margo Kane
1993	Calenture	•• Bruce McManus
	Testing Ground I	Various
	The Story of the Loon	Tukak Teatret (Greenland)
	On The Wings of Change (Goldenrods)	•• Collective, ad. Rosemary De Graff
1994	A Marginal Man	•• Yvette Nolan
	Bag Babies	• Allan Stratton

	Testing Ground II	•• Various
1995	Lion in the Streets	• Judith Thompson
1996	Lonely Planet	Steven Dietz
1997	Between the Lines (touring production)	•• Scott Douglas
	Pandora's Squeezebox	•• Debbie Patterson
	Marg Szkaluba (Pissy's Wife)	• Ron Chambers
1998	Hectic	•• Margaret Sweatman
	I Don't Mind	Le Theatre Parminou CCFM

PRAIRIE THEATRE EXCHANGE

1974	The Princes Who Wanted the Moon	•• Manitoba Puppet Theatre
	Wacky and his Fuddlejig	•• Various
	Pilot TV show (CKY, MTW)	
	Don Cristobel and Miss Rosita	Puppet troupe (Lorca)
	Little Red Riding Hood	
	Quatajorg/Quatajorg Revisited	•• David King
	Let's Go (26 programs) CKY	
	Apple Butter/People Can't Help Sneezing	• James Reaney/Woods
1975	New Canadian Drivel/Finite Junction	•• David King/Confidential Exchange
	I Like Me	•• ad. Deborah Quinn
	Glooscap & The Mighty Bullfrog-Mermaid	
	Ken Fiet, the Fool	• Ken Fiet
	My World (Expectation program)	•• Collective production
	Ahtushmit (Expectation program)	Jeremy Gibson
	The West Show	• Theatre Passe Muraille
	If You're So Good, Why Are You in Saskatoon?	• 25th Street Theatre Collective
1976	Sandhills	•• David King/Confidential Exchange
	Naked on the North Shore	•• Ted Johns/Confidential Exchange
	Gabe	•• Carol Bolt/Confidential Exchange
	A Visitor From Charleston	• Erika Ritter/Confidential Exchange
	What's that got to do with the price of fish?	• Newfoundland Mummers
1977	Quiet Moments—TNT	•• ad. Deborah Quinn
	Dermot's Illustrated Ballad Book	•• B. Richardson/Confidential Exchange
	Hey, Don't Call Me Kid!	•• ad. Deborah Quinn
	Artsfare	
1978	Just Do It—Puppet Tree	Kimmelman
	An Hour of Theatre Magic with Brian Glow	•• Brian Glow
	The Mountain Show	• University of Alberta
	Stories my Grandparents Told Me—TNT	•• ad. Deborah Quinn
	Dud Shuffle—Confidential Exchange	•• Alf Silver
	More of a Family—TNT	•• Alf Silver
	A King's Breakfast of Tall Tales—TNT	Kimmelman
	The Primaries / The Snow Queen	•• Jamie Olivero
1979	Sumigadawa	Kaleidoscope
	You Know What I mean, Eh?	•• David Gillies & •• Charles Wilkins
	A Place to Call Home—Puppet Tree	Kimmelman
	Storybag II	•• Penner/Sundance
	Idiot Strings—TNT	•• Alf Silver
1980	From You to Us to You—TNT	•• Deborah Quinn
	Step Right Up Ladies and Jellybeans	• Merrytime Clown and Puppets
	Nonsensical Senses—Puppet Tree	Kimmelman
	The Great Oompah Machine	•• Jamie Olivero
	Saturday Night—TNT	•• Silver/Bleeks
	Keys—Sundance	•• Penner
	Prairie Voices—TNT	•• ad. D. Quinn & B. Richardson
	The White Raven	Theatre Sans Fil
1981	Dr. Glow's Illustrated Book or Prestidigitation	•• David Gillies, Brian Glow
	It's About Time—Puppet Tree	•• Shawn Kettner
	About Free Lands	Kaleidoscope
	Manitoba At Work—TNT	•• Deborah Quinn
	The Women of Margaret Lawrence	• Margaret Lawrence, ad. Juliana Saxton
	The Ecstasy Of Rita Joe	• George Ryga
	The Snow Queen	H.C. Anderson, •• ad. Robb Paterson
1982	You Are What You Eat—Puppet Tree	•• David Gillies

	The High School Show (Studio Company)	• Rex Deverell
	Flat Out	•• David Gillies
	The Unicorns—Kaleidoscope	• Elizabeth Gorrie
	Playwrights Development Program	
	House	•• Nick Mitchell
	221B Baker Street	•• Martin Reed
	St. Peter's Asylum,	•• William Horrocks
	Climate of the Time	•• Alf Silver
	Fields of Sorrow	•• Rosemary De Graff
	The Promised Land	•• Gordon McCall
	Leavin' the Real World Behind: 3 One-Acts	
	Babel Rap	• John Lazarus
	This Property is Condemned	
	Talk to Me Like the Rain	Tennessee Williams/Studio Company
1982-1983	Last Call—Tamanous Theatre	• Morris Panych
	New Canadian Kid	• Dennis Foon
	Beauty and the Beast	Traditional, •• ad. Robb Paterson
	Cold Comfort	• Jim Garrard
	St. Peter's Asylum	•• William Horrocks
	Straight Ahead / Blind Dancers	• Charles Tidler
1983-1984	Playing the Fool	• Alun Hibbert
	Beyond the End of Your Nose	• Patricia Henderson & Julie Slaverson
	Pinoccio	Carlo Goldoni, •• ad. David Gillies
	Drift	• Rex Deverell
	So You Think You're the Teacher?	Gilles Gauthier
	The Fighting Days	•• Wendy Lill
1984-1985	Sarah's Play	• Rex Deverell
	You Want to Be Grown up, Don't You?	• Rex Deverell
	After Baba's Funeral/Sweet and Sour Pickles	•• Ted Galay
	The Fighting Days	•• Wendy Lill
	Checkin' Out	• Kelly Rebar
	A Prairie Boy's Winter	•• M. Brooks, S. Birdsell, D. Gillies
	Section 23: The French Language Revue	•• D. Arnason, C. Dorge, G. Jean
1985-1986	The Shunning	••Patrick Friesen
	Enemy Graces	• Sharon Stearns
	Section 23: The French Language Revue	•• D. Arnason, C. Dorge, G. Jean
	A Prairie Boy's Winter	•• M. Brooks, S. Birdsell, D. Gillies
	Welcome to Hard Times: The Cultural Cabaret	•• David Arnason & Gerard Jean
	The Occupation of Heather Rose	•• Wendy Lill
1986-1987	The Primrose School District #109	•• Ted Galay
	I Met a Bully on a Hill	•• Martha Brooks, Maureen Hunter
	Fallout	• Rex Deverell
	Bandits	•• David Gillies
	The Revival'	•• Sandra Birdsell
	A Prairie Boy's Winter	•• M. Brooks, S. Birdsell, D. Gillies
	The Paper Bag Princess and Other Stories	• Robert Munsch, Irene Watts
	Schedules	•• Bruce McManus
	Dewline	•• David Arnason
1987-1988	Bordertown Cafe	• Kelly Rebar
	All Over the Map	• Kelly Rebar
	Don't Blame The Bedouins	• René-Daniel Dubois, trans. M. Kevan
	Snowsuits, Birthdays, and Giants	• Robert Munsch
	Talk to Me, Talk to Me	•• Rick Chafe & Bruce McManus
	Boiler Room Suite	• Rex Deverell
	Welcome to the NHL	•• Alan Williams
1988-1989	My Memories of You	•• Wendy Lill
	Andrew's Tree	•• Martha Brooks
	On Your Marks	• Robert Clinton
	The Third Ascent	• Frank Moher
	You Can Do It If You Try!	•• David Gillies
	The Chinese Man Said Goodbye	•• Bruce McManus
	The Mail Order Bride	• Robert Clinton
	Snowsuits, Birthdays, and Giants	• Robert Munsch
1989-1990	Village of Idiots	• John Lazarus
(Portage Place)	Lloyd's Prayer	Kevin Kling
	A Prairie Boy's Winter	•• M. Brooks, S. Birdsell, D. Gillies

	The General	• Robert Morgan
	Section 23: The sequel	•• Arnason, Smith, Dorge & Jean
	Odd Jobs	• Frank Moher
	Cruel Tears	• K. Mitchell, Humphrey & Dumptrucks
	Murmel, Murmel, Mortimer, Munsch	• R. Munsch, •• adapted by K. Selody
1990-1991	The Passion of Narcisse Mondoux	• Gratien Gélinas, • trans. L Gaboriau
	The Fighting Days	•• Wendy Lill
	Sisters	•• Wendy Lill
	Brian Goes Hawaiian (second stage)	• Brian Linds
	More Munsch	• R. Munsch, • adapted by K. McCaw
	Jelly Belly makes Garbage Delight of Alligator Pie	• Dennis Lee, • adapted by K. Selody
	A Day at the Beach	•• The Easy T's
	Amigo's Blue Guitar	• Joan McLeod
	A Flush of Tories	• Allan Stratton
1991-1992	Selkirk Avenue	•• Bruce McManus
	Cornflower Blue	• Kelly Rebar
	Love You Forever and Other Stories	• R. Munsch, •• adapted by K. McCaw
	The Grimm Sisters	•• Tannis Kowalchuk, Lora Schroeder
	On the Go	•• Canadian Content
	Lisa	•• Carol Matas, Per Brask
	The Raft	•• Patrick Friesen
	The End of The World Romance	• Sean Dixon
1992-1993	The Soft Eclipse	• Connie Gault
	Dog and Crow	• Michael Springate
	Let's Do Munsch	• R. Munsch, adapted by B. Poggemiller
	Hansel and Gretel	Manitoba Opera
	Waiting for the Sun	•• N. Jual, S. Kettner, J. Olivero
	Annie and the Old One	• Adapted by Tomson Highway
	Thirteen Hands	•• Carol Shields
	The Stone Angel	•• M. Lawrence, • adapted by J.W. Nichol
Second Stage		
	Gulliver's travels	SIOP collective
	Napalm, the buffoon	• David Craig
	Mermaid in Love / Mary Medusa	•• Shawna Dempsey & Lorri Millan
	Monkey Trials II	•• K. Knight, R. Jenkins, B. Drader
1993-1994	Tin Can Cathedral	•• Nick Mitchell
	Marilyn Mudrow—Odessa (Ukrainian)	Nikolai Koljada
	Marilyn Mudrow (English)	N. Koljada, •• trans. by Arnason & Hryn
	The Snow Queen	Anderson, •• ad. Anderson & Schroeder
	Bondagers	Sue Glover
	Fox	•• Margaret Sweatman
Second Stage		
	Mump & Smoot	• Michael Kennard, John Turner
	Man on the Moon, Woman on the Pill	• Christine Taylor
	The Dark Room	The New Theatre Company
	Moonlight Sonata	••Martha Brooks
	A Promise is a Promise	• Robert Munsch & Michael Kusugak
1994-1995	Pretty Blue	• Ron Chambers
	The Stone Angel	•Margaret Lawrence, •• ad. J. W. Nichol
	InQuest	•• William Harrar
	Cinderella Stories	•• Adapted by Anderson & Schroeder
	Ming Lo Moves the Mountain	A. Lobel, •• adapted by B. Poggemiller
	All Fall Down	• Wendy Lill
	Fashion Power Guilt and the Charity…	•• Carol & Catherine Shields
Second Stage		
	Tough!	• George F. Walker
	The Water Hen	Stanislaw Ignacy Witkewiicz
	Washing Spider Out	•• Ross McMillan/with Adhere & Deny
	Noah's Arc	Magdelena Kazubowska
1995-1996	Someone Who'll Watch Over Me	Frank McGuinness
	Playboy of the West Indies	Mustapha Matura
	The League of Nathans (with WJT)	• Jason Sherman
	fareWel	•• Ian Ross
	A Prairie Boy's Winter	•• M. Brooks, S. Birdsell, D. Gillies
	Munsch—A Whole Buncha Munsch	• R. Munsch, • adapted by K. McCaw
Second Stage		
	Heart of a Dog	• Robert Astle

1996-1997	Crackpot	•• Adele Wiseman, • adapted by R. Wyatt
	My Fair Lady	Lerner & Lowe
	2 Pianos, 4 hands	• Ted Dykstra & Richard Greenblatt
	Marvin's Room	Scott McPherson
	Supreme Dream	• Frank Moher, Rhonda Trodd
	Little Monster	• Jasmine Dubé, trans. M. Labonté
	Zeke and the Indoor Plants	• Ruth Smillie
1997-1998	Mom's the Word	• Carson, Daum, Kelly, Nichol, Pollard, Williams
	Vigil	• Morris Panych
	Jacques Brel is Alive and Well...	E. Blau & M. Shuman, music by Brel
	A Doll's House	H. Ibsen, •• adapted by B. McManus
	Painting Churches	Tina Howe
	Tree house	Martha Johnson, Mark Gane
	Head A Tete	• David S. Craig, Robert Morgan
1998-1999	Still The Night	• Theresa Tova
	The Norbals	•• Brian Drader
	Love and Anger	• George F. Walker
	Speak	• Greg Nelson
	The Paper Bag Princess and Other Stories	• Robert Munsch
	Old Wicked Songs	Jon Marans
1999-2000	For the Pleasure of Seeing Her Again	• Michel Tremblay, • trans. L. Gaboriau
	Godspell	J-M. Tebelak & S. Schwartz
	Love You Forever & More	• Robert Munsch
	Mom, Dad, I'm Living With a White Girl	• Marty Chan
	15 Seconds	• François Archembault
	Walking On Water	• Dave Carley
2000-2001	Salt-Water Moon	• David French
	The Importance of Being Earnest	Oscar Wilde
	Much Munsch	• Robert Munsch
	Kilt	• Jonathan Wilson
	Side by Side by Sondheim	Sondheim, Sherrin
	The Gap	•• Ian Ross
2001-2002	A Room of One's Own	Virginia Woolf, ad. Patrick Garland
	The Glass Menagerie	Tennessee Williams
	Joni Mitchell: River	• Joni Mitchell, ad. Allen MacInnis
	The Rez Sisters	•• Tomson Highway
	Something Drastic	• Colleen Curran
	A Promise is a Promise	• Munsch & Kusugak, ad. Poggemiller

RAINBOW STAGE

1955	Brigadoon	Lerner & Lowe
1956	The Wizard of Oz	L. Frank Baum, Teitjens & Sloane
	Annie Get Your Gun & Pop Concert	Irving Berlin, H & D Fields
	Our Town & August 8th Pop Concert	Thornton Wilder
	Kiss Me Kate	Cole Porter, S. & B. Spewack
1957	Pot O' Gold Variety Show	Jack Phillips
	I Remember Mama	John Van Druten
	Do You Remember	
	Gentlemen Prefer Blondes	Anita Loos & John Emerson
	Pitfalls of Pauline	
	Chu Chin Chow	Frederick Norton & Oscar Ashke
1958	Hell's A Poppin'	
	The King and I	Rogers & Hammerstein
1959	Guys and Dolls	Frank Loesser & Abe Burrows
	Showboat	Jerome Kern & Oscar Hammerstein
	The Wizard of Oz	L. Frank Baum, Teitjens & Sloane
1960	The Pajama Game	Adler, Ross, Abbot & Bissel
	Carousel	Rogers & Hammerstein
	Damn Yankees!	Adler, Ross, Abbot & Wallop
1961	Most Happy Fella	Frank Wesser
	High Button Shoes	Jule Styne & Sammy Cahn
	South Pacific	Rogers & Hammerstein
1962	The Music Man	Meredith Wilson

	The Student Prince	Sigmund Romberg
	Oklahoma!	Rogers & Hammerstein
1963	Bye Bye Birdie	Stewart, Strouse, Adams
	West Side Story	Bernstein, Laurents, & Sondheim
	The King and I	Rogers & Hammerstein
1964	Sound of Music	Rogers & Hammerstein
	Anything Goes	Porter, Wodehouse, Bolton
	Finian's Rainbow	Burton Lane/Y. Harburg
	Gypsy	Sondheim, Styne, Laurents
1965	Guys and Dolls	Frank Loesser & Abe Burrows
	Can Can	Cole Porter
	Annie Get Your Gun	Irving Berlin, H & B Fields
	Flower Drum Song	Rogers & Hammerstein
1966	My Fair Lady	Lerner & Lowe
	South Pacific	Rogers & Hammerstein
	1967	Oliver!
	Sound of Music	Rogers & Hammerstein
1968	Carnival	Merrill, Stewart, Deutch
	Music Man	Meredith Wilson
1969	Funny Girl	Isobel Lennert & Bob Merrill
	The King and I	Rogers & Hammerstein
1970	Wizard of Oz	L. Frank Baum, Teitjens & Sloane
	Hello Dolly!	Stewart, Wilder, Herman
1971	Peter Pan	J. M. Barrie
	Fiddler on the Roof	Bock, Harnick & Stein
1972	Cinderella	Rogers & Hammerstein
	Mame	J. Lawrence, R.E. Lee, Herman
1973	Where's Charlie	George Abbot & Frank Loesser
	Annie Get Your Gun	Irving Berlin, H & B Fields
1974	Sound of Music	Rogers & Hammerstein
	No, No, Nanette	Vincent Yeomans
1975	My Fair Lady	Lerner & Lowe
1976	Oklahoma!	Rogers & Hammerstein
	Brigadoon	Lerner & Lowe
1977	Irene	Montgomery, Tierney, McCarthy
	Fiddler on the Roof	Bock, Harnick & Stein
1978	Oliver!	Lionel Bart
	Hello, Dolly!	Stewart, Wilder, Herman
1979	The King and I	Rogers & Hammerstein
	The Desert Song	Romberg & Hammerstein
	Over the Rainbow 25th Anniversary	
1980	Guys & Dolls	F. Loesser, A. Burrows, J. Swerling
	Showboat	Jerome Kern & Oscar Hammerstein
1981	South Pacific	Rogers & Hammerstein
	Funny Girl	Isobel Lennert & Bob Merrill
1982	The Pajama Game	Adler, Ross, Abbot & Bissel
	The Music Man	Meredith Wilson
1983	The Pirates of Penzance	Gilbert & Sullivan
	Kiss Me Kate	Cole Porter, S. & B. Spewack
1984	Kismet	Lederer, Davis, Wright, & Forbes
	Fiddler on the Roof	Bock, Harnick & Stein
1985	H.M.S. Pinafore	Gilbert & Sullivan
	Mame	J. Lawrence, R. E. Lee, Herman
1986	The Student Prince	Sigmund Romberg
	The Sound of Music	Rogers & Hammerstein
1987	My Fair Lady	Lerner & Lowe
	Annie	Charnin, Strouse, Meehan
1987-198	Anne of Green Gables (at Playhouse)	• Harron, Campbell, Campbell & Moore
1988	Oliver!	Lionel Bart
	Sweet Charity	Cy Coleman & Dorothy Fields

1989	Carousel Peter Pan	Rogers & Hammerstein J. M. Barrie
1990	Anything Goes Say It With Music Cinderella	Porter, Wodehouse, Bolton Irving Berlin
1991	A Funny Thing Happened on the Way... Sondheim The Wizard of Oz	Shevelove, Gelbart, Susan Cox L. Frank Baum, Teitjens & Sloane
1992	The Wizard of Oz Guys & Dolls	L. Frank Baum, Teitjens & Sloane F. Loesser, A. Burrows, J. Swerling
1993	Fiddler on the Roof	Bock, Harnick & Stein
1994	Brigadoon Damn Yankees!	Lerner & Lowe Adler, Ross, Abbot & Wallop
1995	Oklahoma!	Rogers & Hammerstein
1996	Sound of Music	Rogers & Hammerstein
1997	South Pacific	Rogers & Hammerstein
1998	Music Man	Meredith Wilson
1999	Crazy for You	Gershwin, Gershwin & Ludwig
2000	Singin' in the Rain (Pantages) 42nd Street	Betty Comdon & Mark Green Michael Stewart & Mark Bramble
2001	A Chorus Line (Pantages) Big, the Musical	Kirkwood, Dante, Kleban & Hamlisch Richard Maltby, Jr. & David Shire

SHAKESPEARE IN THE RUINS

1994	Romeo and Juliet	William Shakespeare
1995	A Midsummer Night's Dream	William Shakespeare
1996	Macbeth	William Shakespeare
1997	Twelfth Night	William Shakespeare
1998	Much Ado About Nothing	William Shakespeare
1999	Richard III	William Shakespeare
2000	Love's Labour's Lost Odyssey: The Islands	William Shakespeare •• Rick Chafe
2001	The Tempest Odyssey: The Islands	William Shakespeare •• Rick Chafe
2002	Threepenny Opera Hamlet	Bertolt Brecht William Shakespeare

THEATRE PROJECTS MANITOBA

1990-1991	Albertine in Five Times Tickle Trunk/Why the Dishes Can't Wait...	• Michel Tremblay •• Ellen Peterson/David Demchuk
1991-1992	To Kill The Weatherman The Resurrection of Joseph Frum Jewel/Job's Wife The Best of Cockroach	•• Michael Nathanson •• Vern Theissen • Joan McLeod /•• Yvette Nolan •• Alan Williams
1992-1993	Brave Hearts Ce Weekend là Jesus Does Laundry Too See Bob Run	•• Harry Rintoul •• Rick Skene •• Sharon Bajer • Daniel MacIvor
1993-1994	My Old Man Live With It Etienne	•• James Durham •• Elise Moore •• Steve McIntyre
1994-1995	The Real World? Sophie and The Wiener Man The Fruit Machine	• Michel Tremblay •• Carolyn Gray •• Brian Drader
1995-1996	Short Shots (w/ MAP) The Harrowing (w/ Adhere & Deny) Jack of Hearts	•• Various •• Scott Douglas •• Harry Rintoul
1996-1997	Short Shots (w/ MAP) The Tomato King	•• Various •• Laurie Block

1997-1998	Bubba and the Peter Eater (workshop read)	•• Brian Drader
	Short Shots '98	
	Never, Never Mind, Kurt Kurt Cobain	•• Dale Lakevold
1998-1999	Short Shots	
	I do... Do You	•• Dennis Trochim
1999-2000	L-Love's Body/Ordinary Days	•• Dale Lakevold/Bruce McManus
2000-2001	Cruel and Unusual Punishment	•• James Durham
	Flux	•• Margaret Sweatman/Glenn Buhr
2001-2002	PROK	•• Brian Drader
	Hot Shorts	•• Various
	The Colour of Vowels	Jaik Josephson

WINNIPEG JEWISH THEATRE

1987-1988	Hannah Senesh	David Schechter
	Today I Am A Fountain Pen	Israel Horowitz
1988-1989	Lies My Father Told Me	• Ted Allan
	A Shayna Maidel	Barbara Lebow
1989-1990	Cantorial	Ira Levin
	The Golden Land	Zalmen Mlotek & Moishe Rosenfeld
1990-1991	Talley's Folly	Lanford Wilson
	Crossing Delancey	Susan Sandler
1991-1992	Nehemia Persoff's Sholem Aleichem	
	The Rothschilds	J. Bock, S. Harnick & S. Yellen
1992-1993	Shmulnik's Waltz	Allan Knee
	The Escape	•• Carol Matas
	Substance of Fire	Jon Robin Baitz
1993-1994	Chutzpah A Go-Go	David Gail & Randy Vancourt
	The Diary of Anne Frank	F. Goodrich & A. Hackett
1994-1995	The Cemetery Club	Ivan Menchell
	The Always Prayer Shawl	•• Sheldon Oberman
	Beau Jest	James Sherman
1995-1996	Kindertransport	Diane Samuels/Persephone co-prod
	The League of Nathans	• Jason Sherman/PTE co-prod
	Family Secrets	Sherry Glaser & Greg Howells
1996-1997	Too Jewish	Avi Hoffman
	10 X 10 by 10 Canadian Female Playwrights	
	None is Too Many	• Jason Sherman/Warehouse co-prod
1997-1998	Cecil And Cleopaytra	• Dan Libman
	Anne Frank and Me	Cherie Bennett
	That's Life!	Conceived by Helen Butleroff
1998-1999	Make Yourself At Home	Yitzhak Meshel
	The Immigrant	Mark Harelik
	Diary of a Skokie Girl	Caryn Bark
	Ghetto Tango	Zalmen Mlotek & Adrienne Cooper
	Social Security	Andrew Bergman
1999-2000	Visiting Mr. Green	Jeff Baron
	Cote Saint Joe	• Dan Libman
	Last Night of Ballyhoo (With MTC)	Alfred Urhy
2000-2001	Door to Door	• James Sherman
	Hello Muddah, Hello Fadduh!	A. Sherman, ad. Krausz & Bernstein
	The Waltonsteins	• Frannie Sheridan
	The Gathering	Arje Shaw
2001-2002	Sibs	• Richard Greenblatt & Diane Flacks
	Via Dolorosa	David Hare
	Victoria	• Dulcinea Langfelder & Eric Gingras
	Funny Girl	Lennert, Styne, & Merrill

Endnotes

1. One account gives the year as 1866, another 1868, and a third puts it in the 1870s. However, J. J. Hargrave's memoir, *Red River,* published in 1871, gives an eyewitness account and dates the event 1867.

2. Oscar G. Brockett's 1991 *History of the Theatre,* part of the curriculum at the University of Winnipeg, contains no index entry for Manitoba, or for that matter Canada, Michel Tremblay, Kate Reid, or the revered John Hirsch.

Felicia Hardison Londré's *The History of World Theater From the English Restoration to the Present* (Continuum, 1999) similarly has no index entries for Manitoba, John Hirsch, Robert Lepage, or George F. Walker. It does have index entries for Canadian theatre, skipping from garrison theatre to the Stratford Festival, with a passing mention of the Manitoba Theatre Centre (as an outgrowth of Stratford). A cursory discussion of important Canadian theatre artists leaves Manitoba out entirely.

The *Cassell Companion to the Theatre* describes itself as "an all-encompassing companion to the theatre." Other than a reference to the Stratford Festival, Canada does not seem to exist: no entry for Ryga, Gelinas, Michel Tremblay, Robert Lepage, Tomson Highway, George F. Walker, Manitoba, or even Canada.

3. *English Canadian Theatre,* by Benson and Connoly (Oxford Press, 1987) discusses Calgary and Saskatchewan playwriting at length, but gives Manitoba playwrights only a passing mention, and no mention at all after World War II.

The same book cites the Manitoba Theatre Centre only in a discussion of regional theatre's lack of commitment to Canadian plays.

Contemporary Canadian Theatre: New World Vision edited by Anton Wagner (Simon & Pierre, 1985) provides some interesting perspectives. The article on alternative theatre does not mention Manitoba. The article on playwrights does not mention Manitoba playwrights. The article on the Prairie provinces extols prairie playwrights without mentioning one from Manitoba, and it mentions Prairie Theatre Exchange only in passing. The article on training does not mention either the University of Winnipeg or Manitoba as ones that would "stand out for the quality of students who make it to the profession."

In *Love and Whisky* (McClelland & Stewart, 1973), Betty Lee presents a historical sketch of theatre development in Canada. She skips from Ontario to British Columbia.

In *Just the High Points? A Canadian Theatre Chronology* that Ric Knowles prepared for the Playwrights' Union of Canada, there are 169 citations. Nine of these pertain to Manitoba. The Manitoba Theatre Centre receives no mention after its opening. Another instance of central-Canadian myopia? Maybe, but Newfoundland has 12 entries, Alberta and BC both have 15, and the Yukon and Northwest Territories split five between them. One Manitoba entry, about Manitoba native Tomson Highway, concerns his premiere in Toronto. If you deduct that entry, Manitoba has fewer than Nova Scotia. Primus is the only Manitoba entry deemed worthy of two mentions.

4. *The Centennial History of Manitoba* by James A. Jackson, published jointly by the Manitoba Historical Society and McClelland and Stewart, does not mention theatre at all. No entry exists for the Manitoba Theatre Centre, the Walker Theatre, Pantages, Harriet Walker, Lady Tupper, John Hirsch or Tom Hendry.

Margaret McWilliams' 1926 *Manitoba Milestones* (J. M. Dent & Sons) mentions that in the late 19th century amateur theatricals were a diversion. Her "Milestones" entry does not mention theatre at all.

W. L. Morton's *Manitoba: A History* (University of Toronto Press, 1957) gives theatre more attention than other texts. He discusses the lively professional theatre scene early in the 20th century, and laments "that the great days of the theatre were over would not have been so sad, had local talent and local effort been strong enough to take the place of professional productions."

Although he was part owner of the building in which Winnipeg's first theatre performance took place, Alexander Begg does not mention performances there in the journal he kept in 1868-70, although there were certainly performances during that time. He describes sermons he heard in churches of various denominations, balls, and other festivities, but theatre does not seem to him to be worthy of mention. (He does mention the theatre in his volume *Ten Years in Winnipeg*, Times Printing and Publishing, 1879)

Ed Russenholt's *The Heart of the Continent* (MacFarlane Communications Services, 1968), mentions theatre only in passing.

Gerald Friesen's 1987 *The Canadian Prairies: A History* contains only passing mention of theatre.

5. *My Dear Maggie...* by William Wallace, Canadian Plains Research Centre, University of Regina, 1981.

6. *Manitoba Milestones,* by Margaret McWilliams, 1926.

7. *Chippewa Customs*, by Frances Densmore, Minnesota Historical Society Press, 1979.

8. A vestige of this trade route competition today is the port of Churchill's struggle to maintain itself as a grain shipping terminus in competition with the St. Lawrence Seaway. The limited shipping season at Churchill works against it, but the shorter distance (and lower transport costs) work in its favour.

9. *Cambridge Guide to Theatre*, Cambridge University Press, 1992.

10. *My Dear Maggie...* by William Wallace, Canadian Plains Research Centre, University of Regina, 1981.

11. Ibid., introduction.

12. As Cecil Rhodes (1853-1902) said: "Remember that you are an Englishman, and have consequently won first prize in the lottery of life."

13. *Theatre History in Canada*, Spring, 1983.

14. *The Marx Brothers Scrapbook,* by Richard J. Anobile, Darien House, 1973.

15. Nancy Pyper collection, University of Manitoba Achives.

16. *The History of Prairie Theatre* by E. Ross Stewart, Simon & Pierre, 1984.

17. *The W.O. Mitchell Papers: Biocritical Essay,* by Catherine McLay, University of Calgary Press, 1986.

18. *Theatre History in Canada*, Spring/Fall 1982.

19. No written script exists for this play. It is likely that McClung delivered it from memory, since she had heard Roblin give his speech only the day before. Slightly different versions exist in Nellie McClung's autobiographical work, *The Stream Runs Fast*, and in her Novel *Purple Spring,* which she wrote much earlier and which she says is historically accurate regarding this episode. *The Spring Runs Fast* book also quotes *The Free Press* and *Telegram* accounts, which also differ slightly. The version in this book comes from the Parks Canada website, since it is more complete and flows better.

20. McClung gives a good example of the disposable attitude many managers had towards labour during this period. In *The Stream Runs Fast* she describes dragging Premier Rodmond Roblin through a sweatshop. "At one machine a girl worked with a bandaged hand, a badly hurt hand and a very dirty bandage. At another a girl coughed almost continuously." McClung asked the manager why the girl did not get a few days off work with pay to get better. He replied, "The company is not a charitable institution and makes no provision for anything like that. If the girl is sick, she can always quit."

21. Reprinted in *Theatre History in Canada,* edited by Dan Rubin, Oxford University Press, 1996.

22. As late as 1983 the *Oxford Companion to Canadian Literature* did not mention *Eight Men Speak* (published in 1934), as Robin Mathews points out in *Canadian Poetry,* vol 16, Spring/Summer 1985. In April of 2001, the on-line *Canadian Theatre Encyclopedia* did not have a listing for *Eight Men Speak,* Toby Ryan, E. Cecil-Smith, Workers' Theatre, or Theatre of Action.

23. From *A History of the Black Hole Theatre Company and Theatre at the University of Manitoba 1914-89,* web site compiled by Sioban Turner, Wayne Watson, Deanna Schuerbeke Anne-Marie McGinn and Sean Dillon, April 1994.

24. Ibid.

25. Ibid.

26. Ibid.

27. *The W.O. Mitchell Papers: Biocritical Essay,* by Catherine McLay, University of Calgary Press, 1986. This was a particularly outstanding period in the University of Manitoba's history. It was then the third-largest university in Canada, and besides Mitchell, Tween and Morris (Evelyn), it also had among its student body parliamentarian and social activist Stanley Knowles, world-renowned thinker and communications theorist Marshall McLuhan, and historian W.L. Morton.

28. Pyper collection, University of Manitoba Archives.

29. Judith Evelyn file in the *Winnipeg Tribune* collection, University of Manitoba Archives.

30. Ibid.

31. From *A History of the Black Hole Theatre Company and Theatre at the University of Manitoba, 1914-89.*

32. Ibid.

33. Ibid.

34. Ibid.

35. In 1966, students at Kelvin High School began to enjoy the benefits of having Tom Dickens teach them English and History. Those fortunate enough to be in his class that first year got to enjoy not only the depth and breadth of his education, but to learn how their society affected someone completely foreign to it. One day he confessed to the class that our market-driven economy had finally seduced him. "I found myself picking up a tube of Colgate toothpaste," he said, "not because it was a good price, or because I knew it was a good product, but because that Ward Cornell on the commercials seemed like such a pleasant fellow." It is one thing to read about how mass marketing affects people. It is quite another to see it happen before your eyes.

36. From *Standing Naked in the Wings,* collected by Linda Mason Green and Tedde Moore, Oxford University Press, 1997.

37. Reprinted in *Theatre History in Canada,* edited by Dan Rubin, Oxford University Press, 1996.

38. Introduction, *Whittaker's Theatre,* pub. The Whittaker Project, 1985.

39. Prairie Theatre Exchange collection, University of Manitoba Archives.

40. Ibid.

41. "Training for Independence," by Rick Skene, *Canadian Theatre Review*, #66, Spring 1991.

42. "Entering into Intelligent Chaos," by Garth Buchholz, *Theatrum*, #39, Summer 1994.

43. *Bastards and Boneheads,* by Will Ferguson, Douglas & McIntyre, 1999.

44. "Glimpses: Recent Productions That Caught Our Eye," by Kevin Longfield, *Theatrum*, #28, April/May 1992.

45. Ibid.

46. *Winnipeg Free Press*, December 16, 1993.

47. *Theatrum,* "Canadian Plays in Britain," by Malcolm Page, February/March, 1994.

Selected Bibliography

Books

Benson and Conolly. *English Canadian Theatre.* Toronto: Oxford Press, 1987.

Anobile, Richard J. *The Marx Brothers Scrapbook.* New York: Darien House, 1973.

Banham, Martin, Ed. *Cambridge Guide to Theatre.* Cambridge; New York: Cambridge University Press, 1992.

Bartlett, John. *Familiar Quotations.* Boston; Toronto: Little, Brown, 1955.

Begg, Alexander. *Begg's Journal and Other Papers.* Toronto: The Champlain Society, 1956.

Begg, Alexander. *Ten Years in Winnipeg.* Winnipeg: Times Printing and Publishing, 1879.

Brockett, Oscar. *History of the Theatre.* Boston: Allyn & Bacon, 1991.

Bryden, Ronald, Ed. *Whittaker's Theatre.* Greenbank, On: The Whittaker Project, 1985.

Bumsted, J. M. *Dictionary of Manitoba Biography.* Winnipeg: University of Manitoba Press, 1999.

Careless & Brown. *The Canadians: 1867-1967.* Toronto: Grolier, 1967.

Chafe, J. W. *Extraordinary Tales From Early Manitoba.* Toronto: McClelland & Stewart and Manitoba Historical Society, 1973.

Columbo, John Robert. *Columbo's Concise Canadian Quotations.* Edmonton: Hurtig, 1976.

Densmore, Frances. *Chippewa Customs.* Saint Paul: Minnesota Historical Society Press, 1979.

Earl, Marjorie, Ed. *Torch on the Prairies.* Winnipeg: Winnipeg Press Club, 1988.

Edwards, Murray D. *A Stage in Our Past.* Toronto: University of Toronto Press, 1968.

Esselin, Martin, Ed., *Illustrated Encyclopedia of World Theatre.* London: Thames and Hudson, 1977.

Ferguson, Will. *Bastards and Boneheads.* Vancouver: Douglas & McIntyre, 1999.

Ford, Arthur R. *As the World Wags On.* Toronto: Ryerson Press, 1950.

Friesen, Gerald. *The Canadian Prairies: A History.* Toronto: University of Toronto Press, 1987.

Garebian, Keith. *A Well-bred Muse.* Oakville: Mosaic Press, 1991.

Hargrave, J.J. *Red River.* Montreal: Standard, 1871.

Harvey, Ruth. *Curtain Time*. Boston: Houghton Mifflin, 1949.

Healy, William. *Women of Red River*. Winnipeg: Women's Canadian Club, 1923.

Jackson, James A. *The Centennial History of Manitoba*. Toronto: Manitoba Historical Society and McClelland and Stewart, 1970.

Knowles, Ric. *Just the High Points? A Canadian Theatre Chronology*. Toronto: Playwrights Union of Canada, 2000.

Lee, Betty. *Love and Whisky*. Toronto: McClelland and Stewart, 1973.

Linda Mason Green and Tedde Moore, Ed. *Standing Naked in the Wings*. Toronto: Oxford University Press, 1997.

Londré, Felicia Hardison. *The History of World Theater from the English Restoration to the Present*. New York: Continuum, 1999.

Market House Books Staff (Editor). *Cassell Companion to the Theatre*. London: Market House Books, 2000.

McClung. Nellie. *Purple Springs*. Toronto: Ryerson Press, 1926.

McClung, Nellie. *The Stream Runs Fast*. Toronto: T. Allen, 1945.

McMillan, Ala D. *Native Peoples and Cultures of Canada*. Vancouver: Douglas & McIntyre, 1995.

McWilliams, Margaret. *Manitoba Milestones*. Toronto: J. M. Dent & Sons, 1926.

Morgan, Murray C. *Skid Road*. Seattle: Viking Press, 1960.

Morton, W. L. *Manitoba: A History*. Toronto: University of Toronto Press, 1957.

Paterson, Edith. *Tales of Early Manitoba*. Winnipeg: Canadian News, 1970.

Paterson, Edith. *Tales of the Early West*. Winnipeg: Canadian News, 1978.

Pearson, Lester B. *Mike: The Memoirs of the Rt. Hon. Lester B. Pearson, Volume 1*. Toronto: University of Toronto Press, 1972.

Pearson, Lester B. Ed. John A. Munro & Alex I Inglis. *Mike, the Memoirs of the Rt. Hon. Lester B. Pearson, Volume 3*. Toronto: University of Toronto Press, 1975.

Pettipas, Leo. *Aboriginal Migrations*. Winnipeg: Manitoba Museum of Man and Nature, 1996.

Playwrights Union of Canada. *Catalogue of Canadian Plays*. Toronto: Playwrights Union of Canada, 2000, 2001.

Ross, Alexander. *The Red River Settlement*. London: Repr. Hurtig, 1972.

Rubin, Don. *Theatre History in Canada*. Toronto: Oxford University Press, 1996.

Russenholt, Ed. *The Heart of the Continent*. Winnipeg: MacFarlane Communications Services, 1968.

Ryan, Toby Gordon. *Stage Left*. Toronto: York University, 1981.

Spencer, John Peter. *The History and Contribution of the Manitoba Theatre Workshop/ Prairie Theatre Exchange* (Doctoral Thesis). New York: New York University, 1983.

St. George Stubbs, Lewis. *A Majority Of One.* Winnipeg: Queenston House, 1983.

Stewart, E. Ross. *The History of Prairie Theatre.* Toronto: Simon & Pierre, 1984.

Taylor, John Russel. *The Penguin Dictionary of the Theatre.* Middlesex; New York: Penguin, 1970.

Turner, Sioban, Watson, Wayne, Schuerbeke, Deanna, McGinn, Anne-Marie and Dillon, Sean. *A History of the Black Hole Theatre Company and Theatre at the University of Manitoba, 1914-89.* Winnipeg: Black Hole web site, 1994.

Wagner, Anton. *Contemporary Canadian Theatre: New World Vision.* Toronto: Simon & Pierre, 1985.

Wallace, William. *My Dear Maggie...* Regina: Canadian Plains Research Centre, University of Regina, 1981.

Watiuk, Judy. *Stages: Prairie Theatre Exchange Celebrates 25 Years.* Winnipeg: WriteStuff Publishing, 1998.

Wilkins, Charles. *The Winnipeg Book.* Toronto: Key Porter, 1984.

Yates, Sarah. *Manitoba Theatre Centre: The First 20 Years.* Winnipeg: Manitoba Theatre Centre, 1978.

Articles

Arrell, Douglas. "Teaching Aesthetics to Artists." *American Society for Aesthetics Website*: http://www.aesthetics-online.org/ideas/arrell.html, undated.

Arrell, Douglas. "Paradigm Shifts at the Box Office." *Canadian Theatre Review*, Spring, 1991.

Blanchard, Sharon. "Esse Ljungh and the Winnipeg Little Theatre." *Theatre Research in Canada*, Fall 1984.

Brask, Per. "Seizing the Centre." *Canadian Theatre Review*, Spring, 1991.

Buchholz, Garth. "Entering into Intelligent Chaos." *Theatrum*, Summer, 1994.

Budnick, Carol. "Theatre on the Frontier: Winnipeg in the 1880s." *Theatre History in Canada*, Spring, 1983.

Byrd, Kim. *Theatre History in Canada*, Spring/Fall, 1982.

Douglas, John. "Ukrainian Leaders Accuse Minister of Ignoring the Past." *Winnipeg Free Press*, September 23, 1988.

Johnson, Chris. "Wooing Winnipeg: The Manitoba Theatre Centre and the Community." *Canadian Theatre Review*, Spring, 1991.

Johnson, Chris. "Working From the Child's Perspective." *Canadian Theatre Review*, Spring, 1985.

Longfield, Kevin. "Review: Jewel/Job's Wife." *Theatrum*, April/May 1992.

MacLennan, Mary Jane. "Road Show Draws Raves." *Winnipeg Sun*, September 22, 1988.

McLay, Catherine. "The W.O. Mitchell Papers: Biocritical Essay." University of Calgary Press, 1986.

Page, Malcolm. "Canadian Plays in Britain." *Theatrum*, February/March, 1994.

Prokosh, Kevin. "Review: i dreamed i was a baseball card." *Winnipeg Free Press*, July 17, 1994.

Prokosh, Kevin. "Transit of Venus Stunning in England." *Winnipeg Free Press*, December 16, 1993.

Skene, Reg. "Theatre on the Prairies: An Introduction." *Canadian Theatre Review*, Spring, 1985.

Skene, Rick. "Training for Independence." *Canadian Theatre Review*, Spring, 1991.

Templeman, Staff Sgt. Jack. "History of the Winnipeg Police." *City of Winnipeg Web Site*, 2000.

Walker, Morley, "Arts and the Free Press." *Winnipeg Free Press*, 1997.

Index

Kevin Longfield was born in Winnipeg in 1950, and has lived all his life there except for six years in Ottawa in the 70s. He earned a degree in mechanical engineering and worked in manufacturing engineering before starting a career in writing and theatre. A degree in theatre from the University of Winnipeg followed in 1993.

From 1990 to 1995 he was Winnipeg correspondent for *Theatrum* magazine. Kevin and his family are active in the local theatre scene; they are perennial volunteers at the Winnipeg Fringe Festival, and have also worked with Primus, the Manitoba Theatre for Young People and Shakespeare in the Ruins.

Liam Lacey of *The Globe and Mail* said his play *Going Down the River* "manages to evoke an entire set of social and historic problems through one pivotal incident." Kenneth Dyba of the CBC mentions "first-rate characterizations, terrific dialogue, strong story and genuine stage sense..." *Going Down the River* appears in the Simon & Pierre anthology *Canadian Mosaic.*

Kevin divides his time between his day job writing technical documentation for Norsat International and various theatre projects, including producing plays for Theatre Anywhere, a company he founded in 1998 to give local theatre artists more opportunities.

Among the awards Kevin has received are the Allen Sangster Award for dedicated service to the Canadian Authors Association, the 1983 Air Canada Award, an honourable mention in the *Writer's Digest* Scripts competition, the Dorothy White Award from the Ottawa Little Theatre (for *Going Down the River*), an honourable mention in the Ferndale Repertory Theater's New Works Competition (for *Playing by the Rules*), and an Award of Merit from the Society for Technical Communications.

Kevin is also the author of *Dreams For a Winter's Night,* a chapbook of poetry published in 1987 by Southwestern Ontario Poetry.

Quebec, Canada
2001